SOCIAL SEMIOTICS

Key Figures, New Directions

Thomas Hestbæk Andersen, Morten Boeriis, Eva Maagerø, and Elise Seip Tønnessen

Routledge
Taylor & Francis Group

LONDON AND NEW YORK

First published 2015
by Routledge
2 Park Square, Milton Park, Abingdon, Oxon OX14 4RN

and by Routledge
711 Third Avenue, New York, NY 10017

Routledge is an imprint of the Taylor & Francis Group, an informa business

British Library Cataloguing-in-Publication Data
A catalogue record for this book is available from the British Library

Library of Congress Cataloging in Publication Data
Andersen, Thomas Hestbæk.
Social semiotics : key figures, new directions / by Thomas Hestbæk Andersen,
Morten Boeriis, Eva Maagerø, and Elise Seip Tønnessen.
pages cm
1. Semiotics--Social aspects. I. Boeriis, Morten, editor. II. Maagerø, Eva, editor.
III. Tønnessen, Elise Seip, editor. IV. Title.
P99.4.S62A53 2015
302.2--dc23
2014045712

ISBN: 978-0-415-71210-1 (hbk)
ISBN: 978-0-415-71211-8 (pbk)
ISBN: 978-1-3156967-9-9 (ebk)

Typeset in Bembo
by Taylor & Francis Books
Printed in Great Britain by Ashford Colour Press Ltd.

SOCIAL SEMIOTICS

M.A.K. Halliday's work has been hugely influential in linguistics and beyond since the 1960s. This is a collection of interviews with key figures in the generation of social semioticians who have taken Halliday's concept of social semiotics and developed it further in various directions, making their own original contributions to theory and practice. This book highlights their main lines of thought and considers how they relate to both the original concept of social semiotics and to each other. Key themes include:

- linguistic studies, multilinguality and evolution of language
- text, discourse and classroom studies
- digital texts, computer communication and science teaching
- multimodal text and discourse analysis
- education and literacy
- media work and visual and audio modes
- critical discourse analysis.

Featuring interviews with leading figures from linguistics, education and communication studies, a framing introduction and a concluding chapter summing up commonalities and differences, connections and conflicts and key themes, this is essential reading for any scholar or student working in the area of social semiotics and systemic functional linguistics. Additional video resources are available on the Routledge website (www.routledge.com/9780415712101).

Thomas Hestbæk Andersen is Associate Professor, Department of Language and Communication, University of Southern Denmark and is Chairman for the *Nordic Association for SFL & Social Semiotics*.

Morten Boeriis is Associate Professor, Department of Language and Communication, University of Southern Denmark.

Eva Maagerø is Professor, Department of Language Studies, Buskerud and Vestfold University College, Norway.

Elise Seip Tønnessen is Professor, Department of Nordic and Media Studies, University of Agder, Norway.

CONTENTS

ACKNOWLEDGEMENTS

PREFACE

In an interview that two of the editors of this book conducted with Michael A.K. Halliday in 1998 he underlined the importance of a versatile approach to the study of language and semiotic processes. Even though he regarded his systemic functional description of language as a coherent whole, he was well aware that not all aspects were fully developed, and anticipated further work to move in different directions in the future.

This book aims to present ideas from a generation of scholars who have been inspired by Michael Halliday and his social and functional approach to language and semiotics, and who have added their own ideas and academic interests, developing original works of their own. By presenting their thoughts and ideas in the form of interviews, we want to highlight their main lines of thought and discuss how they relate to both the original concept of social semiotics and to each other. It is our hope that the dialogical form of the interview can serve as a door opener to complex theories and make connections across fields. Some of these connections we shall discuss in the final chapter.

The interviews have been carefully prepared, videotaped, transcribed and edited, and in the end the final version of each interview has been approved by the interviewee. We wish to express our profound gratitude to the five scholars who so generously shared their time, knowledge and experiences with us, and responded to our questions in the meticulous follow up procedures. They have strengthened our belief that academic work is not primarily about competition, but rather about sharing.

Thomas Hestbæk Andersen, Morten Boeriis,
Eva Maagerø and Elise Seip Tønnessen
Odense (Denmark), Tønsberg and Kristiansand (Norway)
August 2014

1

INTRODUCTION

Social Semiotics: Key Figures, New Directions contains interviews with five scholars, who have all contributed immensely to the expansion of Michael A. K. Halliday's ideas about semiosis, i.e. human meaning making. What the scholars have in common is that Halliday's theory of a social semiotics has inspired them to do ground breaking work themselves. In other words, the scholars are *key figures* in social semiotics, and their work represents a plurality of *new directions*. The scholars in question are Christian M.I.M. Matthiessen, James R. Martin, Gunther R. Kress, Theo J. van Leeuwen and Jay L. Lemke. In this book, we present their thoughts and ideas in the form of five separate interviews followed by a discussion of their similarities and differences. The dialogical form of an interview is particularly apt for making inroads into complex theories and making connections among the scholars and across fields. With the interviews in this book, we highlight the main lines of thought of each of the fives scholars, and we discuss how they relate to Halliday's original concept of social semiotics, as well as to each other.

In order to establish a context for the remainder of the book, we shall provide below a concise introduction to the intellectual legacy from Michael A. K. Halliday (in the section *What is Halliday's social semiotics?*). This section is no more than a brief outline of the fundamentals of Halliday's social semiotics; the main aim of the book is to present and discuss how our five scholars have taken Halliday's ideas to new frontiers, and how they have redefined and reshaped several of his original ideas, not to present Halliday's ideas themselves. After the brief introduction to Halliday's social semiotics, we shall provide an overview of the academic careers of each of our interviewees (in the section *Who are the scholars?*); in this second section of this introduction, we shall also sketch out their main contributions to social semiotics. The final section of this chapter contains some remarks on the way in which we have gathered and edited the interviews, i.e. some remarks on the methodology behind the book.

What is Halliday's social semiotics?

"Language is as it is because of what it has to do", Halliday states in his *Language as Social Semiotic*, and in a concise and typical Hallidayan down-to-earth way, the statement conveys the axiomatic hypothesis that language (and other semiotic systems) has developed and is as it is because of the meanings that people have perceived the need to create in order to communicate; semiotic systems (such as language) reflect, construe and enact our reality.

In a social semiotic approach, therefore, semiosis is not done by minds, but by social practices in a community. Meanings do not arise in the individual; meaning is a superindividual and intersubjective activity, and consciousness is approached from a Vygotskian perspective, whereby consciousness is a social mode of being. The functionality of any semiotic system is based on a social understanding of meaning and meaning making, as signalled with the notion of social semiotics. The social understanding of meaning is, in fact, also a cultural understanding of meaning, since Halliday – inspired by Malinowski – equates social with cultural, whereby all meanings are cultural. With a social and cultural foundation for semiosis there is no need for the concept of mind, or for the idea of some extra-semiotic knowledge base in the Hallidayan approach. Meanings do not exist or arise in a separate cognitive universe of concepts or ideas; instead Halliday sees them as patterns of semantic organization, which are realized through grammar.

Halliday suggests that a semiotic system can be located as a fourth order of complexity in an evolutionary typology of systems, i.e. in a typology representing the emergence of grammar (through time). The most basic system type is a physical system. If we add life to a physical system, we have a biological system. If we then add value to our biological system, we have a social system. To the social system, we can then add meaning, and thereby the typology culminates in a semiotic system.

A semiotic system is a fourth order of complexity, since it is at the same time semiotic *and* social *and* biological *and* physical. Semiotic systems can be of two kinds: they can be primary, consisting of content/expression pairs (i.e. of signs), or they can be of a higher order, involving a stratification of content into a dual layering of semantics and grammar; language is a higher order semiotic system. Higher order semiotic systems are not systems of signs (pairings of content and expression), they are meaning systems in which entities function along different dimensions in complex "grammatico-semantic" relations to each other.

Being a linguist, Halliday is primarily concerned with language, and he only occasionally reaches out to other semiotics systems. In effect, social semiotics is a notion seldom used by Halliday himself, he prefers the notion of systemic functional linguistics (SFL). Part of the reason is that his original use of the notion of social semiotics was intended to cover only higher order semiotic systems (systems with a distinct grammar) but, in its contemporary use, the notion is associated with any semiotic system, i.e. also with systems that Halliday as a linguist would regard as primary semiotic systems.

Halliday upholds the Whorfian idea of a close connection between thinking and language. Whorf describes this connection as follows:

> … thinking is most mysterious, and by far the greatest light upon it that we have is thrown by the study of language. This study shows that the forms of a person's thoughts are controlled by inexorable laws of pattern of which he is unconscious. These patterns are the unperceived intricate systematizations of his own language (…). And every language is a vast pattern-system, different from others, in which are culturally ordained the forms and categories by which the personality not only communicates, but also analyses nature, notices or neglects types of relationship and phenomena, channels his reasoning, and builds the house of his consciousness.
>
> *(Whorf, 1956, p. 252)*

Halliday's approach is multifaceted and rich in detail, and different aspects of semiosis and different parts of language are described with a varying emphasis on the many different theoretical and descriptive concepts. However, we can single out three major organizing principles, which are crucial in every aspect of his approach: stratification, instantiation and metafunction.

Language is regarded as being stratified, which means that language is organized in four strata: semantics, lexicogrammar (both of these are "content" strata, meaning that they organize the content part of meaning), phonology and phonetics (both of these are "expression" strata, organizing the resources for expressing meaning). Language is context sensitive, both in the sense that its categories are motivated by the (social) context, in which language has a function, and in the sense that its categories reflect back on context by imposing a certain understanding of reality. Halliday therefore embeds the four linguistic strata in a stratum for context, as it is illustrated in Figure 1.1.

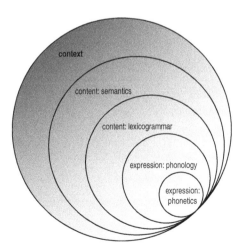

FIGURE 1.1 Stratification (language)

The relationship among the strata is that of realization, so context is realized in semantics, which again is realized in lexicogrammar, and so forth. The realizational relationship has a progressive scope, meaning that context is realized not only in semantics but in the sum of all the linguistic strata, i.e. in all the strata below context. In the same way, semantics and lexicogrammar are realized in the sum of all their lower-level strata. Realization, thus, is accumulative.

Halliday suggests that the realizational relationship between the "content" strata (semantics and lexicogrammar) and the "expression" strata (phonology and phonetics) is arbitrary, while the more internal realizational relationship between the two content strata (between semantics and lexicogrammar), and between the two expression strata (between phonology and phonetics) is natural. Thus, grammar is not just form. Grammar is the wording of semantics, which organizes the meanings – the flux of experience – that are significant for a community. Ultimately, therefore, grammar is motivated by context: it is functional.

The concept of realization holding the strata together is distinct from another major type of relation recognized by Halliday, namely that of instantiation. Instantiation designates the relationship between a semiotic system regarded as an underlying potential, and text. In the light of instantiation, text is understood as a particular instance of the underlying potential, i.e. a text represents a particular actualization of parts of the total (and abstract) semiotic system. From the idea that system and text are the same phenomena seen by different perspectives, Halliday links system and text as poles on a continuum; this is illustrated in Figure 1.2.

Halliday's third major organizing principle is that of metafunction. Halliday sees a semiotic system as diversified into three metafunctions: the interpersonal, the ideational and the textual metafunction. The interpersonal metafunction enacts exchange, which includes expression of personalities and personal feelings on the one hand, and forms of interaction and social interplay with other participants in the communication situation on the other. The ideational metafunction is further subdivided into the experiential and the logical metafunction; the experiential metafunction concerns the way language construes experience, both of the external world and of the inner, mental world, while the logical metafunction organizes basic logical relations. Finally, the textual metafunction enables the speaker to organize ideational and interpersonal meaning in such a way that it makes sense in the context and fulfils its function as a message.

The theoretical inspiration to the metafunctional hypothesis comes from Malinowski, Whorf and Mathesius; Malinowski's work has inspired Halliday to the idea of the interpersonal metafunction, Whorf's work to the idea of the ideational

| System | Text |
| Potential | Instance |

FIGURE 1.2 Instantiation

metafunction, and Mathesius's work to the idea of the textual metafunction. Halliday pays tribute to these scholars as follows:

> For Malinowski, language was a means of action; and since symbols cannot act on things, this meant as means of interaction – acting on other people. Language need not (and often did not) match the reality; but since it derived its meaning potential from use, it typically worked. For Whorf, on the other hand, language was a means of thought. It provided a model of reality; but when the two did not match, since experience was interpreted within the limitations of this model, it could be disastrous in action (...). Mathesius showed how language varied to suit the context. Each sentence of the text was organized by the speaker so as to convey the message he wanted at that juncture, and the total effect was what we recognize as discourse. Their work provides the foundation for a systemic functional semantics.
>
> *(Halliday, 1984, p. 311)*

Halliday's conceptions of stratification, instantiation and metafunction have been used by our five scholars in their work with varying loyalty to Halliday's original formulations; in one scholar's work, the concepts have to a very large extent been adapted as intended by Halliday, in others' work, the concepts have been reshaped (beyond recognition, nearly, in some cases). Common for all, however, is that the three concepts (and Halliday's work at large) have functioned as an undeniable source of inspiration and frame for exploring semiosis.

Who are the scholars?

Christian Matthias Ingemar Martin Matthiessen

Photo by Hong Kong Polytechnic University

Christian Matthiessen was born in Sweden in 1956. He credits his mother, Christine Matthiessen, for inspiring his interest in language, an interest also nurtured by the fact that he grew up in a family whose members were dispersed all over the world, speaking numerous languages. Matthiessen completed his candidate's degree (Phil. Cand.) in English and Linguistics at Lund University in 1980, and he took his MA at UCLA (completed in 1984). He holds a PhD from UCLA (1989); his thesis was entitled *Text generation as a linguistic research task*, and this signifies one of his major interests, namely in computer-helped descriptions of language(s). He held various positions at the Information Sciences Institute at the University of Southern California during his time in Los Angeles, in the years from 1980 to 1988. Whilst there, he met and worked with Halliday, who functioned as a consultant on the Penman project (which produced a large-scale systemic functional grammar of English (the Nigel grammar)), in which Matthiessen was involved; this work was so fruitful and inspiring that he followed in Halliday's footpath and moved to the Department of Linguistics at the University of Sydney (a department originally set up by Halliday in 1976) in 1988, where he worked first as Lecturer, then as Senior Lecturer. He moved to the Department of Linguistics at Macquarie University in 1994 to take up a position as Associate Professor. He became Chair Professor there in 2002, and he worked at Macquarie University until 2008, when he moved to Hong Kong to take up a position as Chair and Head of the Department of English at the Hong Kong Polytechnic University.

Since he moved to Sydney, Christian Matthiessen has been Halliday's closest associate and, in collaboration with Halliday, he has extended and revised Halliday's seminal *An Introduction to Functional Grammar* (*IFG*). Matthiessen's influence on this work, which for the last 30 years has functioned as a reference work for the systemic functional description of English, is clear in the third and fourth edition, which appeared in 2004 and 2014, respectively; in these editions of *An Introduction to Functional Grammar*, Matthiessen's devotion to the system network as a representational tool is apparent, and to a large extent the third (and fourth) edition of IFG incorporates much of the systemic description known from Matthiessen's Lexicogrammatical Cartography: English Systems (1995), albeit still upholding Halliday's more functionally, less systemic oriented disposition in terms of the whole presentation. One could say that Matthiessen is the key exponent of the systemic part of systemic functional linguistics; in all his works, the relational-dimensional thinking is salient. In other words, Matthiessen defines every systemic functional category in terms of its location in a multidimensional network of relationships (its "semiotic address", as he coins it); the dimensions conjoined in this multidimensional network are the global dimensions: stratification, instantiation and metafunction, and the local dimensions: rank, axis and delicacy.

As a systemicist, Christian Matthiessen has approached and worked within a number of linguistic research domains, most notably with (computer-based) grammatical and semantic description of particular languages – not least English – language typology, text and register analysis, and translation.

Below are listed the publications that Matthiessen regards as his most important:

1995. *Lexicogrammatical cartography: English systems*. Tokyo: International Language Sciences Publishers.

1998. Construing processes of consciousness: from the commonsense model to the uncommonsense model of cognitive science. In: J.R. Martin & Robert Veel (eds.), *Reading science: critical and functional perspectives on discourses of science*. London: Routledge, pp. 327–57.

2004. Language typology: a functional perspective. Amsterdam: Benjamins. (With Alice Caffarel & J.R. Martin.)

2006. *Construing experience through meaning: a language-based approach to cognition*. London & New York: Continuum. (With M.A.K Halliday.)

2007. The "architecture" of language according to systemic functional theory: developments since the 1970s. In: Ruqaiya Hasan, Christian M.I.M. Matthiessen & Jonathan Webster (eds.), *Continuing discourse on language*. Volume 2. London: Equinox, pp. 505–61.

2009. Ideas and new directions. In: M.A.K. Halliday & Jonathan J. Webster (eds.), *A companion to systemic functional linguistics*. London & New York: Continuum, pp. 12–58.

2009. Systemic Functional Grammar: A First Step into the Theory. In: Christian M.I.M. Matthiessen & M.A.K. Halliday (eds.), *English and Chinese*. Higher Education Press. Available at http://web.uam.es/departamentos/filoyletras/filoinglesa/Courses/LFC-SFL/FirstStep.html (accessed 6 January 2015).

2010. *Key terms in systemic functional linguistics*. London & New York: Continuum. (With Kazuhiro Teruya & Marvin Lam.)

2014. *Halliday's Introduction to Functional Grammar*. 4th revised edition. London: Routledge. (With M.A.K. Halliday.)

Forthc. *Rhetorical System and Structure Theory: the semantic system of rhetorical relations*. Book MS.

James Robert Martin

Jim Martin was born in Canada in 1950. He enrolled in Glendon College at York University in 1968, wishing to pursue a career in politics or foreign affairs. However, thanks to Michael Gregory, his lecturer in English, he was soon hooked on linguistics. In his interview, Martin says that Glendon College was probably the only place in North America where a Hallidayan perspective on linguistics was taught at that time. Martin completed his BA (hons) from Glendon College and took his MA at the University of Toronto; here his interest in Tagalog began, since this language was used in a course for field methods. In 1974 Martin was awarded a scholarship to study with Halliday; this brought him to Britain, and he completed his PhD at the University of Essex. His thesis was on the development of storytelling by primary school children, focusing on participant identification and conjunction; the thesis lays out two tracks that have been salient in Martin's work ever since: a concern for pedagogy and an interest in cohesion. In 1977 he followed Halliday to Australia, and became first a lecturer and later professor in linguistics at the University of Sydney, where he today holds a personal chair.

Jim Martin participated, as most of the other interviewees in this book, in the Newtown Semiotic Circle in Sydney in the 1980s, where social semiotics came in contact with critical theory and European linguistic thinking. The works of Hjemslev (1899–1965) were discussed and Hjelmslev's ideas had a deep influence on Martin (and on others in the Newtown Semiotic Circle). Hjelmslev stressed the importance of language as a stratified system. Stratification has also been a main issue in Martin's linguistic thinking.

Martin's fields of interests are functional linguistics, systemic theory and discourse semantics. One of his main contributions to SFL has been to rework Halliday's grammatical theory into a theory of discourse semantics. The lexicogrammar has the clause as focus. Martin's primary focus is on the text as the unit of meaning. With his notion of discourse semantics, Martin emphasizes the importance of cohesion in text analysis and text production; at his stratum for discourse semantics, he organizes cohesive resources according to metafunctional diversity. Martin's work on discourse semantics was first published comprehensively in his seminal *English Text: System and Structure*. With his work on context – i.e. with his stratification of context into the two strata: register and genre – he simultaneously reinterprets the notion of register, making it a term for a context stratum and not for linguistic variation (as it is understood by Halliday), and emphasizes purpose and the extrinsic functionality of language as key to understanding language use. He has also developed a linguistic appraisal theory based on SFL together with Peter White.

In 1979 Halliday organized a language in education conference in Sydney where teachers and university professors were brought together. At the conference Martin met Joan Rothery, and they started a long lasting cooperation on writing development in primary school. This was the beginning of genre pedagogy, a genre-based literacy programme that has inspired teachers all around the world. Martin has taken part in several school projects, in recent years most notably with David Rose.

Martin has, in addition, published papers on Tagalog and English, also in an educational context, and on children's picture books. In 2010–12 eight volumes of his collected papers were published by Shanghai Jiaotong University Press, and in April 2014 the Martin Centre for Appliable Linguistics at Shanghai Jiao Tong University was opened.

Below are listed the publications that Martin regards as his most important:

1979. *Crazy Talk: a study of the discourse of schizophrenic speakers.* New York: Plenum (Cognition and Language: a series in psycholinguistics). (With S. Rochester.)
1985. *Factual Writing: exploring and challenging social reality.* Geelong, Vic.: Deakin University Press (ECS806 Sociocultural Aspects of Language and Education).
1992. *English Text: system and structure.* Amsterdam: Benjamins.

1993. *Writing Science: literacy and discursive power.* London: Falmer (Critical perspectives on literacy and education) & Pittsburg: University of Pittsburg Press (Pittsburg Series in Composition, Literacy, and Culture). (With M.A.K. Halliday.)

1997/2010. *Working with Functional Grammar.* London: Arnold. 2nd edition 2010. *Deploying Functional Grammar.* Commercial Press: Beijing (The Halliday Centre Series in Appliable Linguistics). (With C.M.I.M. Matthiessen & C. Painter.)

2003/2007. *Working with Discourse: meaning beyond the clause.* London: Continuum. (With D. Rose.)

2005. *The Language of Evaluation: appraisal in English.* London: Palgrave. (reprinted by Foreign Language Teaching and Research Press. 2008). (With P.R.R. White.)

2008. *Genre relations: mapping culture.* London: Equinox. (With D. Rose.)

2012. *Learning to Write, Reading to Learn: genre, knowledge and pedagogy in the Sydney School.* London: Equinox. (With D. Rose.)

2013. *Reading Visual Narratives: image analysis of children's picture books.* London: Equinox. (With C. Painter & L. Unsworth.)

Gunther Rolf Kress

Photo by Robert Taylor, www.taylor-photo.co.uk

Gunther Kress was born in Germany in 1940, and moved to Australia at the age of 16. Encountering a new language and culture as a teenager, he decided to study English literature "because it seemed most difficult and a challenge", as he puts it. He received his first degree in Literature from the University of Newcastle in Australia, but decided to move on to Linguistics in search for more rigour in his approach to texts. After finishing a second degree in Linguistics with Michael Halliday at University College London, his plans for a PhD with Halliday were stopped when Halliday moved to Australia. Eventually Kress also returned to Australia and obtained his Doctor of Letters (D. Lit.) from the University of New-castle. He also holds an Honorary Doctorate from the University of Technology in Sydney.

Before entering into the academic world Gunther Kress was an apprentice and worked as a furrier, and this has affected his way of thinking within an academic setting, alternating between practical and theoretical perspectives. His first University appointment took him back to Europe to teach English at the University of Kiel. After only a year in an environment dominated by transformational grammar he moved on to work as a research fellow in applied linguistics at the University of Kent in Canterbury, at the same time commuting to London to work with Halliday. His next job was at the University of East Anglia in Norwich, where he met Robert Hodge with whom he co-authored works that proved to become significant steps on his academic path, such as *Language as ideology* (1979) and *Social semiotics* (1988). The cooperation with Hodge continued after they both moved to Australia, Kress in 1978 to take up a position in Adelaide at what is now known as the University of Southern Australia. From there Kress moved to the University of Technology in Sydney, and in his years in Sydney he played a vital part in the Newtown Semiotic Circle. Through his twelve years in Australia Kress worked in departments of Communication and Culture, and also held positions as Dean. This was also where he started his cooperation with Theo van Leeuwen on images and multimodality, which continued when they both moved to Britain, to London and Cardiff respectively.

Coming to London as Professor of Semiotics and Education at the Institute of Education in 1990 led to a certain shift in focus for Gunther Kress. His move into the field of Education at a time of profound social changes in Britain called for an integration of his previous interests in language and social power, with educational matters of vital importance for social futures on a cultural as well as an individual level. Through his years in London, Kress has worked extensively with classroom research, investigating communication and meaning making processes in the science classroom as well as in English teaching. He has worked with text book design and the move from page to screen. Also he has extended the notion of education to new fields, such as the operating theatre.

Looking back, Gunther Kress concludes that his work has been in semiotics more than in linguistics, and that an important aim for him has been to account for the whole domain of meaning. From Hallidayan linguistics he has taken the social foundations and the close connection between form and meaning. This has inspired his approach to the semiotic and social aspects of multimodality. His interest in the social consequences of semiotic change ties in with an engagement with the personal interests involved in meaning making, resulting in a strong commitment in multimodal learning as well as the politics of education.

Below are listed the publications that Kress regards as his most important:

1979. *Language as Ideology*. London & New York: Routledge & Kegan Paul. (With Bob Hodge.)
1982/1994. *Learning to write*. London & New York: Routledge & Kegan Paul. 2nd edition 1994. London: Routledge.
1984/1989. *Linguistics Processes in sociocultural practices*. Oxford: Oxford University Press.
1988. *Social Semiotics*. Cambridge: Polity Press. (With Bob Hodge.)
1993. Against arbitrariness: the social production of the sign as a foundational issue in critical discourse analysis. *Discourse Society*, April 1993, 4(2): 169–91.

1996/2006. *Reading Images*. London & New York: Routledge. (With Theo van Leeuwen.)

1997. *Before Writing: Rethinking Paths to Literacy*. London & New York: Routledge.

2000. *Early spelling: From creativity to convention*. London & New York: Routledge.

2003. *Literacy in the new media age*. London & New York: Routledge.

2010. *Multimodality: A social semiotic approach to contemporary communication*. London & New York: Routledge.

Theodore Jacob van Leeuwen

Theo van Leeuwen was born in the Netherlands in 1947. He was a student of the Dutch National Film School in Amsterdam in the late 1960s, and at that time already interested in the idea of the language of image and film, as well as in doing intellectual work on film. This was not approved by his teachers at the time, who thought that a strong intellectual interest could jeopardize his creativity. Van Leeuwen had his own view of things and maintained a firm belief that creativity and intellect can work in unison. In 1972 he finished his BA in scriptwriting and direction and started working as film editor, writer and producer.

After he married an Australian and moved to Australia in the 1970s, Van Leeuwen experienced difficulties applying his film production skills in the Australian context, which at the time did not appreciate the European film style. So he took on teaching film production at Macquarie University, while at the same time studying linguistics and semiotics in the evenings. In 1980 he studied cinema semiotics at the CETSAS in Paris with Christian Metz.

In 1982 Van Leeuwen completed a research master's thesis about intonation at Macquarie University in Sydney which was examined by Gunther Kress. Not long after they started working together exploring the language of images in which they shared a keen interest. Eventually these explorations led to their influential publications on images and multimodality. Van Leeuwen received his PhD in 1992 at the University of Sydney. He was supervised by Jim

Martin and his thesis was still not on images but on bringing linguistics and social theory together, giving him a grounding in both sociology and systemic linguistics.

Van Leeuwen has been one of the most influential scholars in social semiotics and multimodality and contributed many publications of great impact on very varied topics, such as e.g. discourse analysis, images, sound, typography, kinaesthetic, colour, software design and, not least, general multimodal theory proper.

In his career, van Leeuwen has held numerous prominent positions. He has been Professor of Communication Theory and Head of Research at London College of Communication at London University of the Arts, Professor, Director and Chair in Language and Communication at Cardiff University, and Professor of Media and Communication and Dean at the Faculty of Arts and Social Sciences at the University of Technology in Sydney. Currently he is Professor in Multimodality at the University of Southern Denmark. He holds a number of honorary and visiting professorships at other universities around the world. Van Leeuwen is the founding editor of influential journals such as *Visual Communication* and *Social Semiotics* and he is a member of the editorial boards of several other journals. He has been and still is an active scholar doing plenary talks at conferences all over the world.

Looking back, van Leeuwen considers himself lucky to have been in Sydney at a very good time for social semiotics when the idea of extending Hallidayan social semiotics into multimodality began to blossom and put new ideas into the world. It is clear that van Leeuwen has achieved his goal: he has shown that images and film (and other modes of communication) are as good and important as language, and that creativity and intellect can indeed work in in very productive unison.

Below are listed the publications that van Leeuwen regards as his most important:

1996/2006. *Reading Images: The Grammar of Visual Design*. London & New York: Routledge. (With Gunther Kress.)
1999. *Speech, Music, Sound*. London: Macmillan.
2001. *Multimodal Discourse: The Modes and Media of Contemporary Communication*. London: Arnold. (With Gunther Kress.)
2005. *Introducing Social Semiotics*. London & New York: Routledge.
2006. Towards a Semiotics of Typography. *Information Design Journal* 14(2): 139–55. London: John Benjamins Publishing Company.
2008. *Discourse and Practice: New Tools for Critical Discourse Analysis*. New York: Oxford University Press.
2009. Parametric systems: the case of voice quality. In: C. Jewitt, (ed.), *The Routledge Handbook of Multimodal Analysis*. London & New York: Routledge, pp. 68–78.
2010. The semiotics of decoration. In: K.L. O'Halloran and B.A. Smith, (eds.), *Multimodal Studies: Exploring Issues and Domains*. London & New York: Routledge, pp. 115–31.
2011. *The Language of Colour: An Introduction*. London & New York: Routledge.
2011. The semiotics of texture: from tactile to visual. *Visual Communication* 10(4): 541–64. London: Sage. (With Emilia Djonov.)

Jay L. Lemke

Jay Lemke was born in Chicago in 1946. He entered into social semiotics from a different academic background than the other scholars in this book. He studied mathematics and physics and completed his PhD in theoretical physics at the University of Chicago in 1973; his thesis was entitled *Proton-Antiproton Scattering Near Threshold*. His interests in science education led him to accept a job offer at the City University of New York, where he initiated a research programme in science education. He later moved to the University of Michigan, and then to University of California, San Diego.

The lack of a feasible theory on how to communicate scientific ideas in the classroom led him to Halliday's approach to language, which he found gave him what he needed. His introduction to systemic functional linguistics and social semiotics in 1978–79 became fundamental in his further career working with linguistics and communication as it applied to science education. His contact with Halliday was further developed through several research stays in Sydney through the 1980s and 1990s. During his stays in Sydney he met most of the other interviewees in this book, and he participated in meetings in the Newtown Semiotic Circle. With his American background and broad reading also of theory originating in Europe, he has contributed to social semiotics by bringing concepts such as intertextuality (Rifaterre, Kristeva, Bakhtin) and heteroglossia (Bakhtin) into the discussion, and by applying notions of what is now known as multimodality from Barthes and social theory from Foucault and Bourdieu.

His interests in the field have expanded to the history of mathematical and scientific language on the one hand, and learning processes through other modes than language and in contexts outside the classroom on the other. Around the turn of the century this led to studies of multimodal interactions in computer games. From such experiences with informal learning, Lemke has become very aware of an emotional component in learning, and his most recent work aims at integrating "the analysis of cognitive or ideational dimensions of learning with the affective or emotional and interpersonal dimensions", as he states in his interview.

With his background in a different scientific tradition, Jay Lemke has contributed to the systemic thinking as well as expanding semiotics into new fields of research. A case in point may be his notion of multiplicative meaning in multimodal texts, where he draws his argument from information theory cybernetics. Another example is his concept of meta-redundancy, where he treats the relationship between the signifier and the signified – and between strata – in mathematical terms as a contingent probability relationship.

Below are listed the publications that Lemke regards as his most important:

1990. *Talking Science: Language, Learning, and Values*. Norwood, NJ: Ablex/Praeger Publishing.
1995. *Textual Politics: Discourse and Social Dynamics*. London: Taylor & Francis.
1998. Multiplying Meaning: Visual and Verbal Semiotics in Scientific Text. In: J.R. Martin & R. Veel (eds.), *Reading Science*. London: Routledge, pp. 87–113.
1998. Resources for Attitudinal Meaning: Evaluative Orientations in Text Semantics. *Functions of Language* 5(1): 33–56.
1999. Typological and Topological Meaning in Diagnostic Discourse. *Discourse Processes* 27(2): 173–85.
2000. Opening Up Closure: Semiotics Across Scales. In: J. Chandler & G. van de Vijver (eds.), *Closure: Emergent Organizations and their Dynamics (Volume 901: Annals of the NYAS)*. New York: New York Academy of Science Press, pp. 100–11.
2000. Across the Scales of Time: Artifacts, Activities, and Meanings in Ecosocial Systems. *Mind, Culture, and Activity* 7(4): 273–90.
2002. Travels in Hypermodality. *Visual Communication* 1(3): 299–325.
2012. Analyzing Verbal Data: Principles, Methods, and Problems [revised]. In: Barry J. Fraser, Kenneth Tobin & Campbell J. McRobbie (eds.), *The Second International Handbook of Science Education*. London: Springer, pp. 1471–84.
2013. Feeling and Meaning in the Social Ecology of Learning: Lessons from Play and Games. In: Michael Baker, Jerry Andriessen & Sanna Järvelä (eds.), *Affective Learning Together: The Socio-emotional Turn in Collaborative Learning*. London & New York: Routledge, pp. 71–94.

How were the interviews done?

The interviews have been conducted over a period of eighteen months. The interview with Gunther Kress was conducted in his office at the Institute of Education in London in December 2012; the interview session lasted two hours. The interview with Jim Martin was conducted in an apartment in London in June 2013, and the session lasted approximately two and a half hours. The interview with Christian Matthiessen was conducted in his apartment in Hong Kong in September 2013, and it lasted some three hours. The interview with Theo van Leeuwen was conducted in his apartment in Odense in November 2013, and the session lasted three hours. Finally, the interview with Jay Lemke was conducted in his apartment in San Diego in March 2014, and it lasted two hours.

Prior to each interview, the interviewee had been presented with the interview guide for his interview, and with a short introduction of the book project. All the interviews were recorded on video and, afterwards, they have been transcribed in full. The transcriptions have then been edited into separate book chapters for each of the five scholars. In this process, we have cut away more than a third of each interview, and we have made adjustments to the wording and occasionally to the structure of the arguments. All these adjustments have been made with the purpose of clarifying; ensuring that what was originally a set of multimodal texts with gestures, pauses, stress, facial expressions, etc. is also understandable as a set of monomodal written accounts of the spoken texts. After our editing, the interviewees have all been asked to approve and where necessary contribute with clarifications and modifications to their interview. They have all done so, and we thank them all for contributing immensely and fruitfully not only to the interview session itself but also to the editing process.

References

Halliday, Michael A.K., 1984. On the Ineffability of Grammatical Categories. In: Michael A. K. Halliday, 2002, *On grammar*. Vol. 1 in the collected works of M.A.K. Halliday. London: Continuum, pp. 291–322.

Whorf, Benjamin Lee, 1956. *Language, Thought, and Reality*. Boston, MA: The MIT Press.

2

CHRISTIAN M.I.M. MATTHIESSEN

Background

How were you introduced to systemics or social semiotics?

This goes back to around 1976, the beginning of my undergraduate days at Lund University in the departments of Linguistics and English. I had already become interested in linguistics during my years in high school, reading Otto Jespersen and Bertil Malmberg, whose work gave me insight into European structuralism, and also Alvar Ellegård's account of generative semantics, which was fascinating because it showed the relationship between grammar and meaning. I was in the mathematics and natural sciences stream in high school, so the technicality in the accounts was not a barrier for me. As undergraduate students in linguistics at Lund University, we were of course trained in the then current fashion of Chomsky's version of generative linguistics, which was the Extended Standard Theory. But, at the same time, we were very much encouraged to read around, first by Bertil Malmberg and then by his successor, Bengt Sigurd. I read Tagmemics, Stratification Linguistics, Generative Semantics and the European tradition (including Gustave Guillaume – not so easy but stimulating, and resonant with SFL in certain respects as I came to realize later), and so on. I read Louis Hjelmslev in Danish, and Arne Næss in Norwegian. In Linguistics, we were lucky enough to have an expert on the Prague School, Milan Bílý, doing his PhD in the Department. And people came to visit – André Martinet, I remember, and also John Sinclair, Geoffrey Leech – and there was still an echo of Glossematics and Louis Hjelmslev (as students, we were taken on a "field trip" to meet linguists at Copenhagen University, and Eli Fischer-Jørgensen was given an honorary doctorate at Lund University while I was there). Among the theories I encountered, there was something about systemic functional linguistics that really caught my attention; I think the first book

I read was Halliday's *Explorations in the Functions of Language*, published in 1973. System networks had a major role to play in getting me hooked, but it was the idea of illuminating language through meaning, and coming to understand the grammar through meaning, that really got me hooked. And I was studying Modern Standard Arabic, and discovering systemic functional linguistics helped me considerably in my attempt to come to terms with the language as a learner – just as it did with my effort to expand my mastery of English. Then Halliday's and Hasan's *Cohesion in English* arrived in 1976, and people got very interested in cohesion studies.

Another influence was Jan Svartvik, who had been trained in London and had fairly recently taken over as Chair Professor of English language. He brought the whole corpus methodology to Lund University and the corpus-based involvement with the survey of English usage. It was very exciting.

SFL and social semiotics

In your view, what is the difference between the terms social semiotics and systemic functional linguistics?

Well, I think I came across social semiotics a little bit later than systemic functional linguistics, in 1978 when Halliday's book was published – "LASS", as he calls it – *Language as Social Semiotic*. Later on he told me that he had taken the term "social semiotics" from Greimas. Halliday wanted to articulate a complementary approach to cognitive science, which had become quite fashionable and dominant at the time. Personally, it took me quite a while to understand how deep his idea of social semiotics was – including the socio-semiotic interactive development of persons; I remember this process clearly because I was also reading Wallace Chafe at the time, and I remember thinking "well, ultimately, you need the cognitive component", so the significance of putting language at the centre and of linking it to the brain rather than the mind, and the significance of the interactive foundation had not broken through to my dense brain. That took a while. But gradually I came to appreciate the notion of social semiotics and, for me, the culmination of employing a social semiotic perspective is Halliday's and my book *Construing Experience through Experience*, first published in 1999.

After the publication of Halliday's *Language as Social Semiotic*, the notion became very popular and, together with van Leeuwen and a couple of other people, I was involved in starting up the journal *Social Semiotics* in the early 1990s. I was very much a junior member, and it was not my initiative, but it was exciting. But then, the notion of social semiotics drifted a bit – drifted away from systemic functional linguistics. In a positive way, it expanded the field of vision and took on semiotic systems other than language, which could still be done in a systemic functional way, but in a somewhat unfortunate way, it became less technical, explicit and systemic (in the sense of being based on the description of a semiotic system) and more like commentary on the text – whatever semiotic system it instantiated – a sort of "explication de texte" approach.

Is there a cognitive component in our theory – and if so, how?

The issue is clearly very interesting, and it is important to realize that different scholars and researchers have explored this in different ways. Robin Fawcett has tried from the beginning to build in the cognitive framework together with the interactive orientation. Halliday has done it differently. To explain this, we need to reverse a bit in time: in the 1960s, when Halliday was starting to develop his theory of language as a social semiotic, the prevailing atmosphere did not resonate with his ideas having to do with meaning in interaction. This was because the kind of cognitive science that was around at that time – the classical cognitive science coming out of the 1950s – saw the mind as isolated, floating somewhere with no connection to anything (the real possibility for grounding cognitive models in neuroscience came later as techniques for observing the brain became more sophisticated), and memory was seen as a kind of container: you put things into it, you retrieve things from it, and so on. This was an uncritical grafting of computational metaphors onto the folk model of the mind, as careful analysis of the discourse of mainstream cognitive science reveals (cf. Matthiessen, 1993, 1998; Halliday & Matthiessen, 2006). So it was very different from anything that had to do with humans interacting. If you look at how people have tried to repair this classical mainstream approach in cognitive science since the 1960s, you see that they have edged closer to a socio-interactive standpoint: they have talked about interaction and the cognitive; they have talked about the embodied mind (see, e.g. Varela, Thompson & Rosch, 1991). But in the 1960s and even the 1970s there was not very much for Halliday to resonate with. Scholars like Colwyn Trevarthen, who emphasized intersubjectivity in psychological research, were not part of mainstream cognitive science (e.g. Trevarthen, 1987). If you then fast forward, the situation has changed considerably, even dramatically. One change was that Vygotsky was discovered. He had first been published in English in the early 1960s, but it took quite a while for him to become a real source of insight and inspiration for Western scholars. Another change was that neuroscience took off: techniques for observing and scanning the brain were improved, so there was no longer any excuse for postulating cognitive models without any grounding in evidence from neuroscience (cf. Gerald Edelman's, e.g. 1982, detailed critique of AI models that are not informed by insights from brain research). Halliday and I relate language directly to the brain, but we put the mind aside, and we try to explain the functioning of the brain through language instead of assuming something like the mind or cognition, and using that to explain language. I think our approach resonates with ideas developed by a number of neuroscientists – obvious examples would be Gerald Edelman and Terrence Deacon (e.g. Edelman, 1992; Deacon, 1997). What has emerged is the insight that the one human system that connects all regions of the brain is language – so it integrates us, neurologically in a sense. I think that is quite an exciting development, and so a number of us have tried to make contact with people like Gerald Edelman, Terrence Deacon, Michael Arbib, and so on (cf. Williams, 2005, and the work by Jim Benson and Bill Greaves, and Paul Thibault).

So, how do brain and language evolve together?

Terry Deacon talks about the co-evolution of language and the brain. I have looked at it more in an amateurish way, but it seems to me that if you examine what scholars, based on the fossil record, have been able to suggest about major spurts in the growth of the brain, then one could line this up with a kind of phylogenetic version of Halliday's ontogenetic account of emergence of complexity in language from a simple system, protolanguage (see Matthiessen, 2004). So, I suspect that the transition from homo habilis to homo erectus (on the order of 1.8 to 2.2 million years ago) is probably the transition from something that was like protolanguage to something that, in terms of Halliday's and Clare Painter's study of language development, was like a transition period. In language development, the transition period to the post-infancy adult language is fairly short, but that is because there is a model around for young children to make a transition to – the mother tongue spoken by the people that the infant interacts with. So, I suspect, in human history it took much longer. Then, a second major spurt in the growth of the brain was part of the evolution from archaic homo sapiens to modern homo sapiens: anatomically modern humans (on the order of 150,000 to 200,000 years ago). I suspect that this is when something that we could call modern language emerged. So when our colleagues in other disciplines talk about anatomically modern humans (AMHs), I think we also need to conceptualize these ancestors as linguistically modern humans (LMHs), or semiotically modern humans (SMHs). And with respect to other parts of the body that were co-opted for language (in the normal fashion of evolution), like the vocal tract, again the fossil record suggests that they were in place by then. If you have this sense of gradual increase in complexity, with a "dialogue" between language and the brain, but also a "dialogue" between human culture in society, the tasks language was put to, and the growing power of language, this makes excellent sense (and this view is also supported by non-systemic work, e.g. the contributions on level formation by Luc Steels, e.g. Steels, 1998). And it makes much more sense than the notion that a dramatic kind of mutation was suddenly introduced – you know: syntax as the result of a mutation.

So, language and the evolution of the brain is a social endeavour?

Very much, and very important, and there is a very interesting great historian, one of the few historians who look into deep human history, David Christian, who published a book in 2004 (Christian, 2004), who gives language a very central place: he suggests that people make the mistake of comparing one chimpanzee brain with one human brain. He says that what you should do is compare one chimpanzee brain with hundreds of human brains because language makes collective intelligence possible. He is pointing out that evolution shifted from being essentially biological to being social and also semiotic; positing the idea of a collective brain. So regarding the question; yes, absolutely, the social, the interactive is central and essential.

Communication, text and code

Let's go to a number of basic concepts: communication, text and code. First communication: how would you define the concept of communication?

Well, where does communication come in? I remember a discussion I had around 1980 with Michael Halliday and Bill Mann. Halliday and I both got involved in computational linguistic research, in a succession of text generation projects led by Bill Mann. Bill Mann had come out of the mainstream understanding of the duality of mind and language, and then he had come across Wittgenstein, and reading Wittgenstein had changed all that. So Wittgenstein had softened him up for systemic functional linguistics (just as Wittgenstein later served as a kind of gateway to SFL for Michio Sugeno). Bill Mann regarded communication as absolutely central, and Halliday was not all that enthusiastic about it. I think one reason was simply that when people link language and communication they tend to operate with this notion that language is there to 'clothe' ideas that arise somewhere else, so it leaves out the ideational component; it misses out on what Whorf has emphasized: language as a resource for construing experience. Communication is the exchange of meanings, and part of what meanings do is to construe our experience. Naturally work in communication studies is often relevant, but from a linguistic point of view it does not tend to truly engage with language, as we have found in our work on healthcare communication.

How would you define "text"?

It seems to me that if you think of systemic functional theory as being a way of exploring language and other semiotic systems, then what is central is relational-dimensional thinking. This means that you understand things by seeing where they are located, in terms of dimensions that intersect. Everything is defined by its location in terms of different dimensions – its "semiotic address" in David Butt's terms. A text, therefore, is simply a location along different dimensions. One dimension is the cline of instantiation, where the text is located at the instance end. Another dimension is the hierarchy of stratification, where the text is located as a unit in semantics, which is in turn realized as acts of wording – so a text is not only meaning, it is also wording, which is in turn realized as sounding – and the meaning and the wording are located within context. So text is meaning, or content, unfolding in a context of situation: language functioning in context, as Halliday & Hasan (1976) put it.

Is the concept of code a useful concept, and if it is what is the place for the concept of code in systemic functional linguistics?

There have been at least two different senses of code. One of course comes from Basil Bernstein: code as in restricted and elaborated code, where it is one of the domains of variation in language. But then there is also code in the sense of the system; code in this sense comes from general semiotics and linguistics. In the paper *Language as code and language as behavior: the nature and ontogenesis of dialogue* (1984), Halliday uses code simply as another way of talking about the system. Code in this sense is located at the potential pole of the cline of instantiation. Now, whether we need "code" as a separate technical term in addition to "potential" and "system", I am not so sure.

Language description

Let us turn to language description, one of your main areas of interest. You have for many years worked closely with Halliday, and you have been co-authoring the last two editions of *An Introduction to Functional Grammar (IFG)*. What have been the major developments in the four editions of *An Introduction to Functional Grammar* we now have? The first edition was seminal, and what happened then in number two, three and four, in your view?

It is nice that it has become a living document, and I think one of the interesting things from the first to the now fourth edition is that the academic context has changed in very positive ways. When Halliday published the first edition, that was it, essentially; there were no other comparable books around. But now we have all these great complementary contributions like Geoff Thompson's *Introducing Functional Grammar* and Suzanne Eggins' book; books by Bloor and Bloor and by Graham Lock, serving different potential readerships, and of course the workbook that Clare Painter, Jim Martin and I produced, and the Using Functional Grammar by David Butt and the team at Macquarie, and my own *Lexicogrammatical Cartography*, which I wrote as a systemic complement to *IFG*. So, in that sense, the whole environment of publications has changed quite considerably, and this has given some more space for *IFG* to grow, to become thicker, and to move towards a reference work, and that is one motif in the changes. The second edition was an expansion of the first edition that simply provided answers to questions that had come up through text analysis and other contexts of use. For the third edition, one thing that we really wanted to do was to add system networks, so they came into the third edition, but it mainly retained its original structure in terms of the whole presentation. Now, in my *Lexicogrammatical Cartography* (Matthiessen, 1995), the system network is the navigational tool, whereas *IFG* is organized more in terms of pedagogic reasoning because it is not slavishly tied to step-by-step reporting on the system network. I think both are useful; both are needed. Probably the biggest change has been from the second edition to the third edition. For the fourth edition, one of the things that seemed to me to be helpful was to introduce a more systematic indexing of text, and that was also in the knowledge that there would be a web companion. So you will find in the fourth edition, in the first chapter, a way of sorting texts based on field of activity and mode in the first instance, so all short text examples in the print version can be located within this, and then the idea is for the web companion to have longer examples, and I have been working on this. What is gradually emerging from this effort is an awareness of register-variation in the lexicogrammar. My view is that if you really want to get a sense of registerial variation in the grammar, you need to take several steps further in deli-cacy in the differentiation of registers (beyond broad categories such as media dis-course, academic discourse and spoken discourse that have been used in many studies), and doing this amounts to a long-term research programme. I see the fourth edition of *IFG* as a tool to help with that. It is not a reference grammar yet, but thanks to the web companion I think it can grow, and I hope that it can encourage people to undertake further work, extending the account in delicacy.

One thing I am very keen on is to make sure that we have a dialogue between the analysis of texts and the description of the system. I am a bit concerned that we should not lose the momentum of the huge effort of describing languages. We should not fall into the trap of using existing descriptions without feeding back into them. One way of expanding descriptions – of testing descriptions – is certainly manual text analysis. This is very important for the future of description. That complements what happens in corpus linguistics because in manual text analysis you have to exhaust a text in terms of the description, in a way you never do in purely corpus-based work. I think methodologically people have missed the importance of sustained extensive manual text analysis based on systemic descrip-tions, partly because they have tended to focus only on the contrast between "corpus-based" and "corpus-driven" description. I would like to see much more manual text analysis in the service of language description, and for researchers to use it when they turn to languages that have not previously been described at all, or not previously been described in systemic functional terms.

What has the work on language typology, and languages other than English, meant for SFL?

I think it has been very useful. There have been obvious pay-offs like the ability to do text/discourse analysis in more communities operating with different languages. I think that is incredibly important. But you can also relate it to an account of the main activities in linguistics, and I have modelled these as a hierarchy of difficulty in the sense of how much linguistic territory you have to cover in a given type of activity. The first step is text analysis; what do you do in text analysis? Well, you engage with a relatively small domain of whatever texts you have, and you are given a description, which means that you operate in terms of the description you have been given, and then you relate that to text instances. The next step is description; that means you have to move up the cline of instantiation, you have to engage with a potential, or at least a sub-potential – that means you have to engage with much more of language – as you have to have lots of texts in order to make descriptive generalizations. If you are really describing a language, you have to have some notion of a reference corpus. So what you are responsible for is much bigger. The next step is contrast and comparison; meaning you have to take in still more: not just a description of one language, but descriptions of a number of languages. The scope is thus extended quite considerably, and generalizing this would be typology as generalized comparison. This is the way that people like Michael Halliday, Jeffrey Ellis and Ian Catford thought about language typology from the 1950s into the 1960s. Yet another step is theory. When you construct theory – and in our case it is a theory of language as a human system – in principle, you have to have detailed descriptions of a considerable number of typologically different languages to ensure that the theory has general validity and appliability. You cannot have a theory of a system such as theme, transitivity, mood or appraisal based on English or on another particular language; such systems are posited as descriptions, not as theories.

We have to be very humble about the development of theory, given the relatively small number of languages we have actually engaged with in any kind of detail and depth; you need to be fairly adamant that you need to get your theory right. When Halliday worked on the development of the theory, he could draw on all the work that had been done in different corners of the world – certainly the Firthian engagement with different languages – you might say the different languages of the British Empire. You could also say the American anthropological linguistics – sort of what flowed from the European colonization of the Americas and then from the US American colonization of North America, but then also other languages in the Americas. You got this sense of description, and the value of description, and that I think was very important in the early theory-making. Now we can begin to ask questions based on the accumulation of descriptions of different languages and, for example, the work on Norwegian and the work on Danish: these new contributions are very important. One question could be: should Mood-Residue be part of the theory? If you look across different languages and make generalized comparison, you see very clearly that it should not be part of the theory – and it never was, of course. It is part of something you posit in the description of particular languages as you explore the grammar of dialogue. From the work on language typology, we now know that the Mood-Residue structure is actually exotic (cf. Halliday, 1959–60), and it is essentially limited to Germanic languages, and languages that have been in some sort of *Sprachbund* with them – like possibly French.

To me, the development of typological databases and the whole project that in some sense is manifested in and reflected in, but also recorded in, WALS (World Atlas of Language Structures) is very exciting. In the research on typology, I would like to see much more complementarity in work involving automated analysis of large samples of text – what you think of as corpus linguistics – and manual analysis. If we push the work in both ways, very exciting things can be done. And I would also say I think it's time to return to contrastive linguistics in the service of studies in second and foreign language education; we should use the conception of language as a meaning potential and explore a multilingual meaning potential, explore how language learners are learning how to mean in a second or foreign language.

In what way would you say the computer is useful or necessary in language description?

It is the technological part of a potential breakthrough to a modern science of language and other semiotic systems – not the theoretical part, but the technological part. It makes it possible to hear things you cannot hear with the naked ear, and see things you cannot see with the naked eye. And there is the volume of data that it makes possible for us to process. I think that the current technological potential for huge volumes of data, "big data", is theoretically fascinating and important. Again, as an aside, to look at what people are doing elsewhere, outside SFL: Deb Roy and his wife, for example, who are not from linguistics but come from a background of AI, machine learning and cognitive modelling; before they had their first child, they wired up their whole house with video and audio in virtually every room, and when their son was born – and he went from infant to toddler and so on – they recorded his development, so they could trace what they take to be his gradual approximations of saying "water" through the house, and where in the house he engaged with caregivers. This is an extraordinary example of what technology can offer. But technology must be combined with theory, as Galileo did in his investigation of physical systems. If you can combine the technological potential for tracking infants and recording virtually all their interactions with the Hallidayan theory of language development and linguistic insight, I think that would be absolutely explosively powerful: a contextual understanding of learning how to mean, not only in different material settings, but also (and more significantly) in different semiotic contexts as well. So I think colleagues in other disciplines may very well have tools that are much more sophisticated than what we have, but they have not got the linguistic theory that is absolutely essential. The challenge is to dialogue with them and to relate huge volumes of data to sophisticated theory, but I think it is extraordinary what the current and future potential is.

It seems to me that the one person who has given us the key to a truly modern science of, and scientific understanding of, language, and of semiotic systems in general, is indeed Michael Halliday. One central part of this key is his notion of the cline of instantiation that treats language not in terms of dichotomies such as *langue* and *parole* or competence and performance, but as a continuum extending along the cline of instantiation. And you have a way of reasoning about how you connect data at the instance pole to what you theorize as system at the potential pole.

Are there systems on all strata? Are there system-structure cycles on all strata, or do we only find them in lexicogrammar? Can we find them in semantics as well?

Very interesting question and I often think of what Halliday said in the foreword to the book by de Joia and Stenton (*Terms in Systemic Linguistics*, 1980). In his foreword he talks about systemic functional theory as a sort of flexi-model. Heuristically, if you assume that you have axes – the syntagmatic and the paradigmatic, with the paradigmatic as the organizing principle across all strata – then that will push us really to explore the question you have posed, and I think that is a useful kind of push: an invitation to look for more phenomena rather than be content with fewer phenomena. Whether in fact the mode of representation turns out across all strata to be system networks for paradigmatic organization, and function structure for syntagmatic organization, is a separate question, and an important one. Even from our work on lexicogrammar, we know of issues with system networks that do not quite allow us to say what we feel we understand theoretically (as becomes clear in computational modelling; cf. Matthiessen, 1988). One issue is: how do you splice in probability? Another issue is: how do you cope with clines? This comes up in the interpersonal area, certainly. Yet another issue is: how do you cope with logical systems that are to be treated as recursive systems (cf. Bateman, 1989)? I think that nobody has cracked it. In a sense we continue to pretend that networks work because they do up to a point. Now, I personally think it is important to at least try with semantic system networks. With all networks, it is critically important to be explicit about the realizations. Otherwise, you are sort of just hand-waving. I think it is a big challenge to map out a paradigmatic organization of semantics; doing it for context is a huge challenge, certainly. Possibly even bigger, because when you get into context you have to take responsibility for all semiotic systems and also for social systems, and for the question of how you integrate them. And you have to really grapple with what colleagues in anthropology and, to some extent, sociology and social psychology have worked on, for example under the heading of culture. There is lots of work to be done there.

Dialects of SFL

There exist different dialects of systemic functional grammar. Most would know that there are major differences between the Cardiff grammar and the Sydney grammar. How is the Sydney dialect of SFL better than the Cardiff dialect?

You often hear claims that the Cardiff grammar is better than the Sydney grammar, but not the other way around! It is interesting if these are metalinguistic dialects – and indeed people have talked about them in these terms. You could also explore them as metalinguistic registers, meaning that they do somewhat different things. So, if you look at the range of applications that people have used these different models for, I think there are significant differences – and similarities too, of course. One could spend a lot of time dialoguing about similarities and differences – it is important to understand them – and also saying where one is better. I have had some discussion with Robin Fawcett over the decades. I think he would like to have more dialogue, and I acknowledge this. But at the same time I also think that it is very important to dialogue with other folks. I have tried to dialogue with West Coast functionalists, for instance, though I cannot say that my effort has been a success. To some extent I have tried to dialogue with computational linguistics. How many dialogue interfaces is it possible for one scholar or even one group of scholars to maintain? To me, there is often considerable value in looking outside of

SFL for ideas – not only to Cardiff, but outside SFL entirely. I could give a very specific example: I think it is important to look at what people have done in construction grammar. And relate constructions to the continuum between grammar and lexis, showing colleagues working on constructions where they are located in a comprehensive description of a language, bringing out the value of interpreting and modelling them not only structurally but also (and primarily) systemically.

Now, to me, a key difference between the Cardiff grammar and the Sydney grammar is that in Halliday's grammar it is dimensions all the way. I find the relational-dimensional thinking very appealing. It contrasts fundamentally with modular thinking that has been prominent in many different linguistic models and theories since the 1950s, such as different versions of Chomsky's generative linguistics, alternatives to his versions conceived within the broad tradition of generative linguistics (e.g. Relational Grammar, Lexical Functional Grammar, Generalized Phrase Structure Grammar) and also frameworks that are a bit further away (e.g. Functional Grammar, Role and Reference Grammar, Construction Grammar): the "architectures" of these frameworks tend to be represented as modules that are conceived of as components in their own right standing in varied relationships to one another; these architectures look like (informal versions of) software architecture diagrams. In contrast, I think the great power of relational-dimensional thinking is that you have to work out how everything is placed in relation to everything else in terms of a small well-defined set of dimensions, and if you posit something, then you have to see how it relates to other phenomena both in terms of the global dimensions: stratification, instantiation and metafunction, and in terms of the local dimensions: axis, rank and delicacy. The nature of the phenomena modelled in this way is inherent in their relationships, as is clear already in Halliday (1961), brought out by his notion of shunting. This kind of modelling is very productive, and it is a way of testing whether you have thought things through. If I look at the Cardiff model, it seems to me that it is much more like the modular thinking that I am familiar with from various generative approaches.

There is also great value in the holistic thinking that is so prominent with what Halliday has done, where he takes in language in the round, in context and is now relating language to other semiotic systems, and also to systems of lower orders of complexity. He introduced the idea of an ordered typology of systems, and he and I worked on it (e.g. Halliday & Matthiessen, 2006; Halliday, 2005; Matthiessen, 2007), and it seems to me to be very valuable. What we do is to ask: if you have a systemic functional account of language, what does it mean? Well, it means that you try to theorize language as a higher order – a fourth order – semiotic system. From this follows a whole research paradigm, where you need to ask: what does language inherit by virtue of also being a social system (as well as a semiotic system)? And by being a biological system and a physical system? What do systems of different orders have in common? How does complexity emerge in systems of different orders? Questions like these constitute a very productive long-term research paradigm, as work by Chris Cléirigh has shown, and one that is an invitation to transdisciplinarity.

I also find the deep functional meaning orientation of Halliday's grammar very attractive: if you posit something in the lexicogrammatical description, then that description is also a part of the explanation; you produce a thick description that will also allow you to explain it. This distinguishes SFL from many other traditions. I talked before about the changing intellectual academic context and if you look at the things Halliday has been working on, and often introduced first in the 1960s, there are so many areas where in the 1960s, he was just plain "weird" – really weird – from the standpoint of mainstream linguistics at the time. Now, 50 years later, he is not so weird any longer! I mean: there is much more resonance in various current approaches with his positions – positions that were previously regarded as absurd. Take a simple thing like the continuity between grammar and lexis; virtually nobody would have thought of that in the 1960s except Halliday – generative linguists had basically taken over Bloomfield's view of the lexicon. Or take things like the exploration of phenomena through the corpus and the value of probability. A language description has to be comprehensive, and that has been the goal for lots of systemic functional work, and Fawcett, Gordon Tucker and their colleagues and research students have, of course, done extraordinary work to expand the description. But at the same time the description has to be of explanatory nature. It seems to me that if you take a number of key points, then Halliday's account is much "weirder" in the sense of departing from the established view, whereas Fawcett's account is much closer to the tradition in some sense. Take for example what you do with hypotaxis versus embedding: Fawcett's position is closer to the received one, e.g. with respect to the embedding of complement clauses, while Halliday has this "weird" notion that you need to differentiate between embedding (downranking) and hypotaxis. Now if you explore work on grammaticalization, there are so many phenomena that can be interpreted in Hallidayan terms, for example the move from a clause complex/verbal group complex to a verbal group; such clines that one can see in his work resonate strongly with the growing evidence from grammaticalization supported by discourse-based investigations of lexicogrammar (cf. Matthiessen & Thompson, 1988, on Halliday's notion of hypotaxis in relation to the semantic organization of discourse – an account that has been picked up in work on grammaticalization). What I am saying is that the description has to have a built-in potential for explanation.

Then you can add the range of applications that depend critically on Halliday's account: to me the work of language development by Michael Halliday, Clare Painter, Jane Torr, Beverly Derewianka and others is so important; and you are able to link Hallidayan accounts to an understanding of deep human history (cf. Matthiessen, 2004; Halliday, 2010). Of course, I have always been fascinated by language typology, and also here, the Hallidayan account is very inspirational.

These are all considerations that are typically not a part of the discussion of Cardiff versus Sydney grammar. But they are part of my considerations. I think there is value in saying "There aren't many folks like Michael Halliday who adopted these 'weird' conceptions – why not give them some space, why not explore them? There are enough people working on mainstream accounts." I think that it is worth the effort, and it seems to me that there has been enormous pay-off already.

Context and genre

Another diversity is between a Martin way of doing things, and a Matthiessen/ Halliday way of doing things – to you, what are the major differences?

The "Sydney School" has come to mean what Martin and his group have done with the genre model, with the description of appraisal in English, with the development of a language-based pedagogy, with multimodality – within SFL – and some people are not so happy about the use of the term because they say: "we have been working in Sydney, but we are not part of the Sydney School"; and people outside Australia often think, quite naturally, that everything that is undertaken in SFL in Sydney is part of the "Sydney School". I think we must understand the naming of the "Sydney School" in strategic terms: in order to survive during a very difficult extended period within Sydney University as a linguistics department and as an SFL group, Martin and his colleagues had to adopt various strategies to convince senior management that what they were doing was unique and very valuable, and therefore worth preserving and investing in. Probably part of the context was to talk about the "Sydney School". People have asked me: "what about the Hong Kong school?" I answered "no way", because personally I do not think that these labels are very helpful – actually, quite the contrary (for one thing, they tend to obscure or efface rich contributions from other parts of the world that may not, unfortunately, be on people's radar unless they are working there). Now, I think it is helpful within SFL to have a sort of flexi-model to be able to explore different ways of setting the variables that the general theory provides us with in a heuristic, exploratory way. My sense of it is that in the 1980s when Martin and Joan Rothery, Frances Christie and others were really struggling to develop an account that would be a tremendous resource in education, much more work was needed on semantics and context. In a sense, the interim report on the extraordinarily productive 1980s work was Martin's 1992 book *English Text*. A more recent account of a number of key theoretical issues is Bednarek & Martin (2010), and Martin & Rose (2012) provide an overview of the educational linguistic work in the Sydney School.

When Martin and his colleagues were exploring the questions of context, ideology, genre and register, they were doing it in terms of one dimension: the hierarchy of stratification. They asked how genre is related to culture and ideology and so on, and the answer was explored in terms of locations along the hierarchy of stratification; so in that particular sense, the modelling was one-dimensional. I think if you go back to much earlier work by Michael Halliday, like *Explorations in the Functions of Language* (Halliday, 1973), where he talks about "potential" and "actual", and about "can mean" / "means", there is another dimension that is also highly relevant, and that is the cline of instantiation. So I think, yes, it is true of

Michael Halliday, Ruqaiya Hasan and a number of us, that we have not stratified context, but instead, in our work, context is, just like language, extended along the cline of instantiation; it is extended from the context of culture at the potential pole of the cline via institutional and subcultural domains and situation types to contexts of situation at the instance pole (see, e.g. Halliday, 2002). So, different contextual patterns have different locations along the cline of instantiation; interpreted contextually, genre corresponds roughly to the range of the cline of instantiation explored under the heading of situation type (for further discussion, see Matthiessen, 2013). This is a way of exploring the same territory, but in a two-dimensional way. I think in later work, Martin and others have also used the cline of instantiation productively (see, e.g. Bednarek & Martin, 2010), but if you go back to the sense of differences, I think that you have a source of origin in the 1980s.

In recent publications about context, you have a circle with different fields of activity (see Figure 2.1). Is this where you place purpose in your methodological approach to text analysis, or where would you place purpose?

The question about purpose goes back to discussions around 1980–81. Purpose came up in discussions with Jim Martin, as he and his team were working on the notion of genre – drawing on Michael Gregory's concept of functional tenor; but in the particular environment I was working in, at the Information Sciences Institute, purpose was even more prominent, because we were trying to develop a model of how to generate text by computer and the notion of the purpose or goal of a text was central to the planning of a text to be generated.

FIGURE 2.1 Description of fields of activity within the field parameter of context

From the 1970s, there were these different models of planning and goal pursuit, and these models were quite explicit and detailed – one influential model was designed by Earl Sacerdoti (e.g. Sacerdoti, 1977) and it had to do with the sequencing of goals that comes from the logic of the activity. I think one of his examples was: "If your goal is to paint a room, how do you work out a plan in the pursuit of this goal?" And there are details, for example: "You paint the ceiling before you paint the floor." Why? Because if you paint the ceiling first, paint will drip down on the floor, so to avoid having to paint it again, you don't paint the floor first. Another line of exploration of goals and plans in AI came from Roger Schank and his colleagues, their work on scripts and semantic representation (e.g. Schank & Abelson, 1977). I think there is reason to take the notion of scripts more seriously than it has been in SFL – you could say theoretically it seems a bit naïve and so on, but instead let's look at where the value lies: maybe not so much in the theory, but the value may lie in the attempt to work something out as an explicit representation. And then I like to translate findings into systemic functional terms, since I am not very fond of eclectic models – Frankenstein models where you are not quite sure how the parts fit together – but once the insights have been translated into SFL, I know how they fit into the overall model.

How is this related to goals and purpose? Well, one of the insights that came through in the work on goal pursuit was a distinction between what was called achievement goals and maintenance goals. Achievement goals are like the Sacerdoti way of painting a room, where you say that there is a desirable state that has not been achieved, and then you map out a plan, and at the execution of the final act or activity, you achieve the goal, and you have brought about a change of state. Maintenance goals are goals that can never be achieved – you have to keep working at them. Now, if you then translate this into systemic functional terms, achievement goals are field-based goals – meaning you have some activity, and you can say that you have a starting point, and then you have the steps of the activity, and the end point. The context of instructing somebody in a procedure has very clearly got achievement goals. Maintenance goals are tenor-based goals; they have to do with values, with interpersonal relations. These are things you have to keep working at – they are never achieved. Wonderful examples come from the work on casual conversation by Diana Slade and Suzanne Eggins (see Eggins & Slade, 2005; Eggins, 1990; Slade, 1996); Eggins on dinner table conversation among close friends, Slade on gossip also among close friends, but also in the workplace. It is so clear that what drives casual conversation in general, and what they have been looking at in particular, are maintenance goals. People keep talking; people keep sharing experiences and values. People keep negotiating relationships, acquaint-anceships, workmateships or friendships. From the point of view of tenor, people have to maintain what we in *Construing Experience through Meaning* (Halliday & Matthiessen, 2006) call interactant models: people have to create, and keep up to date, models of one another, and that includes knowing important events – and also unimportant ones – and the values attached to them. People have a sense of both similarity and difference; difference is like the fuel, the energy of the friend-ship – it sort of keeps it going. In other words, I think there are goals that derive from field, and there are goals that derive from tenor; and, in different contexts, one may be more prominent than the other.

So when you place for example narrating, arguing, describing, explaining and persuading, as part of different fields of activity in model of field, you could also see them in tenor?

Yes, I think so. Coming back to genre, my sense of genre is that it is not a separate phenomenon. There is a terminological problem in the changing sense of the term register (see, e.g. Matthiessen, 2013); I mean register was a functional variety of language in terms of what you do relative to settings of contextual variables – field, tenor and mode (e.g. Halliday, McIntosh & Strevens, 1964; Halliday, 1978). A particular setting of field, tenor and mode values is what Hasan has called "con-textual configuration". I tend to not use "configuration" because it is primarily associated with the syntagmatic axis (as the experiential mode of expression), so I prefer "contextual setting", in the sense of the setting of values of contextual vari-ables. But then Martin exported the term register up to context, and took register to mean field, tenor and mode, rather than the functional variation that lives in the environment of varying settings of values of field, tenor and mode (see Martin, 1992). And that then became register. And then he said: "we need something that coordinates these different field, tenor and mode values", so he posited genre as something higher, as something that would handle recurrent combinations of field, tenor and mode values.

There are just a couple of problems with this change. One problem is that the purposes are functionally diversified, not unified as in genre theory. So I think there is insight into exploring them in terms of field, tenor and mode: it is certainly clear that achievement goals derive from field and maintenance goals derive from tenor; and we should let goal-pursuit modellers know about mode! Another prob-lem is that, until someone has worked out a very explicit model of how genre actually relates to field, tenor and mode, I would hesitate to reify the stratification of genre and "register" (in Martin's contextual sense) in the model. In fact, let me go further: when we probe them, I think genre and "register" collapse into one contextual stratum (see Matthiessen, 2013).

In Martin's work, there is supposed to be an account of certain combinations of genres occurring together with certain combinations of field, tenor and mode. I think there are other ways of accounting for co-occurrence. To me, genre dissolves; genre and "register" collapse into one contextual stratum as I just put it. The clo-sest to genre seems to me to be situation types, which are somewhere mid-region on the cline of instantiation, between context of culture and context of situation. I am more comfortable with that, because there is tendency for genre to become synonymous with text structure. I think it is important to conceive of contextual structure – structure of situation type as opposed to text structure – keeping the two clearly distinct, and to talk about the realization here: genre structure is realized by text structure. The confusion is not Martin's fault – he has kept them clearly distinct – but the way people have talked about genre, they tend to blur the stratal distinction a bit.

Now, Kazuhiro Teruya and I have played around with fields of activity, i.e. the activity part of field, the goings-on, as we say (e.g. Matthiessen & Teruya, 2014). We call them socio-semiotic processes because they can be social and/or semiotic – if they are semiotic they are also social, but there are ones that are primarily behaviour, so only social. If you look at these, you can actually take all that fantastic, very rich work that comes from the description of genres and genre agnation in the "Sydney School", and you can sort the genres into contexts characterized by different fields of activity: some are expounding, some are exploring, some sharing, some enabling and so on. You can read this in different ways. I think (recalling a conversation with him in New Orleans) that Martin reads this as saying what we have here are very general genres – expounding and so on. My reading is different. My reading is that the account of genre in these terms is very much field-oriented and there is a kind of complementary account based on tenor, and another one based on mode; but this reading obviously means that "genre" is in fact not a higher stratum within context, rather it is a field-based view of context (see further Matthiessen, 2013).

Martin says that there is too much clause semantics in SFL. What do you think about this?

I would say: "not too much clause semantics, but too little text semantics" – meaning, we need all the clause semantics there is and lots more actually, but it needs to be complemented. One way of putting it is in terms of Halliday's trinocularity. Certainly a lot of semantics has been developed by pushing up from the meaning-oriented functional descriptions of the grammar; grammatical accounts have been restated in semantic terms, and we can characterize this approach to the description of semantics as being "from below" (bottom-up). I think it is important to develop semantic descriptions "from above" (top-down), from context, as well, but I do not actually see much of that happening: truly locating oneself in context and thinking about semantics strategically, thinking in terms of context, but also in terms of other systems, including sensory motor systems – sort of semantics as strategies for transforming what is not meaning into meaning. A sense of semantics as an inter-level (see Halliday, 1973). I think it is doable, and I think the work by John Bateman is very exciting: e.g. in Bremen, where he has worked with engineers in robotics on a semantic model of space (e.g. Bateman et al., 2010). We need much more of that kind of research. That would be truly coming in from outside, or at least it would involve dialoguing with external accounts. So, I think, at least as far as accounts of semantics are concerned, we have to find a way to make them as detailed and explicit – as "hanging together" – as accounts of lexicogrammar; if we are serious about our understanding of the centrality of language, if, as Martin said to me over three decades ago "I don't think we think, we mean" – and that is a very important insight. If that is the case – if reasoning and thinking are really semantic processes, semiotic processes (cf. Halliday & Matthiessen, 2006) – then we have to have accounts of semantics that are explicit enough to support this. And accounts that can live up to these demands on the semantic system, in the kind of ecological contextualized understanding of what meaning making is all about. There has been a certain tendency among SFL researchers not to value explicitness and modelling of this kind, and this has been detrimental to progress in work on semantics and context.

Meaning

So, is meaning the same as knowing, or do we know something that is outside the realm of language?

I think we do, but what Halliday and I are trying to suggest in *Construing Experience through Meaning* (Halliday & Matthiessen, 2006) is that these are not essentially different phenomena, but rather different metaphors for the same phenomenon: different ways of thinking about the same phenomenon. Certainly, I think, you can "know" in other semiotic systems, but I do have the sense that knowing and thinking are semiotic processes. From this follows a semiotic understanding of sensory motor systems: they are embodied, they are interactive, and they may also involve other people: we learn to perceive, we learn to move with other people.

We certainly know things in other semiotic systems as well. I think probably people vary in terms of the nature of the complementarity of the semiotic systems they operate with, but obviously there has been research into image schemata and so on, and I think mathematics is a way of knowing. It is obvious that these semiotic systems differ considerably in terms of the extent to which we share them across the human family. Some are very specialized in terms of human cultures and the division of labour within a given culture, while others are much more general: language is a very general kind of semiotic system.

Mode and multi-semiotic work

Your remarks on different and multiple semiotic systems lead us to the issue of multimodality. Let's start with a fundamental question: how would you define the term mode?

Well, I like the term that Eija Ventola uses, and I have adopted it – she talks about multi-semiotic systems. There are a couple of reasons for this. One is that "mode" has come to have so many senses: it is one of the variables in context, but we also have modes of meaning, modes of expression; and we have it in linguistic description – we talk about modes of a verb. Another is that it is helpful to be explicit about the theoretical interpretation of "modalities" as semiotic systems in their own right. And that, to me, then, invites consideration of semiotic systems themselves. One thing I would like to see is much more of thinking about different kinds of semiotic system in some sense of a typology of semiotic systems. Drawing on Edelman (1992), Halliday has made a distinction between primary semiotic systems and higher order semiotic systems, language being the prototype of higher-order ones; this was designed to deal with the ontogenesis of language, where protolanguage is primary, and adult language is higher order. This may not be the only way of typologizing semiotic systems, but it seems important to keep such typologies as part of the core agenda for thinking about semiotic systems and multi-semiotic systems, as well as with the multi-semiotic in the special sense of different semiotic systems working alongside each other in the process of meaning making, which of course people have turned to more and more over the last decade or decade and a half.

Now, in multi-semiotic work, I would plead for more detailed, much more explicit accounts. Of course, it is important to focus on the content plane, but I think we need to work on the expression plane, too, and work on the affordances of the materiality of what has been co-opted as expression plane. It seems to me there is a lot of interesting work to be done there. For example: What are the affordances of olfactory semiotics? I do not know if anyone has worked on it. What is the difference in the expression plane between what is available to us visually, and what is available to us through our noses? One difference is obviously temporal in nature, which I would expect would lead to some differences in the nature meaning; visually, we can cope with very rapid change but not in terms of our olfactory sense, because we cannot get rid of fragrances and smells very quickly – they tend to linger. I would like to see more work of the kind that Theo van Leeuwen and others have done on colours and on music, and other expressive resources. In short, we need accounts of the expressive resources of different semiotic systems that are as explicit and comprehensive as the accounts of the phonological systems of different languages.

Going into the content plane – there are discussions on whether the content plane is stratified in other modes or other semiotic systems than language. Can we find differences between semantic and lexicogrammatical resources in, for example, images?

This is a key question. Sometimes it is useful to be challenging just to be proven wrong – and/or to get work done – so I will throw this out as a challenge: there has been lots of fantastic, very rich work on the content plane of different semiotic systems, but let me say this, I am not aware of anybody that has done the work that would allow us to decide about the stratification of the content planes of semiotic systems other than language. In order to decide whether we need to stratify it or not in the description of a given semiotic system, we need accounts with the kind of explicitness and detail we have in the accounts of languages.

If you look at the development of language ontogenetically, you get quite a clear picture of when the stratification of the content plane starts, and I think one could use this ontogenetic perspective to reason about the issue of the stratification of the content plane of other semiotic systems. Now, if you take protolanguage, one of the interesting things about the description of protolanguage (for example Halliday's case study of Nigel as well as Clare Painter's and Jane Torr's case studies) is that protolanguage is inherently multimodal – meaning simply that the expression plane involves either vocalization or gesture. Now, in Halliday's analysis, there is a tendency for vocalization to go with different meanings from those realized by gestures. Obviously, we would need more case studies to see how general this tendency is, but my point is simply this: in the transition from protolanguage to post-infancy adult language, what happens is that what was one system – protolanguage – is split into at least two systems – language and gesture – opening up the possibility for them to become more independently variable. If one can go back to that and reason about it, I think that that would be helpful in describing and modelling language and gesture as distinct but related semiotic systems. And then one could – not to be slavishly always modelling on language – find a way of reasoning about gesture itself, that would shed light on the question of whether the content plane of gesture is stratified or not, if that is the right way of thinking about it. And this could work for the interpretation of other semiotic systems as well. Scholars have talked about the "grammar" of semiotic systems other than language, like the "grammar of film"; but here we must be very careful and be clear about what is meant by grammar: John Bateman has shown that it does not make sense to talk about the "grammar of film" with "grammar" in a technical, scientific sense as the second of two content strata.

In the development of multimodal studies, I think it would have been helpful to start with face-to-face interaction, sorting out the theoretical foundations in terms of the "embodied" semiotic systems that constitute the resources of all meaning-making persons from a very young age. Now, a number of studies started, of course, with multisemiosis in terms of the printed page, but if we can study multisemiosis as it is embodied in the spontaneous "performance" of face-to-face interaction, then we can explore the origins of multisemiosis developmentally.

Another issue in semiotic systems other than language is the degree to which the rank scales on the content plane and the expression plane are congruent or incongruent with each other, related to what André Martinet called double articulation; is that an insight into differences among semiotic systems? Think about it in relation to drawing, for example: to what extent is it possible to operate on the expression plane in drawing, without at the same time representing experience? Once you have an object on the expression plane in a drawing, is it content free? Like phonemes such as *a*, *i*, *o* in principle are. There is also the question of independent variation across the metafunctions. In language, we have the Saussurean line of arbitrariness between the content of different metafunctions and the mode of expression (although the line is subject to natural correlations, as first brought out by Halliday, 1979), so the metafunctions can be mapped onto each other very independently. But what about other semiotic systems? Again, we can think about visual semiotics. If you take a traditional landscape painting: you have beautiful scenery; you will maybe have a family picnicking; you will have rays of the sun coming down, illuminating them; they are likely to figure somewhere central in the composition and so on. Now, representationally (ideationally), we know what this means: picnic, sunny day, out somewhere in nature and so on, but do we know what it means textually? And what about interpersonal meaning? We could say that there is a sense of warmth in terms of the hue of colours and so on and that the family is made textually prominent, but these different metafunctional contributions come as a package; it is not so easy to vary the metafunctional meanings independently: how would you achieve it on a typical Hong Kong day – totally grey, no differentiation and light across the landscape, because it is just foggy and grey? Such questions are fundamental issues that would need working out – and maybe they have been – but these are sort of the questions I would ask as part of understanding semiotic systems according to some sense of typology of semiotic systems.

SFL and language teaching

We will now briefly touch upon SFL and language teaching. SFL has had an extensive impact in schools. Why do you think it is so? What are the strengths of the SFL approach to primary school teaching?

Educational linguistics is not an area where I have been very active; I have labelled myself as a resource person for educators and educational linguists, someone producing accounts that are hopefully useful to them. I think the impact you refer to is due to a combination of factors. One is clearly that the engagement with education issues was very central from early on; it was very much part of what those who were members of the linguistic group in the British communist party were concerned with. They were concerned with what Halliday has now found a term for: appliable linguistics – meaning that linguistics, just like other branches of science and scholarship, could actually have an engineering application, address problems in the community and make a positive difference to the human condition. It was part of the thinking from the beginning that SFL should be scientific in the theoretical sense, but also in the engineering sense and, as Halliday said somewhere along the line, there should be more emphasis on the engineering sense of science than the philosophy sense of science. In that sense, it was appliable, and so it should be appliable to the education context. I think there are other factors. One is that it was a time when people were fed up with traditional grammar: traditional grammar was thrown out of the curriculum because it was not good enough; it did not meet the need. Another factor is the emphasis on education in many places after the Second World War.

Later on in the 1980s, people came from education with real expertise in education and worked with Martin, Halliday and Hasan. I am thinking of people like

Joan Rothery, Frances Christie, Beverly Derewianka, Geoff Williams, Len Unsworth and a number of other people. These are people who worked specifically on what got identified as educational linguistics. So you had very good conditions for a dialogue between different areas of expertise, and you had people who understood the important and essential move from basic research to the development of materials to implementation. I think understanding these phases is very important, also for other areas. Then you had also some luck with people at the more administrative levels in schools, who were sympathetic and understood the need for something new. So, various factors came together, and you need several factors to come together at the same time for new initiatives to succeed. Change needs to be facilitated trinocularly – both from below and from above but also from round-about. Top-down reforms tend to be doomed to fail, and grassroots movements need help from above. Effective change requires trinocular resonance.

One thing that is interesting to me is that genre pedagogy is gradually being taken up in second-language teaching. One person who is really moving this forward is Heidi Byrnes at Georgetown University. To me it would be one of the important developments now to take what we have learned from the genre-based curriculum and make that a model for development in second-language teaching. If you look at the Sydney School of genre, what is so potent and powerful is that it is part of the total model; it is part of a holistic model. If you take other traditions, they are more standalone, and of course you can do a lot with them, but what you cannot do is to have a holistic hookup with all the other aspects of language in context and other semiotic systems. I would, incidentally, say the same about purpose-built frameworks, for example critical linguistics and critical discourse analysis. I think SFL is so much more powerful than these precisely because it is not purpose built – it has a much wider range of applications, and to me that is so important, because then you can get cross-fertilization.

The future

A look into the future: what will be the main challenges for SFL and social semiotics in the next decade or so?

I think there is a combination of challenge and excitement (cf. Matthiessen, 2009). I think there is obviously much positive going on, both continued development of existing areas of strength – areas where there is a continuity going back to the 1960s such as the tremendous developments in educational linguistics – and fresh development of new areas, sometimes unexpected and opportunistic, in a good sense. Other areas that are more recent, but which now have an established history are the multi-semiotic work, the cumulative effect of the language descriptions, knowing more about different languages, and also reaching other communities in terms of what one can do with appliable descriptions – moving into new areas like healthcare communication work, research that Di Slade and others have done, and forensic linguistics. All these developments are very positive, and many of them involve professions where language is a key resource, as in Slade's recently established International Research Centre for Communication in Healthcare (IRCCH).

In the 1950s and into the 1960s, systemic functional linguists were ridiculed because SFL was seen as impure linguistics, and in the 1960s, to be taken seriously by the emerging mainstream in "theoretical linguistics", you had to be theoretical in their sense, and anything that smacked of application was a "no-no", and there was lots of funding for theoretical linguistics. Theoretical linguistics and applied linguistics drifted apart. Now the situation has changed quite dramatically, both in terms of funding sources, and in terms of how universities have to justify themselves, so now what was seen as a weakness has become a strength. And there is financial value put on appliability in a number of areas, and I think that it is very important to work with that. What worries me is that you get very few people then working on language description, even English. I think that is a potential tragedy. If there is no new investment in this, what will we apply in the future?

Another consideration is the location of SFL relative to other disciplines in universities, and possibly also other institutions. One of the strengths of SFL has been to operate outside of mainstream linguistics. This has been a real asset, because it has enriched the influences, engagement with scholars, potential to do good, areas of application and so on. But what will happen in the next ten years? We need to ensure that people continue to do descriptions of grammar, people continue to worry about transitivity, and people take up descriptions of new languages, like the work on Norwegian, the work on Danish and so on. These tasks are challenging, and sometimes much harder than doing a CDA (critical discourse analysis) of something that is very visible. But I think they are very important. Who will be doing that kind of SFL research on the core systems?

In the Humanities in general, there is a sense that research is now driven in a different way, and it depends on many things, including funding sources, and to what extent research is project-based, lab-based and so on. If you look at various project- and lab-based disciplines, like computer science, construction engineering and electrical engineering, there is much more of an expectation that when new PhD students come in, they will probably be assigned a PhD topic. It will not be something that through agony they think up for themselves, as tends to happen in the Humanities. I think we have a sense – those of us coming from a different era – that the last thing we should do is to impose a topic on somebody, because developing a topic of research is such an important part of learning, of becoming an apprentice, of becoming a researcher. But at the same time, things are changing. And I wonder if we should collectively have a much clearer sense of what our research agenda is: what are the areas that really need work? What would actually fill holes in our knowledge? What would make a difference?

So it is the usual mixture of being excited and being concerned, and one thing that I think is now possible, not only in SFL but in linguistics in general, is the breakthrough to modern science. Maybe we have already broken through? I do not quite think so, but as I noted above, Halliday is the one linguist who has given us the key. So I think it is a very exciting time from that point of view, too.

References

Bateman, John, 1989. Dynamic systemic-functional grammar: a new frontier. *Word* 40(1–2): 263–87.

Bateman, John A., Joana Hois, Robert Ross & Thora Tenbrink, 2010. A linguistic ontology of space for natural language processing. *Artificial Intelligence* 174: 1027–71.

Bednarek, Monika & J.R. Martin, (2010). *New discourse on language: functional perspectives on multimodality, identity, and affiliation.* London: Continuum.

Christian, David, 2004. *Maps of time: an introduction to big history.* Berkeley, Los Angeles & London: University of California Press.

Deacon, Terrence, 1997. *The symbolic species: the co-evolution of language and the human brain.* Harmondsworth: Penguin Books.

Edelman, Gerald, 1992. *Bright air, brilliant fire: on the matter of the mind.* New York: Basic Books.

Eggins, Suzanne, 1990. *Conversational structure: a systemic-functional analysis of interpersonal and logical meaning in multiparty sustained talk.* Department of Linguistics, University of Sydney: PhD thesis.

Eggins, Suzanne & Diana Slade, 2005. *Analysing casual conversation.* London: Equinox.

Halliday, M.A.K, 1959–60. Typology and the exotic. Combination of two lectures, one delivered at the Linguistics Association Conference, Hull, in May 1959, the other to the St. Andrews Linguistic Society, in May 1960. In: M.A.K. Halliday & Angus McIntosh, 1966. *Patterns of language: papers in general, descriptive and applied linguistics.* London: Longman, pp. 165–82.

——, 1961. Categories of the theory of grammar. *Word* 17(3): 242–92. Reprinted in Halliday, M.A.K, 2002. *On grammar.* Volume 1 of Collected Works of M.A.K. Halliday. Edited by Jonathan J. Webster. London & New York: Continuum, pp. 37–94.

——, 1973. *Explorations in the Functions of Language.* London: Edward Arnold.

——, 1978. *Language as social semiotic: the social interpretation of language and meaning.* London: Edward Arnold.

——, 1979. Modes of meaning and modes of expression: types of grammatical structure and their determination by different semantic functions. In: D.J. Allerton, Edward Carney & David Holdcroft (eds.), *Function and context in linguistic analysis: a Festschrift for William Haas.* Cambridge: Cambridge University Press, pp. 57–79. Reprinted in Halliday, M.A.K, 2002. *On grammar.* Volume 1 of Collected Works of M.A.K. Halliday. Edited by Jonathan J. Webster. London & New York: Continuum, pp. 196–218.

——, 1984. Language as code and language as behaviour: a systemic-functional interpretation of the nature and ontogenesis of dialogue. In: M.A.K. Halliday, Robin P. Fawcett, Sydney Lamb & Adam Makkai (eds.), *The semiotics of language and culture.* London: Frances Pinter. Volume 1: pp. 3–35. Reprinted in Halliday, M.A.K, 2003. *On Language and Linguistics.* Volume 3 of Collected Works of M.A.K. Halliday. Edited by Jonathan Webster. London & New York: Continuum, pp. 226–50.

——, 2002. Computing meanings: some reflections on past experience and present prospects. In: Guowen Huang & Zongyan Wang (eds.), *Discourse and Language Functions.* Shanghai: Foreign Language Teaching and Research Press, pp. 3–25. Reprinted in M.A. K. Halliday, 2005. *Computational and quantitative studies.* Volume 6 in the Collected Works of M.A.K. Halliday, edited by Jonathan Webster. London & New York: Continuum, pp. 239–67.

——, 2005. On matter and meaning: the two realms of human experience. *Linguistics and the Human Sciences* 1(1): 59–82.

——2010. Language evolving: some systemic functional reflections on the history of meaning. Manuscript of plenary given at ISFC 37, UBC Vancouver, Canada, July 2010. Published as Chapter 16 of Halliday, M.A.K, 2013. *Halliday in the 21st century*. Volume 11 in the Collected Works of M.A.K. Halliday, edited by Jonathan J. Webster. London: Bloomsbury Academic.

Halliday, M.A.K. & Ruqaiya Hasan, 1976. *Cohesion in English*. London: Longman.

Halliday, M.A.K., Angus McIntosh & Peter Strevens, 1964. *The linguistic sciences and language teaching*. London: Longman.

Halliday, M.A.K. & Christian M.I.M. Matthiessen, 2006. *Construing experience through meaning: a language-based approach to cognition*. London & New York: Continuum.

Martin, J.R., 1992. *English text: system and structure*. Amsterdam: Benjamins.

Martin, J.R. & David Rose, 2012. *Learning to Write, Reading to Learn: Genre, Knowledge and Pedagogy in the Sydney School* (Equinox Textbooks & Surveys in Linguistics). London: Equinox.

Matthiessen, Christian M.I.M., 1988. Representational issues in systemic functional grammar. In: James D. Benson & William S. Greaves (eds.), *Systemic Functional perspectives on Discourse*. Norwood, NJ: Ablex, pp. 136–75.

——, 1993. The object of study in cognitive science in relation to its construal and enactment in language. In: *Language as Cultural Dynamic* (Special issue of Cultural Dynamics) VI (1–2): 187–243.

——, 1995. *Lexicogrammatical cartography: English systems*. Tokyo: International Language Sciences Publishers.

——, 1998. Construing processes of consciousness: from the commonsense model to the uncommonsense model of cognitive science. In: J.R. Martin & Robert Veel (eds.), *Reading science: critical and functional perspectives on discourses of science*. London: Routledge, pp. 327–57.

——, 2004. The evolution of language: a systemic functional exploration of phylogenetic phases. In: Geoff Williams & Annabelle Lukin (eds.), *Language development: functional perspectives on evolution and ontogenesis*. London: Continuum, pp. 45–90.

——, 2007. The "architecture" of language according to systemic functional theory: developments since the 1970s. In: Ruqaiya Hasan, Christian M.I.M. Matthiessen & Jonathan Webster (eds.), *Continuing discourse on language*. Volume 2. London: Equinox, pp. 505–61.

——, 2009. Ideas and new directions. In: M.A.K. Halliday & Jonathan J. Webster (eds.), *A companion to systemic functional linguistics*. London & New York: Continuum, pp. 12–58.

——, 2013. Modelling context and register: the long-term project of registerial cartography. Manuscript of book chapter submitted to Leila Barbara & Sara Cabral (eds.), *Teoria Sistêmico-Funcional para brasileiros* (Systemic Functional Theory for Brazilians). PPGL: Programa de Pós-Graduação em Letras. Universidade Federal de Santa Maria – UFSM: Santa Maria, Brazil.

Matthiessen, Christian M.I.M. & Kazuhiro Teruya, 2014. Registerial hybridity: indeterminacy among fields of activity. In: Donna Miller & Paul Bayley (eds.), *Permeable contexts and hybrid discourses*. London: Equinox.

Matthiessen, Christian M.I.M. & Sandra A. Thompson, 1988. The structure of discourse and "subordination". In: John Haiman & Sandra A. Thompson (eds.), *Clause combining in grammar and discourse*. Amsterdam: Benjamins, pp. 275–329.

Sacerdoti, Earl D., 1977. *Structure for Plans and Behaviour*. Amsterdam: Elsevier.

Schank, Roger C. & Robert P. Abelson, 1977. *Scripts, plans, goals and understanding: an inquiry into human knowledge structures*. Hillsdale, NJ: Lawrence Erlbaum.

Slade, Diana M., 1996. *The texture of casual conversation in English*. University of Sydney: PhD thesis.

Steels, Luc, 1998. Synthesizing the origins of language and meaning using coevolution, self-organization and level formation. In: James R. Hurford, Michael Studdert-Kennedy & Chris Knight (eds.), *Approaches to the evolution of language: social and cognitive bases*. Cambridge: Cambridge University Press, pp. 384–404.

Trevarthen, Colwyn, 1987. Sharing making sense: intersubjectivity and the making of an infant's meaning. In: Ross Steele & Terry Threadgold (ed.), *Language topics. Essays in honour of Michael Halliday.* Amsterdam: Benjamins, pp. 177–99.

Varela, Francisco J., Evan Thompson & Eleanor Rosch, 1991. *The embodied mind: cognitive science and human experience.* Cambridge, MA: The MIT Press.

Williams, Geoff, 2005. Language, brain, culture. *Linguistics and the Human Sciences* 1(3): 147–50.

3

JIM R. MARTIN

Background

How were you introduced to social semiotics?

I will start back in Canada. I did my BA at Glendon College, at York University in Toronto. Glendon was a small bilingual college (English and French), especially designed for a cohort of students who would become civil servants, diplomats, politicians and the like. I was at that time very inspired by Pierre Trudeau, our prime minister, who was elected the year I went to college. He was a superstar, a kind of pop star in fact (the term "Trudeaumania" was in fact coined, without apologies to the Beatles); attractive, intellectual, sporty – all these things I admired. I would have liked to be a person like him and I went to York University because of that. As students in a bilingual college we all had to do the two national languages, English and French. My English professor was Michael Gregory. He was a colleague of Halliday, so I had a very unusual training for North America at the time. It was probably the only place in North America where you could have been introduced to Firthian/Hallidayan perspectives on language. This was the sixties. Gregory had just built up a Department of English from scratch. He designed a programme that focused on stylistics, drama and linguistics, and all students were trained in all those disciplines. So to my surprise I got lectures in linguistics. I had no idea what linguistics was at that time.

Gregory himself had developed a grammar of English that was based on Halliday's 1961 article: "Categories of the theory of grammar." It has only recently been published (de Villiers & Stainton, 2009). Gregory had also hired Waldemar Gutwinski to teach us North-American linguistics, including Chomsky's transformational generative grammar and also stratificational linguistics. Gutwinski, who had worked with Gleason, was a cohesion specialist – drawing in part on Halliday's (e.g. 1964) work on "Leda and the Swan". So I did cohesion analyses on texts with him. This was 1968, and since then my great love has been to figure out how texts work in society and how to interpret discourse. That was one major input.

The influence of Gunther Kress was also important. I was very inspired by the work that he and his colleagues had done in East Anglia in critical linguistics (Fowler *et al.*, 1979). I met Kress in Adelaide in Australia when he arrived there, in 1979 I believe. Then in the early eighties he moved up to Sydney, to the University of Technology. He started to work on genre in England (e.g. Kress, 1982) at roughly the same time as I did in Australia, and as Swales and Miller did in America. Genre work came up as a common interest in all these places at the same time. Later on in the 1980s, a number of people from cultural studies, primarily influenced by Bakhtin, and SFL people like Kress, Theo van Leeuwen, myself and others, formed what we called the "Newtown Semiotic Circle" – so named because several of us, including Gunther Kress who was the main host, lived in and around Newtown at that time. About 1988, we started having meetings, and that was the beginning of the dialogue between SFL and critical theory. Kress and Hodge (1988) had published their social semiotics book by then, but the idea was to bring SFL into dialogue with the more European, especially French, thinking at that time. I suppose that was my real initiation into social semiotics. Kress and van Leeuwen presented their very first work on images to that group in '88 or '89 (Kress & van Leeuwen, 1990, 1996, 2006). I had of course read Halliday's book, *Language as Social Semiotic* (1978), and Gregory had introduced us to Halliday's work at Glendon College. In senior seminars we had worked through his recent papers, in mimeo versions hot off the press. Gregory would do a running commentary, going through the papers paragraph by paragraph. He thus inspired my dream of studying with Halliday. I got a scholarship to do that in 1974, beginning at Essex in the UK; and I followed Halliday to Australia, to Sydney, in 1977.

We have talked about your personal background and inspiration. What about inspiration and motivation from practice?

Several people at Glendon College were interested in applications of linguistics, and my very first job in linguistics was working on a project where I was part of a team led by Jonathan Fine; we were studying primary school language. I think that I have always been inspired by the idea that we should have a socially responsible linguistics (cf. Halliday, 1993). I am a person from the sixties. I was exposed to the radical students' politics of the time, and it was the time of the Vietnam War and all the protests. That was probably one reason why the East Anglia work was inspiring to me and also the critical discourse analysis work that followed on from that (e.g. Fairclough, 1995/2010). I think I was someone who wanted to make a contribution to society through my linguistics, and Halliday's aspiration to have a socially responsible linguistics motivated me.

I worked first in clinical contexts on schizophrenic discourse, in a project led by Sherry Rochester (from 1973; Rochester & Martin, 1979). We were trying to understand how the psychiatrists made a diagnosis of schizophrenia. I used the discourse analysis I was evolving to interpret that. This was not so we could help the patients; rather it was an attempt to analyse what was going on in their discourse. There were psychiatrists working with us who were quite interested in what we were doing as ways of thinking about why they were diagnosing patients in the way they were.

Later on in 1979 Halliday organized a language in education conference in Sydney and brought some teachers and linguists together. He wanted to kick off the kind of work that had happened in London in the sixties. Joan Rothery was there, and we began working together on writing in primary school. All sorts of things grew from that. I found this work really interesting, and both politically and theoretically challenging. It was a stimulating context for me to develop ideas and theory and new ways of thinking about language and semiosis to face the challenges that you confront when you try to improve literacy outcomes in a more democratic way in school.

More recently, I have been working on a project in which we are studying diversionary justice, involving adolescent offenders in my state, New South Wales; the programme is called Youth Justice Conferencing (Martin, 2012b). In this programme they set up a kind of mediation group with a convener, the young offender and their victim, their support persons, the arresting officer and a police liaison officer; and both victim and offender seem to be satisfied with the outcome of this kind of process. It is not that you can be sure that it is better than court and a custodial sentence, in terms of stopping people from re-offending, but generally the programme in New South Wales and comparable programmes around the world have been rated positively by those involved in the process. We have been trying to understand how such a programme works.

I have always wanted my linguistics to do something in the world. This is different from Chomsky, who is very famous for his politics but claims his linguistics has nothing to do with that work. Gregory was, in a way, similar. He apparently sold left-wing newspapers on the corner every Saturday morning, but we never heard a word of politics in his courses (although he was always outspoken in support of our student radicals in their rallies and meetings). Halliday, too, was never very explicit about his own aspirations to develop a Marxist linguistics until he retired, and given the things that happened to him during his life, that is quite understandable. But his interest in a socially accountable linguistics is clearly there in the background of his writing well before that time.

Basic concepts

How do you consider the relation between SFL and other social semiotic directions?

I see SFL as one language-based way of approaching social semiotics. I think that Halliday, and Kress and Hodge, and others have tried to distinguish their work from a line of European structuralist semiotics that had derived from Saussure's work. They wanted something that was much more attuned to variation in language, both variation according to uses of language (the whole register and context orientation), and also the users of language (something that was sensitive to the social background of the language users). They focused on both uses and users. So I think SFL is a language-based theory of social semiotics in principle, and under the influence of Kress and van Leeuwen there is also systemic functional semiotics now. There is both a language-based and multimodally based approach to the social semiotic enterprise.

Has Kress' and van Leeuwen's work made multimodality more systemic functional?

Yes. Theo took my courses in Sydney, and I think that the system networks and structures you find in Kress and van Leeuwen's versions of *Reading Images* are obviously inspired by SFL. I find that these systems and structures are a very substantial part of what they have done and something that has made their work very successful compared to the work of O'Toole (1994) on images (which lacks explicit system/structure cycles and is based more on Halliday's earlier scale and category modelling). Kress has generally taken up a position whereby he talks as if he is moving beyond SFL and into multimodality. I get that flavour from his discourse a lot of the time. But for me, *Reading Images* was simply taking the SFL theory and applying it to another modality, just as if you applied the theory to another language. It is a natural development out of SFL into another modality following on from the general inspiration of Saussure and Hjelmslev. We have to see language as one semiotic system and automatically we then have to explore the other systems in order to understand language. Certainly as a discourse analyst you cannot avoid the fact that texts are multimodal.

Is there a cognitive component in social semiotics?

I think the issue here is whether you need to have a tripartite model of what is going on when you are making meaning. Do you need a view of the world where you have a brain, a mind and language? That is generally what people think. You can, however, have a more ambitious Hallidayan project, which develops a rich theory of social semiosis alongside a rich theory of neurobiology and interfaces those two directly. I think that there are two distinct projects here. My reading of the people who work on cognition and the mind is that their work does not interface with a rich functional model of language. It generally interfaces with a more formal model of language. I think that their interface with a formalist theory of language is not the appropriate model for trying to understand what they think of as the mind. My impression is that the cognitivists talk about the brain, but when it comes to referring to the work of neurobiologists, like Edelman for example, there is no real connection. I'm not sure that they really do address neurobiology.

I am not particularly impressed with what the cognitive approach has to offer. Many people think that you have to supplement a social semiotic approach and a neurobiological approach with a cognitive approach. I think that a cognitive approach is rather an alternative way of describing semiosis (of describing meaning). I do not think that you need a supplemental cognitive model for semiosis.

A lot of linguists call themselves cognitive linguists to distinguish themselves from formal linguists. They say that they are interested in meaning and function, and this interest is aligning them with the SFL enterprise. They are in their opinion fellow travellers. I would say, however, that they are misguided allies. We *could* dialogue with them, but, on the other hand, they think that our social semiotic approach is inadequate because we do not have a theory of mind. For my part, I think that they are not appreciating the significance of what we are doing. You could look at this in phylogenetic terms. The world starts as physical matter. Biological systems arise out of that, and social semiotic systems evolve in some biological species. I think that there are several things to worry about here. The critical question is how the brain is geared to negotiate meaning. For me, putting the mind between the brain and language is an obstacle to understanding this. The mind is not something that we need to supplement our understanding of either neurobiology or social semiosis, in my opinion.

We should not put the mind between the brain and semiosis. Rather we should generalize the kind of social semiotics that would account for language and other kinds of modalities of communication and try to understand how the brain has evolved to manage such an emergent form of complexity. Our job is to provide a model of social semiosis that can help to describe this evolution. I personally like to bring as much as I can into our orbit so that we can use the tools that we have evolved to describe it. I am not comfortable in this discussion we have at the moment of handing over responsibility on an interdisciplinary basis to psychologists and whoever we think can do the work to understand the mind. I do not think that this is productive.

What is communication?

Communication is using your semiosis, using your semiotic systems to negotiate meaning. I think you can go for a simple answer like that. It is performing semiosis through language and other modalities of communication.

Stratification

One crucial concept in your work is stratification. How do you understand this concept?

I was trained by a stratificational linguist, Gutwinski, at Glendon College, and I did my MA with Henry Allan Gleason, Jr. and Peter Reich at the University of Toronto. They are both stratificational linguists, and through them I read Lamb, and through Lamb, I turned to Hjelmslev. Hjelmslev's retake on Saussure, arguing that language is not a system of signs, but a stratified system of signs, influenced me. Lamb of course knew Hockett's work in the United States, where the realization relationship between morphology and phonology was getting sorted out. So I have always had this stratificational thinking in my mind, and coming to SFL I thought there was work to be done in sorting out how we would manage the concept of stratification in systemic linguistics.

There was quite a lot of ambiguity in Halliday's writing about strata during the seventies. You could perhaps see the ambiguity reflected in the Cardiff grammar tradition, where the difference between semantics and grammar is conflated with the difference between system and structure. That is a reasonable reading of some of Halliday's writing in the seventies. What perhaps evolved under my influence, and under the influence of Christian Matthiessen in Sydney, was distinct system/structure cycles on the different levels of language. Firth was a phonologist. Halliday reworked his ideas into grammar. What I tried to do was to rework Halliday's grammatical theory into theory of discourse semantics (Martin, 1992). And if you are a discourse analyst you have to push on and worry about context; co-text is not enough. My interest in register and genre is part of that concern.

Do we have system structure cycles on all strata?

For me, by definition that will have to be the case. I would insist that there are distinct system/structure cycles on all levels, and that is how you will have to explore and find the strata in SFL. SFL has a very special way of setting up the strata, because SFL strata have more power than in other models. In SFL it's not simply a matter of having one layer of structure or several layers of structure on a given level. On a given stratum, alongside constituency layering (organized by rank), you may have simultaneous tiers of structure (organized by metafunctions), and you have system/structure cycles (both paradigmatic and syntagmatic axes). This is a lot of descriptive power. It enables you to cover a whole lot of things that can get pushed to other strata in other approaches (to semantics and pragmatics, for example, in formal syntax-based models).

The rich extravagant grammar that this affords is important. What Halliday has packed into the grammar of English, for example, seen from the point of view of discourse, is barely enough. It is just barely enough for beginning to work productively with discourse semantics. Keep in mind that Gleason also had a stratified approach and his semiology was called discourse (Gleason, 1968). His way of thinking had an influence on me. It of course encouraged me to look beyond the meaning of the clause and take whole texts into account. I think my approach to discourse is a blend of Halliday and Gleason. I take Halliday's work on cohesion and rearticulate it on a deeper stratum and call it discourse semantics.

How does Lemke fit in? He came up with the notion of meta-redundancy.

Jay Lemke came to Sydney in the late seventies and early eighties. He had moved from physics into science education and had projects studying science discourse in school. His book, *Talking Science* (1990), comes from those projects. He was informed by Shirley Brice Heath's ethnographic approach and wanted to add on a more linguistic perspective. Lemke had read deeply into information theory and influenced us theoretically in Sydney at that time. I think that his term meta-redundancy comes from information theory – the basic idea of patterns of patterns (Lemke 1984). This idea seems to be a useful way to interpret further what stratification really means when you layer it up like Hjelmslev, Lamb and Halliday do when they say that there is a hierarchy of abstractions rising up from the phonology. Redundancy in itself just means that there is a co-occurrence pattern set up. I have never really used the idea of meta-redundancy to explore inter-rank relations, but I think you could. Inter-stratally, the idea is that you reconsider the syllables as morphemes, and then grammatical classes as discourse moves and then phases of discourse as genre stages. This is all part of saying that there is emergent complexity above and beyond the redundancy we find at a single level of abstraction. It is a very challenging concept to explain.

I think that we are still theoretically rather weak in picking up what we really mean by stratification. It is sorted out differently in different models, and you have to articulate what it means in each model. I think Hjelmslev made important contributions to this way of thinking. His content/expression complementarity is a way of saying that language is a stratified system, not a simple system of signs, and his connotative and denotative distinction is a way of saying that there are connotative systems that do not have their own expression plane, and denotative systems that do. The relation between context in the Hallidayan model (register and genre register in my stratified model of context) and language is that of a connotative to a denotative semiotic in Hjelmslev's terms. We need to be careful not to over-generalize and treat every pattern of pattern border as involving exactly the same kind of realization. If we stratify Hjelmslev's content plane as we do in Sydney SFL (as lexicogrammar and discourse semantics) there is certain kind of relation; and if we stratify context (as genre and register), there is another relationship again. It is still problematic in SFL how we interpret how each of those borders work differently (Martin, 2013a).

Just to make it clear, the relationship between text and context is not the same relationship as between discourse semantics and lexicogrammar?

It is not "grammatical" for me to talk about the relationship between text and context. Context for me is a higher stratum of meaning on the realization hierarchy; and if we stratify context, we are looking at genre as a pattern of register patterns, register as a pattern of discourse semantics, discourse semantics as a pattern of grammatical patterns, grammatical patterns as patterns of phonological or graphological or gestural patterns as we come down. There is no text there. We are just at the level of system all the way down. The system/structure cycles are specifying the syntagmatic output of the choices on different levels. You have to move to the instantiation hierarchy to talk about the text in relation to system. The text is an instance of all these systems, an instance of every one of them. It is not just an instance of context (of register and genre). A text instantiates register and genre as realized discourse semantically, grammatically and phonologically. We have to be clearer than we were in the writing of the seventies and eighties about the difference of those two perspectives. Halliday and Matthiessen (e.g. Halliday, 2002) have published matrixes that set up the instantiation hierarchy on one plane and the stratification on another. The text is a unit on the instantiation hierarchy and context for me is a unit on the stratification hierarchy. I do not call it context, however, but register and genre. In our education work this is all simplified, so the idea of text in context is a typical way of modelling there. You will see all kinds of diagrams in the education work with the text surrounded by field, tenor and mode, surrounded by the context; this is workable and productive in school. But the theory is in fact more complex than that.

You talk in your theories about a circumvenient and a supervenient perspective. Could you explain these perspectives?

The circumvenient/supervenient distinction was introduced by Chris Cleirigh in a book that he has been writing for many years; I was inspired by his ideas and I have to credit Chris for that (Martin, 2013a). In fact he has abandoned the terms now. Via the term supervenient he tried to capture the realization notion that we have been discussing – the notion of emergent complexity (patterns of patterns), with lower orders of meaning realizing higher order ones. If we position, say, context (in Halliday's terms) as a higher level of meaning, it is then supervenient to language that realizes it. The circumvenient perspective on the other hand is the more common sense way that we think about language in context. From this perspective, language is embedded in and thus is part of an extra-linguistic reality. This extra-linguistic reality may be physical or biological, or it might involve other modalities of communication (alternative semiosis). People often used concentric circles to model this circumvenient perspective. You have language in the middle and these other things around. That is a completely different perspective on context from the supervenient one that I am interested in and that has been developed by Halliday and others in SFL. The circumvenient perspective means that you hand over to someone who is not a linguist to describe extra-linguistic reality for you – to physicists and biologists, or, if you think the extra-linguistics includes the mind, to psychologists. If you think that the extra-linguistics is culture and society, you would hand it over to anthropologists, sociologists and cultural theorists. Working from a supervenient perspective, I do not want to hand over anything until I have theorized and described what the person I am handing over to is interested in. Then we can talk.

Teun van Dijk is someone who has included a lot of things into his discourse studies. In an email he said that SFL had totally misunderstood what the word context means. He claims that it is not a stratum of discourse. What do you say to this objection?

We are getting into issues of faith here, and van Dijk is someone who holds very strongly to the circumvenient perspective. I have written to him in the past trying to explain that the supervenient perspective is a productive alternative to the circumvenient one, but I have not been able to engage him in a dialogue. He considers the idea of a supervenient perspective preposterous. So we have to look into what he has to say about context with his circumvenient model and what we have to say with our supervenient register (field/mode/tenor) and genre theory. I do not have any problem with deciding who is doing something more interesting. Van Dijk also defends the tripartite model of language, brain and mind, and believes that if you do not have a cognitive theory as part of your approach to semiosis then your approach is inadequate. He cannot accept a perspective in which cognition is an alternative way of approaching semiosis; he insists on cognition as supplemental. Well, if somebody believes in the mind, just as if they believe in God, or the Subject, what can you do? We have this difference in SFL also, between the Cardiff grammar approach inspired by Fawcett and the Sydney SFL approach. Halliday is more tolerant of cognitive approaches than I am. He has tried to position his relationship with Lamb as a complementarity; but I am a radical Hallidayan, so I do not do that.

Context

Could we go into your context model? What differences are there between Halliday's model and yours?

There is a lot of confusion in this area, and part of it is purely terminological, which is unfortunate. Historically, a problem arose from about 1983 when I went down to Deakin University near Melbourne. Frances Christie wanted me to write up the context model that we were developing at that time for an education audience. When you work for Fran, you know that you are going to be locked in a room for a couple of days and that you cannot come out until you have done your writing. So I tried to write up our language, register and genre model for this teacher education audience (Martin, 1984). In the middle of that article I thought it would be helpful to make a gesture towards Malinowski's terminology. I suggested an analogy to Malinowski's context of situation as a way of thinking about field, mode and tenor, and to his context of culture (as there is something more abstract by Malinowski there) as a way of thinking about genre. I repeated the same kind of analogy a couple of times after that in publications over a ten-year period. Since then I have tried not to use the terms context of situation and context of culture in discussions of my model. These terms are not a formal part of my theory. However, in our *Language in Education* (2012a) the Deakin paper was taken as foundational, and my model is typically presented in the "Sydney School" education tradition as text, in its context of situation (including field, mode and tenor), in its context of culture (genre); and that is how it is taught. A lot of people read my theory through that lens.

During the eighties I did not really appreciate what Halliday intended when he adopted the same terms from Malinowski and said that the relation between context of culture and context of situation was not a stratal relationship, but an instantiation relationship, with context of situation instantiating context of culture (cf. Matthiessen, 1993). Part of the problem was that in the seventies and eighties many of us were using the term realization for both stratification and instantiation. So context was discussed as realized in text, and also discussed as realized through language (discourse semantics, lexicogrammar and phonology/graphology). These are two very different things. I think we are very careful now to try to use realization for the strata hierarchy and instantiation for the hierarchy of generalization. Halliday (e.g. 2002) does formally think of context of culture as instantiated in context of situation, and I have no problem with that. I don't use the terms formally, and he is welcome to them.

I could not call my approach to context "context", because I have two strata. Halliday has one, so he calls it context. I had split it up and so had to give the levels different names. I chose genre and register to be those two names. A further confusion arises here in that, for Halliday, the term register refers to language, not to context; for Halliday, register refers to the way in which systemic probabilities in language (discourse semantics and lexicogrammar, in particular) are pushed about by the connotative semiotic (his context of culture – meaning field, mode and tenor systems). It is only the realizations of his context stratum that he calls register. So there is terminological variation. The only really substantial issue is whether you stratify context or not. I do; Halliday does not. That is what we have to focus on.

Why do we need to stratify context?

That is another piece of history. Since I was studying with Michael Gregory in Toronto, we were from the first year trained in his approach to register. He had four categories, as other people within SFL also had (e.g. Gregory & Carroll, 1978). Gregory used field and mode, and split tenor into personal tenor and functional tenor. Halliday would be the exception with his model of three categories. Halliday, MacIntosh and Strevens had in their 1964 book field, mode and style; and later, since style was confusing in relation to stylistics, Halliday adopted Gregory's term tenor for that dimension. When I started to teach in the MA Applied Linguistics programme in Sydney, I had a course called "Functional varieties of language". I reached back to my undergraduate training and introduced Gregory's model. We worked with field, mode, personal tenor and functional tenor. Halliday used in his courses field, mode and tenor. Students do not like such differences when they are learning a theory at the beginning. They find alternative views confusing. Two students addressed me on this: Joan Rothery and Guenter Plum. Joan was working with school writing, partly with me, and Guenter Plum was very interested in genres and analysis of sociolinguistic style (Plum, 1988). Joan and Guenter suggested pushing functional tenor deeper because it seemed to influence all of ideational, interpersonal and textual meaning, not just one metafunction. They wanted to hang on to Halliday's notion of ideational meaning construing field, interpersonal meaning enacting tenor, and textual meaning composing mode. That was proving difficult if purpose (functional tenor) got in the way. They persuaded me that stratifying would be a good idea. Then we had two terms, personal tenor and functional tenor, on two different levels of abstraction, with functional tenor realized through field, personal tenor and mode. That was not ideal. It was still confusing. So we changed the functional tenor term to genre.

We were also influenced by Mitchell's (1957) and Hasan's (1979) work on buying and selling encounters. And we were working on the structure of the spoken and written texts that Joan collected in school and Guenter from socio-linguistic interviews. We took the idea of staging (text structure) and reconceived it in terms of a system/structure cycle, so that we had an axial perspective on genre. I referred to text structure as schematic structure and was trying thereby to make a connection to the kind of work that van Dijk was doing with Walter Kintsch – the work they and others were doing on schema theory or script theory. That is, how the stratified model of context evolved.

The important point is the motivation: Why did we do this? For one thing, we wanted to hang on to the idea of intrinsic and extrinsic functionality mapping on to each other (as foregrounded in Halliday, 1978). If you are going to treat func-tional tenor or genre as part of the variables field, or mode or tenor, then experi-ence tells us that an elegant formulation of Halliday's metafunction and context variable hookup is not sustainable. A genre is a configuration of all three kinds of meaning, and the configurations themselves can then be organized into systems. Their relations to one another can be explored typologically or topologically (cf. Martin & Rose, 2008), and we can thus map a level of emergent complexity beyond field, mode and tenor and articulate a culture as a system of genres. We used that in our school work to map the primary school curriculum and the sec-ondary school subject areas. The alternative approach is that you describe these relationships we have been working on as a part of field, or mode or tenor. Hasan's (e.g. 1999) and Matthiessen's choice is to make these relations part of field. Hasan has in a few publications showed sketches of these kinds of relations in field. Mat-thiessen has more recently developed a "pie model" where he maps the genre relations as slices of a field pie. As he does that, I read him as saying that there is ideational integration of some kind for each of the slices of the pie (genre families in my terms); that assumes, of course, that he is being Hallidayan and saying that idea-tional meaning by and large construes field. I think that decades of work show that ideational integration of genre families of this kind is not the case. The slices are not tied together because they are ideationally related; they are tied together as configurations of all three kinds of meaning. So either you stratify context and stop trying to put genre into one of the three register categories or you give up the intrinsic and extrinsic functionality hookup notion. I want to hang on to this hookup as part of our heritage. In addition it has always seemed clear to me that as you move through the stages of a genre, the field, mode and tenor variables may be shifting too. If the genre category itself is part of any of the variables, the question is then how you can account for these changes? I think there is a theo-retical problem there, and to my mind Hasan and Matthiessen are not dealing adequately with this problem yet. In short, I think my colleagues and I have pushed harder at the question of genre relations. As we pushed, the systems of relations started to sort themselves out as four systems, not three, and with one system (genre) as more abstract than the others (field, tenor and mode).

Semantics

Let us talk about semantics. You published *English Text* in 1992 where you write about discourse semantics. Why this publication?

That was my attempt to consolidate the work on discourse that I had started back in 1974. My project was to reconceptualise Halliday & Hasan's work on cohesion as discourse, including both system and structure. I began early on in my clinical linguistics work with what *Cohesion in English* calls reference, but used Gleason's (1968) term identification when trying to recontextualize it as part of discourse semantics. I later tried to extend conjunction analysis to include considerations of implicit relations and worked on ways of more clearly modelling the overall shape and structure of conjunctive relations in text. It was a similar kind of project to that undertaken later on by rhetorical structure theory (which developed later on in the eighties). If you look at Halliday's model, you see cohesion placed at the level of grammar, as non-structural textual meaning. What I do is to try to reinterpret cohesion as a higher stratum of meaning. This is different from Halliday's "grammar and glue" model. He is a grammarian and as a grammarian you work with clauses, and you naturally think beyond grammar in terms of how you can stick those clauses together. This gives rise to what I think of as the grammar and glue perspective. I think not in terms of glue sticking clauses together, but in terms of discourse semantic system/structure cycles realized through lexicogrammar. The unit of meaning we need to worry about in semantics is the text, an unfolding discourse, so we need to think about systems at that level. That opens up a number of possibilities.

You can, for example, look at this discourse semantic stratum and ask whether you think it is metafunctionally organized. I think it is. You can see the conjunction systems as ideational, the appraisal and negotiation as interpersonal and identification as textual. I think you can see metafunctional organization there, so the idea that all these dimensions of cohesion are textual is reinterpreted. If there is a metafunctionally organized discourse semantics between lexicogrammar, register and genre, this has huge influence in how you reason about intrinsic and extrinsic functionality, and in how you see the relationships between field, mode, tenor and language. It is a very different perspective. You are essentially arguing that a text is not a bag of clauses. Rather there is an intermediate level of organization that you must consider before you move to study context. Most systemic work considers, however, texts to be bags of clauses. People analyse the clauses and add up the results and divide them by the number of clauses, and think they have the meaning of the text. That is rather ridiculous, but it is standard practice in SFL meetings. It comes in part from Halliday's comment in his grammar book that if you are not doing a grammatical analysis of the text, you are just doing a running commentary on the text. Beyond this I have been designing system/structure cycles for text analysis (Martin, 1992). Once you have these, you need to attend to both lexicogrammar and discourse semantics to interpret a text.

I'm not suggesting for a moment we give up SFL work on TRANSITIVITY, MOOD, THEME, nominal group, verbal group and so on. All that is there. But when you build on this it is important to refocus on texts as your unit of meaning. If you only have a clause semantics, I think you have something quite limiting. When Halliday and Matthiessen were writing the book *Construing Experience through Meaning* I was criticizing them, saying that they were not taking co-textual relations into account as they mapped the semantics. And thinking from above, they were not really taking responsibility for field and giving us something abstract enough to go up and look at field with. They advised me to criticize the book after they had finished it. We were, however, working on different projects. They were trying to build a semantics that might convince cognitive linguists and psychologists that the semiotic project is a reasonable alternative. To my mind that project was never going to succeed because people believe in the mind; they can't be approached rationally. You will never convince the people who believe in the mind that there is no mind. You cannot succeed in that. My feeling is that their ideational semantics is severely compromised because it does not reason enough from around (the co-text) and from above (field). It mainly reasons from below (chiefly from ideational meaning in the grammar of clauses and nominal groups).

Is this what you mean when you say that there is too much clause semantics floating around in SFL?

Yes. Sometimes you are in a specific project, however, where clause analysis is what you need to do. An example would be Hasan's work in the eighties when she was exploring Bernstein's ideas and looking at users of language in certain contexts of use (Hasan, 2009). She was exploring gender and class and predispositions to meaning when children are being socialized into their culture before school. She decided that her basic units of analysis should be the message, and designed networks formalizing the meaning of clauses. On the basis of these networks she coded her data and came up with very interesting results in terms of how mothers talk differently to boys and girls, and how working-class and middle-class mothers talk differently. So I think there might be specific projects where clause semantics is a practical way to proceed. In Halliday and Matthiessen's project of construing experience through meaning they articulated their work essentially as clause semantics, and the networks they came up with are very similar to grammar networks. The grammar categories are basically simply renamed. My perspective has always been that semantics has to do with texts. Halliday and Hasan clearly concur with that (e.g. in their *Cohesion in English* book); and Hasan's work on the texture and structure of a text is clearly in this tradition (e.g. Hasan, 1985). I wanted to take the notion of text semantics seriously and say that if you stratify the content plane and move to semantics, you need to set your horizons wider as well (thus a discourse semantics not a clause semantics). You take the text as the unit of analysis and not the clause. For me clause semantics is just a first step. We need to push on. *English Text* is my attempt to show what more semantics can do.

Appraisal

Let us go to appraisal (Martin & White, 2005). Could you give a historical overview and introduction to how you came to that concept?

Historically it came out of the work that Joan Rothery and Guenter Plum were doing on genre. One genre family they collected was the story family. Guenter had a range of spoken genres – what we now call anecdote, exemplum, observation and recount (e.g. Martin & Rose, 2008). Joan had another range of genres from her analyses of school writing – narratives, recounts, observations, and what she called thematic narratives (the more literary narratives that have an underlying message). From Labov's work, we took the idea that in successful stories the way in which interpersonal meaning mapped on to the ideational meaning made the point of the story. Labov had long lists of things he called evaluation (or intensity). We wanted to do better than a list, because much of the genre theory was still hanging on these interpersonal patterns that we did not have a theory of. So from the late eighties we were trying to build a theory of feeling inspired by this work on story genres.

Then we began working on a project in secondary school and workplace discourse (the Write it Right Project). A part of the project involved workplace literacy, and one focus there was media discourse. Peter White, a former journalist, worked with us on that project, and he was interested in differences between news stories, editorials and features and the different kinds of evaluation that were possible within the different media genres. We had started with just one kind of feeling and called it AFFECT (as outlined in Chapter 7 of *English Text*). Then as part of the work on media discourse we realized that we had to separate the negotiation of emotions from JUDGEMENTS that were made of people's character and behaviour, because those two kinds of feeling distinguished different kinds of stance in media discourse. In the same project Joan Rothery, Maree Stenglin and Mary Macken-Horarik were working on English in secondary school discourse, and Caroline Coffin was working on history. Joan was also working in visual arts – on texts responding critically to art, sculpture and architecture. There you had to describe semiotic phenomena, and so APPRECIATION fell out as the third dimension of types of feeling. That was as far as we got with that typology, and to my surprise it seems to have survived now for about fifteen years without anybody trying to tear it to pieces. It is a kind of emotion, ethics and aesthetics framework recontextualized in functional linguistics.

Then there was the question of who the feelings come from – whose feelings you are looking at. In narratives this is complicated in terms of focalization and point of view. In media discourse, there are constraints to what the reporter can say or report. What we called ENGAGEMENT systems came out of this work. This was in particular Peter White's interest. Then we had the question of the strength of feelings, which we looked at originally as amplification. Some further advances arose from work academic discourse where you play with ENGAGEMENT and GRA-DUATION to position your research. Sue Hood (2010) took it further there, developing GRADUATION as delicate FORCE and FOCUS systems. That would be the general set of factors that led to the evolution of the APPRAISAL framework. And perhaps I should stress here that we need to be careful when we refer to appraisal "theory". There have been some misunderstandings. SFL is the theory, and APPRAISAL is a discourse semantic system developed within that theory. It is not separate from SFL; it is a part of the theory. It is a discourse semantic system.

Appraisal comes from the study of language. What about multimodal appraisal?

As people have started to work on multimodality they naturally ask questions about APPRAISAL as they analogize between the linguistic system and systems in other modalities (just as Kress and van Leeuwen did in relation to SFL grammar). The question is whether there are feeling systems that are actually describable in terms of ATTITUDE, JUDGEMENT, APPRECIATION, ENGAGEMENT and GRADUATION in other modalities. For example, can you inscribe any more than AFFECT in an image? Is inscribing JUDGEMENT or APPRECIATION possible? I do not think it is. Of course once there is ideation, you cannot resist judging – you do make judgements as a reader; but they are not inscribed for you. To take another example, in our work on children's picture books, Claire Painter and I tried to account for colour (Painter *et al.*, 2013). We suggested that colour does create a feeling, and colour is quite important in children's picture books and may be used in different ways as stories unfold. And different styles of children's picture books use different kinds of colours. So there is a system of feeling there (which we called AMBIENCE), but its realization, how we are viewing it and the kind of choices we have are very different from APPRAISAL in language. Colour is, we suggest, interacting with APPRAISAL in language, and that raises a big issue in multimodal analyses having to do with how we describe interaction between modalities. APPRAISAL and AMBIENCE are working together in the same text, but they are coming from different realization hierarchies. By and large I think there may be bits of APPRAISAL where we could recognize similar system/structure cycles across modalities; but generally we are looking at different resources to negotiate feeling when we get into music, space grammar and image, and even paralanguage (including facial expression). We cannot expect to find the same *valeur* as we move from one modality to another.

Multimodality

What is a mode?

I am sure I have used that term in different ways over the years, and I will try not to do that now. For me, mode is a register category (cf. Chapter 7, Martin, 1992). It refers to the semiotics of the texture of discourse as influenced by the channel of communication (a register pattern of a pattern of discourse semantic meaning, in other words) – sensitive to whether the channel is writing or face-to-face communication, or emailing, texting or posting, or any other ways that communication is electronically mediated. Mode also has to do with the role that language is playing – how much work language is doing in relation to other modalities. Is language doing most of the work and thereby constituting what is going on, or sharing the work, or doing less work with other modalities doing most of the job? That is what I use the register variable mode for.

Semiotic systems alongside language I refer to as modalities of communication. Of course there is a problem, because Halliday uses modality for probability, usuality and that kind of meaning. I have complained to him that he should pay a carbon tax on his use of terminology, because he has used up so much terminology in his rich grammar that we need elsewhere. He has, however, refused to pay, commenting that we should take the terms back if we need them. So I think that can be taken as a licence for using the term modality as it is used in multimodal discourse analysis. John Bateman (2011) uses the term "semiotic mode" for what I am calling a modality here; that then creates a possible confusion with the register variable mode. The problem is that we haven't inherited anywhere near enough terms from traditional rhetoric to cover our needs.

What is special about language as a mean of communication?

I accept a point that Halliday often makes, namely that language is the only modality that can talk about the other modalities (that can construe them, ideationally speaking). That is something that is significantly different compared to other semiotic systems. He also suggests that the other modalities could not have arisen without language. I do not know how you can explore that or argue for that. But Halliday is usually right, so I think that this probably is the case, and so there is a difference in terms of the evolution of these resources. If we are serious about stratification and rank and metafunction as systemic functional semioticians, and we are using our system/structure cycles as the basis for whether we actually have two strata or two ranks or two different metafunctions, then language would be special as it is the only modality that is a stratified system. So far, that's what people have demonstrated. Some people take secondary concepts like rank, metafunction and strata and impose them on the other modalities without any system/structure justification. But we really only have system/structure cycles for images, and we only have one metafunctionally diversified cycle of system and structure there, so there is only evidence for one stratum in modalities outside of language at present (Martin, 2011a).

I really think that discussion of the presence of strata is the most responsible way to approach the modalities in terms of SFL or SFS (Systemic Functional Semiotics). There are other criteria that people use, and Halliday uses different criteria obviously in his characterization of protolanguage. When he retrospectively looks back at protolanguage from adult language, he starts with a stratified model (phonology and semantics) and treats grammar as emerging between phonology and semantics (nowhere providing three strata of system/structure cycles, or even two). I would prefer to say that the protolanguage is a single stratum, comprising one system/structure cycle. For me, the interesting question to ask is how a child's developing meaning potential gets too complicated to handle in a single stratum. When do ranks emerge? When do the metafunctions emerge? When do we have to stratify? These are the interesting questions looking at language as it develops, adopting a child's perspective. Halliday looks down from the adult perspective when he analyses protolanguage; he is not using independently motivated strata of system/structure cycles to model what is going on.

Most people working on multimodality aren't working with independently motivated strata of system-structure cycles either. For my part I do not want to immediately transfer too much theoretical baggage from language. It was incredibly productive to take metafunctions as point of departure for analysing images as Kress and van Leeuwen did. But this strategy is less productive when you turn to music, and attempt to take the textual, the interpersonal and the ideational over (though perhaps this was easier to do in earlier stages of the evolution of music). On the other hand, if you go from the question of types of structure (Halliday, 1979), perhaps it is easier to see particular prosodic, periodic patterns in music. When you move between languages or modalities, you cannot pretend that you do not know how the language or modality you have already worked on works. But you need to be cautious as well and ultimately the system/structure cycle should decide what is going on for you, if – and this is a very big if – you are a systemicist.

SFL dialects

There are at least two different SFL dialects, as Robin Fawcett calls it, the Cardiff grammar and the Sydney grammar. What are the main differences between these two dialects?

Let us remember what a dialect is. A dialect involves a regional or social difference; essentially we are looking at different ways of saying the same thing. I think that the difference between the Sydney perspective and the Cardiff grammar is definitely not that. Minimally, it is a register difference; they are meaning different things, though with a common history. The last time I tried to explore the differences critically I suggested they are not different dialects or registers, but different languages – because of a general lack of mutual intelligibility (Martin, 2011b). The crucial point here is whether positing a stratum depends on proposing a distinct set of system/structure cycles. Sydney grammar proposes distinct system/structure cycles for semantics and grammar; Cardiff grammar conflates axis and stratification (with system conflated with semantics and structure with grammar). Of course if we do stratify and have system/structure cycles on the two strata, we can have either clause semantics or text semantics. But if we conflate axis with stratification as in the Cardiff model we can only have a clause semantics.

The crucial thing comes down to this question: Is one stratum of system/structure cycles for language enough? I think there are all kinds of reasons to argue that it is not enough. I have tried to be specific about this argument in relation to grammatical metaphor (e.g. Martin, 2008), in terms of how we need to have systems on the two levels, in tension with each other, to interpret interpersonal and ideational metaphor. If a model cannot handle this, it is of no use in education or many other contexts of application. If you look carefully, Fawcett's systems for MOOD and TRANSITIVITY, or whatever he calls them in a particular phase of his research, are not based on or motivated by structure (in the way that they are for Halliday and Matthiessen and others). In his recent MOOD networks for example (e.g. Fawcett, 2008), he has speech function labels for what Halliday would classify as imperative, interrogative, declarative and exclamative clauses. But these features do not make generalizations about structural patterns; a wide variety of grammatical syntagms realize most of Fawcett's features; and there is no co-textual reasoning either, in terms of the discourse semantics of exchange structure (we are dealing with clause semantics here). So we seem, in fact, to be dealing with a kind of speech act theory. We have a philosophical notional perspective on meaning, not a social semiotic one, and, of course, naturally enough, this is set in a cognitive framework.

I think the Cardiff model is a very inadequate model of language because it collapses axis and stratification, two things that have to be kept theoretically and descriptively distinct. You can't afford to do this if you want enough power to describe what language is. Particularly if you want to have a model you can use in education, grammatical metaphor is a fundamental concept – both interpersonal metaphor, when you look at the classroom practice, and ideational metaphor, for an understanding the nature of knowledge and how it is configured differently in different subject areas. So there is just not enough room in the Cardiff model for what we need in education. I have written about this in many places. I have just finished a book where I introduce readers to system network writing. I have prepared it as a bilingual book (English and Chinese) to follow up on Halliday and Matthiessen's book *Systemic functional grammar: a first step into the theory*. It is called *Systemic functional grammar: a next step into the theory* (Martin, 2013b). In this book I have tried to apprentice people carefully into the kind of argumentation that Halliday and others developed in the sixties, which treats system/structure relations (i.e. axis) as a yin and yang relationship. There is no meaning if there is no structural realization. Those things are tied together. I have tried to do my best to show in that book how the argumentation works, and I have also tried to show as explicitly as I can what the consequences are if you untie this nexus, and create the possibility of Cardiff grammar. The book explores some of the consequences of giving up the axial argumentation on which IFG style grammars are based.

Genre pedagogy

Let us go to SFL and education. Can you tell us the story of genre pedagogy?

I mentioned Joan Rothery earlier. I started to work with her in 1979, and over the years she gathered a large collection of student writing from all levels of school.

She tried to sort them out, initially using a field, mode, personal tenor and functional tenor approach, and as I mentioned earlier genre theory in part arises from this work. Other people, like Guenter Plum, working on his interview data, and Suzanne Eggins, working on her dinner table conversations with her friends, were also interested in genre. You could say that it was under the influence of education that people got to hear about the stratified model of context, although it arose from work on many contexts (Ventola, 1987; Eggins & Slade, 1997; Plum, 1988).

The stratified model of context was the model that we used when we tried to change the practice in schools at that time (the 1980s). In Australia, process writing was the dominant paradigm as far as teaching literacy was concerned. It was itself a radical protest against traditional approaches to reading and writing, which basically involved "phonics", some knowledge of traditional school grammar (parts of speech) and some formal exercises. Process writing was an approach where teachers changed from teaching the students to guiding them. They let the children write in any form they chose about any topic they liked, and they argued that this was a good strategy because this is how children learn to talk (it was justified as "natural" language learning). The idea was that if teachers surrounded the students with writing (meaning a few texts posted around the classroom), then they would learn to write. This is a complete misunderstanding of early language development, based on Chomsky. These progressivist educators removed all knowledge about language from the curriculum in Australia, and they argued that knowledge of language was useless and even harmful as far as learning to read and write was concerned.

We studied the effect of that method and found that, by and large, what the children did was to write down the genres they had learned at home before they came to school. They wrote short observations about what they did on the weekend or on their holidays. They also wrote recounts (unproblematically unfolding stories of experiences they had been involved in). And they finished primary school and headed off to secondary school without any knowledge about language. We felt that this was a poor preparation for secondary school. It was also a very poor preparation for reading and writing across the curriculum in primary school, where the students study science and social science. We were working in so-called disadvantaged schools, where the main population of students had working-class, migrant and indigenous backgrounds, and we could see that the students needed more, both for their school work and, in some cases, for mediating on behalf of their families in the community (families in which they would have been the most literate or only literate member). We wanted to broaden the range of writing undertaken, so we used our genre theory to integrate various kinds of factual writing into the curriculum. We categorized those factual genres into reports, explanations, expositions, discussions and so forth.

When we introduced those ideas into school, we quickly came to understand that we had as well to design a new pedagogy for teaching writing. Halliday's and Painter's work on language development was the inspiration. They looked at how adults were scaffolding young children into language as they enact various kinds of genres as the child is growing up. The general idea of the pedagogy was that you need a model text, and then you would, as a teacher, jointly construct the text with the students. A general principle, also inspired by Vygotsky, was that what you can do with someone is more than you can do on your own. Another principle was that you should never ask anybody to write something until you have shown them what you want and undertaken a comparable task jointly with them. We also knew from Halliday's and Painter's work that talking about language is a part of learning language, and we wanted to reintroduce knowledge about language in the school. We introduced our genre theory, technical terms for the names of the different genres, elements of discourse semantics and some lexicogrammar, so that we could talk about the texts. We wanted the students to have resources of knowledge that they could draw on.

Has the genre pedagogy changed during the years?

I think it has constantly evolved. One big change came when David Rose became more involved and addressed the problems of the building of field and the deconstruction of model texts if the students cannot read. The students cannot do research on a topic or study a model text if they cannot read. David had to recontextualize the teaching/learning cycles, so that they included an explicit focus on reading. David has also been very concerned to foreground the importance of reading as a foundation for schooled learning. The book I recently published with David Rose is called *Learning to Write, Reading to Learn* (Rose & Martin, 2012). It describes the evolution of the reading and writing focused cycles that incorporate earlier work into a more complex set of cycles.

The other major change introduced in David's pedagogy is the focus on the micro-interaction between teacher and student. Initially we just tried to change the teacher practice globally (by designing curriculum macro-genres; Christie, 2002). David's *Reading to Learn* model goes right down into the micro-interactions – to the exchange structures when teacher and students jointly construct meaning – and shows how these exchanges can most effectively be done.

Is genre pedagogy only for the subject English?

Remember we were not just teaching mother-tongue kids. Everything was designed in schools where students had learned some English (perhaps indigenous or migrant dialects of English), before or very soon after they came to school; but they didn't speak a standard variety. Nor did they know how to write or read in English. We tried to build a kid-proof pedagogy – one where it does not matter what your social background is; and it does not matter what your language background is. There is flexibility in the model to deal with students who have different kind of needs. David Rose's teaching/learning cycles have been designed in part for very early literacy, with infants at the very beginning of school. He includes cycles that have to do with building basic grammar resources, and working on the spelling and word structure – and so there is space for working on graphology and lexicogrammar in the model, in an ESL (English as a second language) or EFL (English as a foreign language) context.

Is it also a pedagogy that can be used in subjects like science and social science?

The pedagogy is designed not only for language teaching. If you look at the cycles you will see that there is always a point, or various points, where you build the field in terms of register theory. If you do not have something to write about, you cannot write. If you do not understand the knowledge structure of the texts you are reading, you will not be able to interpret them. The model is designed for any subject and works best as an embedded literacy programme (cf. Martin & Matthiessen, 2014). If we move to secondary school it is a question of working out what are the key genres that the students need to read and write in biology, in physics or mathematics, and in English, history or geography. The model helps in teaching the children to read these academic discourses that they have not faced before, and to write the genres that the curriculum will use to assess their progress. The needs of every discipline are different. Every discipline has a different kind of academic discourse – different genres, and within the genres very different uses of discourse semantics and grammatical metaphors to construct the knowledge of each genre. So the content teachers have to take the responsibility for reading and writing in their own subject. Our new national curriculum in Australia is advocating this view and legislating nationally for each content area to take responsibility for language and literacy.

Would you say that this kind of pedagogy could be a way of developing democracy by giving all children a voice in society through literacy skills?

Sure. In the disadvantaged schools that we began to work in, we took advantage of a special kind of federal funding that was devoted to more democratic outcomes in terms of education for those kinds of students. Run by boards of parents, teachers and politically active citizens, the Disadvantaged Schools Program centres aimed for a pedagogy and curriculum that would mean that the students' social background was not a factor in terms of success in schooling. We were motivated by this agenda. For us it was part of Halliday's vision of a socially responsible linguistics, and part of his conception of how a Marxist linguistics can evolve. That is perhaps something that made the project controversial from the beginning.

How is multimodality built into the genre pedagogy?

Well, this is a crisis. If we assume a supervenient perspective, and we set up genre as our highest meaning-making stratum, we are then interested in how genre configures linguistic choices. On the other hand, from the point of view of instantiation, we know that generally we have a multimodal text, so there is more than one stratification hierarchy involved (Bateman, 2008). We know that a textual instance is able to draw on different realization hierarchies and blend them together in this perfectly coherent unfolding multimodal discourse. I think that the crisis here is how we describe and model multimodality as a logogenetic process (Martin, 2013a). We have very little theory as far as the instantiation hierarchy is concerned. We have been working for a hundred years on realization, trying to sort out axis, rank, strata and metafunction and all these ideas, but the fleshing out of instantiation is just beginning.

For me the exciting work in this area is coming from translation rather than multimodality; there you have the question of how we get from one language to another in the process of translation. One of my students, Ladjane de Souza (2010), has been interpreting translation as an interlingual re-instantiation process. I think that there are exciting ideas here: thinking of translation as a process of moving back up the instantiation hierarchy, opening up choices, finding the points when we cross over into the other language and coming back down again with, of course, not quite the same meaning, but a related one. You could analogize this to intermodality. If we are going to incorporate another modality, the space grammar, the paralanguage or whatever, into the multimodal text and blend it, then there must be a point where language choices are less particularized, and where we re-distribute the meaning into the gesture, the image, the music or the movement, and then have that come down instantially, seamlessly into the text. Kress and van Leeuwen opened up this area of multimodality, and now you cannot be a discourse analyst without being multimodal. It is just not conceivable. But the theory has not yet caught up with that challenge.

The future

You have talked about challenges and problems, and you talked about strengths. What are the current trends for making changes in SFL? What do we do, and what will we see in the next decades of systemic functional linguistics?

I think we already touched upon one major challenge: the intermodality issue. We have created a huge crisis for ourselves by proposing simultaneous realization hierarchies for the different modalities, and then you are faced with the problem that you have a multimodal text. How can it be that these different hierarchies of abstraction come together? That is a huge challenge. How can we build the theory that enables us to understand how the meanings from different modalities come together into a single text as it unfolds? That raises all kinds of questions of representational challenge as well. Our representations of system and instance right now are very static and synoptic. We use essentially a two-dimensional page to configure the systems, and a two-dimensional page to show the structure of a text – both as synoptic "fait accompli". We are stuck in our linguistic theory now, and I think we have fallen far behind where the biological and physical sciences are in terms of animated modelling and multidimensional visualization. We have a brilliant student in Sydney at the moment, Bandar Almutairi (2013), working on visualization. It is a very challenging enterprise. It might change the whole nature of the training of linguists. He is someone who, in one person, combines knowledge of mathematics, programming and linguistics. We also have visualization projects in Singapore (now Perth) with the group Kay O'Halloran established there and with Jonathan Webster in Hong Kong. Interestingly, in Singapore, Kay O'Halloran did not have anyone with all the skills needed in one person, so she had to assemble a team of programmers, mathematicians and linguists that could work together.

Before such modelling you have to tag the texts, and of course you want to tag texts automatically, because the manual tagging is so slow. Then you have to understand the mathematics and the programming enough to turn the tagging into a picture of what goes on, and know what the visualization possibilities are. Perceptually, we can then see in appropriate visualizations what we cannot see when we are using the form of analysis that systemic linguists often use, where by the time we have annotated the text for all the different systems we think are relevant, you cannot see anything. It is too complex. The detail is overwhelming. What kind of visualizations can we produce and train people to view that will let us see what unfolding texts really look like, and how intermodal cohesion really works? The answer will probably involve two- and three-dimensional animated representations that people come up with over the next generation or two. I think that one of my worst nightmares is that linguistics becomes like economics. In economics you have to spend most of your training studying mathematics, and the discipline tends to lose contact with the real world. Will linguistics head in a similar direction? I am sure that we are all going to be challenged by the progress in this area. I think that multimodal discourse analysis is going to be an exciting frontier to monitor.

For me, the eighties was a decade of genre, the nineties of appraisal, and then multimodality in the noughts; I wonder what is coming now? I have imagined that in this postcolonial globalizing world, identity would become a major issue. Questions of identity have been around all the time, but I think we have now been able to develop resources to work more seriously with identity. I am not sure, however, if they are good enough yet for talking about how people are negotiating their identity through discourse. In the special issue of *Text and Talk* that Geoff Thompson recently edited (2013), we see the direction that this kind of work might take. It is hard to predict right now whether it is going to take off and become a dominant trend in SFL work.

On the education side, the teaching of foreign languages is a huge issue. We have not penetrated into that area very far at all. Heidi Byrnes has done very exciting work in German in Georgetown (Byrnes *et al.*, 2010), showing what can be done if you adopt a genre-based programme in foreign language teaching. In the universities in a lot of the English-speaking world, they do not think much about teaching language in context. The language teaching departments are distinctly divided into language teachers and culture teachers, and the language teachers are lower down in the hierarchy and the culture teachers are higher up. Shockingly to me, the culture teachers often teach in English about foreign languages like Spanish and German; and the students often write in English about Spanish and German culture in their course. And the language teachers are left to teach the language skills. Heidi Byrnes threw all that away and introduced a genre-based programme that means that the students can actually do the work in German that culture people want them to do. The students can graduate from the undergraduate programme and go to Germany and do a MA and survive there, which was not happening before. We need tons more work in this area.

I think translation and interpreting is another area. It is the same problem. Translation is basically now an "art". You interpret and translate as a gift. Translation is going to be much more important, mainly because of China. China is the main economic power in the world right now. It will, during the next decades, become the major intellectual power as well, and most of the new knowledge in the world will be generated in China, which will then have to be translated from Chinese into many different languages. This is going to be very difficult as long as translation and interpreting is seen as an art. There will have to be machine translation, properly theorized on the basis of relevant knowledge about language, and translators and interpreters will have to be trained in knowledge about language in order to do their work more efficiently in the future. So SFL work has to happen here as well.

There are currently huge growth areas for SFL in China and Latin America, so I think that one challenge is to get enough theory there to support what is going on. This is a challenge even in England. I have just been to England for a conference where education people are building up the linguistics – educational linguistics for interventions in schools – but there are not enough SFL linguists left in England to support the work, and nowhere near enough teacher/linguist consultants. This is a kind of crisis. With all that interest, how can you get enough theory into China and Latin America and elsewhere to support what they want to be able to do in the future?

I think that the last challenge is a more personal one. Halliday is not going to be with us for another generation. He has been the centre of this SFL community and his character and manner and his ability to hold people together have been of great importance. Life without him is going to be a big challenge. How will the community re-configure when he is not there as the guru holding everything together? I do not know. Maybe we will become a much more federal enterprise. That is already happening with the work and conferencing in Scandinavia, China, Latin America, Indonesia and even in the United States (something which I thought I would never see in my lifetime). Things may start to go in different directions in different places in response to different needs. I hope we can keep talking to each other, and I think interviews like those conducted in this volume will help.

References

Almutairi, Bandar A.A., 2013. Visualising patterns of appraisal in texts and corpora. *Text & Talk* 33(4/5): 691–723.

Bateman, John, 2008. *Multimodality and Genre: a foundation for the systematic analysis of multimodal documents*. London: Palgrave Macmillan.

——, 2011. The decomposability of semiotic modes. In: Kay O'Halloran & Bradley A. Smith (eds.), *Multimodal Studies: exploring issues and domains*. London: Routledge, pp. 17–38.

Bednarek, Monika, 2010. Corpus Linguistics and Systemic-Functional Linguistics interpersonal meaning, identity and bonding in popular culture. In: Monika Bednarek & Jim Martin (eds.), *New Discourse on Language: functional perspectives on multimodality, identity and affiliation*. London: Continuum, pp. 237–66.

Byrnes, Heidi, Hiram H. Maxim & John M. Norris, 2010. Realizing Advanced Foreign Language Writing Development in Collegiate Education: curricular design, pedagogy, assessment. *The Modern Language Journal* 94 (supplement).

Christie, Frances, 2002. *Classroom Discourse Analysis*. London: Continuum.

de Souza, Ladjane M.F., 2010. *Interlingual re-instantiation: a model for a new and more comprehensive systemic functional perspective on translation*. PhD Thesis. Universidade Federal de Santa Catarina, Brazil.

de Villiers, Jessica & Robert J. Stainton (eds.), 2009. *Michael Gregory's Proposals for a Communication Linguistics* (Vol. 2 of *Communication in Linguistics*). Toronto: Éditions du GREF.

Eggins, Suzanne & Diana Slade, 1997. *Analysing Casual Conversation*. London: Cassell (reprinted Equinox, 2005).

Fairclough, Norman, 1995. *Critical Discourse Analysis: the critical study of language*. London: Routledge (2nd edition, 2010).

Fawcett, Robin, 2008. *Invitation to Systemic Functional Linguistics through the Cardiff Grammar*. London: Equinox.

Fowler, Roger, Bob Hodge, Gunther Kress & Tony Trew, 1979. *Language and Control*. London: Routledge & Kegan Paul.

Ghadessy, Mohsen, 1999 (ed.). *Text and Context in Functional Linguistics*. Amsterdam: Benjamins (CILT Series IV).

Gleason, Henry A. Jr., 1968. Contrastive analysis in discourse structure. *Monograph Series on Languages and Linguistics* 21 (Georgetown University Institute of Languages and Linguistics) (reprinted in Adam Makkai & David G. Lockwood, 1973. *Readings in Stratificational Linguistics*. University, Al: Alabama University Press, pp. 258–76).

Gregory, Michael & Susanne Carroll, 1978. *Language and Situation: language varieties and their social contexts*. London: Routledge & Kegan Paul.

Halliday, Michael A.K., 1961. Categories of the theory of grammar. *Word* 17: 241–92.

——1964. Descriptive linguistics in literary studies. In: Angus McIntosh & Michael A.K. Halliday, 1966. *Patterns of Language: papers in general, descriptive and applied linguistics*. London: Longman pp. 56–69.

——, 1978. *Language as Social Semiotic: the social interpretation of language and meaning*. London: Edward Arnold.

——, 1979. Modes of meaning and modes of expression: types of grammatical structure, and their determination by different semantic functions. In: David J. Allerton, Edward Carney & David Holcroft (eds.), *Function and Context in Linguistics Analysis: essays offers to William Haas*. Cambridge: Cambridge University Press, pp. 57–79.

——, 1993. Language in a changing world. In: Michael A.K. Halliday, 1993. *Language in a Changing World*. Canberra: Applied Linguistics Association of Australia (Occasional Paper 13), pp. 62–81.

——, 2002. Computing meaning: some reflections on past experience and present prospects. In: Guo W. Huang & Zong Y. Wang (eds.), *Discourse and Language Functions*. Shanghai: Foreign Language Teaching and Research Press, pp. 3–25.

Halliday, Michael A.K. & Ruqaiya Hasan, 1976. *Cohesion in English*. London: Longman (English Language Series 9).

Halliday, Michael A.K. & Christian M.I.M. Matthiessen, 1999. *Construing Experience through Language: a language-based approach to cognition*. London: Cassell.

Halliday, Michael A.K., Angus McIntosh & Peter Strevens, 1964. *The Linguistic Sciences and Language Teaching*. London: Longmans.

Hasan, Ruqaiya, 1979. On the notion of text. In: Sándor J. Petöfi (ed.), *Text vs Sentence: basic questions of textlinguistics* (Papers in Textlinguistics 20.2) Hamburg: Helmet Buske, pp. 369–90.

——, 1985. The structure of a text. In: Michael A.K. Halliday & Ruqaiya Hasan *Language, Context and Text: aspects of language in a social-semiotic perspective*. Geelong, Vic.: Deakin University Press. Republished by Oxford University Press 1989, pp. 52–69.

——, 1999. Speaking with reference to context. In Ghadessy, Mohsen (ed.) *Text and Context in Functional Linguistics*. Amsterdam: Benjamins (CILT Series IV) pp. 219–328.

——, 2009. *Semantic Variation: meaning in society and sociolinguistics*. London: Equinox (The Collected Works of Ruqaiya Hasan, edited by Jonathon Webster, Vol. 2).

Hood, Susan, 2010. *Appraising Research: evaluation in academic writing*. London: Palgrave.

Kress, Gunther, 1982. *Learning to Write*. London: Routledge.

Kress, Gunther & Bob Hodge, 1988. *Social Semiotics*. Cambridge: Polity Press.

Kress, Gunther & Theo van Leeuwen, 1990. *Reading Images*. Geelong, Vic.: Deakin University Press. (Revised as *Reading Images: the grammar of visual design*. London: Routledge, 1996). (Revised second edition, 2006).

Lemke, Jay, 1984. *Semiotics and Education*. Toronto: Toronto Semiotic Circle (Monographs, Working Papers and Publications 2).

——, 1990. *Talking Science: language. learning and values*. Norwood, NJ: Ablex.

Martin, Jim R., 1984. Language, register and genre. In: Frances Christie (ed.), *Children Writing: reader*. Geelong, Vic.: Deakin University Press (ECT Language Studies: children writing) 1984, pp. 21–30.

——, 1992. *English text: system and structure*. Amsterdam: Benjamins.

——, 2008. Incongruent and proud: de/vilifying 'nominalisation'. *Discourse & Society* 19(6): 801–10.

——, 2011a. Multimodal Semiotics: theoretical challenges. In: Shoshana Dreyfus, Susan Hood & Maree Stenglin (eds.), *Semiotic Margins: reclaiming meaning*. London: Continuum, pp. 243–27.

——, 2011b. Metalinguistic divergence: centrifugal dimensionality in SFL. *Annual Review of Functional Linguistics* (Higher Education Press, Beijing) 3: 8–32.

——, 2012a. *Language in Education*. (Vol. 7: Collected Works of J. R. Martin edited by Wang Zhenhua). Shanghai: Shanghai Jiao Tong University Press.

——, 2012b. *Forensic Linguistics*. (Vol. 8: Collected Works of J. R. Martin edited by Wang Zhenhua). Shanghai: Shanghai Jiao Tong University Press.

——, 2013a Modelling context: matter as meaning. In: C. Gouveia & M. Alexandre (eds.), *Languages, metalanguages, modalities, cultures: functional and socio-discursive perspectives*. Lisbon: BonD & ILTEC, pp. 10–64.

——, 2013b. *Systemic Functional Grammar: a next step into the theory – axial relations*. (Jim R. Martin; Chinese translation and extensions by Wang Pin & Zhu Yongsheng). Beijing: Higher Education Press.

Martin, Jim R. & Christian M.I.M. Matthiessen, 2014. Modelling and mentoring: teaching and learning from home through school. In: Ahmar Mahboob & Leslie Barratt (eds.), *English in a Multilingual Context*. London: Springer, pp. 137–64.

Martin, Jim R. & David Rose, 2008. *Genre Relations: mapping culture*. London: Equinox.

Martin, Jim R. & Peter R.R. White, 2005. *The Language of Evaluation: appraisal in English*. London: Palgrave.

Matthiessen, Christian M.I.M., 1993. Register in the round: diversity in a unified theory of register analysis. In: Mohsen Ghadessy (ed.), *Register Analysis: theory and practice*. London: Pinter, pp. 221–92.

Mitchell, T.F., 1957. The language of buying and selling in Cyrenaica: a situational statement. *Hespéris: Archives Berbères et Bulletin de l'Institut des Hautes-Études Marocaines*. pp. 31–71.

O'Toole, Michael, 1994. *The Language of Displayed Art*. London: Leicester University Press (2nd revised edition Routledge, 2011).

Painter, Clare, Jim R. Martin & Len Unsworth, 2013. *Reading Visual Narratives: image analysis in children's picture books*. London: Equinox.

Plum, Guenter, 1988. *Text and contextual conditioning in spoken English: A genre-based approach*. Vols 1 & 2. Nottingham: Department of English Studies, University of Nottingham (Monographs in Systemic Linguistics).

Rochester, Sherry & Jim R. Martin, 1979. *Crazy Talk: a study of the discourse of schizophrenic speakers*. New York: Plenum.

Rose, David & Jim R. Martin, 2012. *Learning to Write, Reading to Learn: genre, knowledge and pedagogy in the Sydney School*. London: Equinox.

Thompson, Geoff (ed.), 2013. *Text & Talk* 33: 4–5. (Special Issue in Honour of Michael Halliday).

Ventola, Eija, 1987. *The Structure of Social Interaction*. London: Pinter.

Zappavigna, Michele, 2011. Visualizing logogenesis: preserving the dynamics of meaning. In: Shoshana Dreyfus, Susan Hood & Maree Stenglin (eds.), *Semiotic Margins: reclaiming meaning*. London: Continuum, pp. 211–28.

4

GUNTHER KRESS

Background and beginnings

Could you start by telling us a little bit about your background and how you came to engage in social semiotics?

Well, I was not born with an interest in social semiotics. I was born in Germany, and lived there until the age of sixteen. I left school at the age of fourteen and became an apprentice in what was then still very much the intact medieval guild system. And I think, for myself, that it had a lot of effect on how I see the world, because I was an apprentice in an apprentice workshop, which was led by a master in the trade. There was always an introduction of some kind of issue, and talk about what kind of resources you would need and what should be done: a kind of quasi-theoretical framing. Then you were given things to do with the tools and, once you had done them, what you had done would be pegged up on a board, and the Master and all the apprentices in the workshop would come round and discuss it. That, I think, has stayed with me in a way: the relation between a problem in the world and a kind of theoretical framing, or the tools, but also the materiality of the stuff you work on with those tools. So I explain my interest in the materiality of stuff and the detail of stuff as having been laid down quite early in that. And I enjoyed it; it was a good experience.

At the age of sixteen my parents decided to emigrate to Australia, and because in those days sixteen-year-olds could not make any decisions about their lives, I had to go with them, which meant learning a new culture and a new language. I had been an apprentice – as a furrier – so although I could speak no English, I managed to get a job. And I learned English "on the job", as it were, in a workshop which had several teenage girls working there too. They would tease me mercilessly about my English. It was an intense and very effective way of learning a language.

And then, maybe two or three years in, when I could speak English, there was a slight incident at work. My foreman had asked me what I was doing with a particular job. I responded: "Oh, I thought I would … " though before I could finish he said, "You're not paid to think". I thought: "If I'm not paid to think, what am I doing here?" So I decided to do evening classes toward matriculation. When I had passed, I thought I might as well continue. That was in Newcastle in Australia. It was possible to complete a university course with evening classes only, so I worked during the day and in the evening I marched off to do my university course. So that was my kind of background.

Because it seemed most difficult and a challenge, I thought I would study English literature for my first degree. That became important in lots of ways. I found out, for instance, about the differences in writing between German and English. I also found out that if you leave school at fourteen you haven't really had a chance to learn academic forms of writing, and that was a bit of a problem. And that stayed with me; that you need to learn to *write* a language, as a separate issue from learning to *speak* a language. I also found a kind of dissatisfaction with what "literary studies" – "doing Literature" – was at that time. For me, it wasn't theoretical enough, not grounded enough in theory, or so I thought. That led me to think that, although still working as a furrier, I would do something which would give me the grounding to support the kind of things I ought to know and be able to say about literature. So I did linguistics.

Linguistics did not turn out to help me very much to understand literature. I think linguistics does not have much to say about literature. But it does give you tools of a very specific kind, which are generally applicable. The linguistics that I learned was transformational generative grammar; that was in 1966. I had just had a year of my post-graduate life, starting with using transformational generative grammar, and then one of my teachers said, "If you like, I could get you a job at a university in Germany as a lector". As you know, lectors teach their native language. The native language in this case was going to be English, and in ten years I had acquired sufficient English to be a passable native speaker of English – Australian English, of course. It got me a job at the University of Kiel in Germany.

So that took me back to Europe. After a year I saw an advertisement for a job in England and I applied for the job, at the University of Kent, as a research fellow in applied linguistics. In the year in Kiel I had fallen in with a group of "Assistenten", all receiving the latest mimeos – the most up-to-date stuff from MIT – on Chomskian linguistics. So my first grounding really was in Chomskian linguistics. But I was unhappy with Chomskian linguistics because of the separation of meaning and form, and then later on in *Aspects of the theory of syntax* (Chomsky, 1965), with meaning bolted on as a sort of afterthought. When I was in Canterbury, after two years of doing applied linguistics, I began to read stuff of Michael Halliday's, because my job was a research fellow in a language centre. I thought I would do a degree with him, and so I used to commute up to London two days a week, and did a two-year degree in Halliday's department at University College, London. And Halliday's linguistics, from the very first moment, seemed to me to be the right kind of linguistics. There wasn't a separation of form and meaning in the way that there was in transformational grammar. I could see that it was a socially founded theory, and it satisfied the kinds of things that had left me dissatisfied with the linguistics I had encountered before. So I did this Post-Graduate Diploma, a kind of Hallidayan foundation course, and that was the start of my future career in linguistics.

Politics and semiotics

The term social semiotics came much later. While I was there doing a PhD with Halliday I said to him: "You know, Michael, there isn't a book that sets out your theory." Because at that time, 1971 or maybe 1970, there were just articles, lots of articles. And he said to me: "OUP[1] has asked me to do an edition of some of my papers, but I haven't got time because I am writing this big grammar of English. Would you like to do it?" I said yes, and so he very generously gave me a large stack of all the papers he had, and I produced a book called *Halliday: system and function in language*, which was a kind of selection from his papers, setting out his theory of language. My contribution, as I see it, was that at the time the theory was called either "system and structure", "system structure theory" or "system function theory", and I thought to myself: if this is about anything, it is about function. And so I chose the title *System and function in language*, and it stuck. And I think from then on there was no further debate on what it should be. I think Halliday's kind of linguistics had always been semiotically organized linguistics, but I think his book *Language as Social Semiotic* (1978) post-dates that particular period.

Immediately I thought that this was a Marxist linguistics, although he never talked about that at all. But the way it is set up with a *chooser* on one side of the system network, and a kind of formed utterance on the other, is actually a combination of the social with the, let us call it linguistic, because semiotics wasn't being talked about at that time. That appealed to me: the social was combined with the other. At that time I had started a new job at the University of East Anglia, and there I joined colleagues who had started a group, studying Marxist readings focused on Literature. And I thought: well, language is also a super-structural category. That shaped my idea. And then with a friend and colleague, Bob Hodge, we began discussing what a kind of Marxist linguistics would look like, where you could trace the relations between the forms and the social base that gave rise to these forms. Somebody then said, at the time when we had published a paper – a small paper outlining the book which was to become *Language as ideology* (1979) – that that was the most significant semiotic publication in that year. And we were both astonished. But the relation of base and superstructure, which is sort of fundamental – it is called "realization" in Halliday's linguistics – is a semiotic kind of relation.

So the first step really was politically motivated; we were saying "you can see that in this particular interview here, or in this publication there, power is at issue". And how does power express itself through the resources of language? That was our question: could we show how power manifests itself in speech or in writing?

By showing that, we would give people the means to change their relations to power. We thought we could reform linguistics! Two ambitious goals, neither of which have happened, of course. So in East Anglia we started something called critical linguistics.

And then in 1976 Bob Hodge went back to Australia, to Perth. We had a long walk somewhere along the north Norfolk coast – with our families – and we said: "Well, what haven't we done?" We were quite happy with *Language as Ideology* (1979). But we said: "We haven't talked about all the other ways in which meaning is made, which co-occur with the linguistic." And then two years later I went to Adelaide, and so the distance wasn't quite so large, and we began working together again. In 1983, quite a long time after, I had moved to Sydney and Bob was on a visit, and we talked about writing a book. What should we call this book, which would look at all the other ways in which meanings were made? And we thought that one of the fundamentals of *Language as ideology* was Halliday's conception of language. As a tribute to his influence in our work, we should call it *Social semiotics*. We sent a proposal off to Polity Press and they accepted it, and from then on we talked about social semiotics. From then on, it was a term which other people sort of took up, even though, of course, it came from the title of Halliday's book. That was for me then a kind of decisive step. Really, now, I was doing semiotics more than linguistics. Because linguistics could not provide the tools that we needed in order to account for the whole domain of meaning.

How does your form of semiotics relate to other forms of semiotics, like that of Ferdinand de Saussure, Charles Sanders Peirce or Roland Barthes?

When staying, for a start, in a Hallidayian frame, I was most struck by the relations between base and superstructure. The person located in the social, making choices in the resources that are available to her or him, producing utterances. That was an overarching frame. And then Bob and I actually began to talk about signs. But the notion of arbitrariness in the Saussurian sign just didn't fit with a social notion. It fitted in one respect, namely that the power of the social was essential to keep the relation of form and meaning together. So we kept the conventional part, and we developed the notion that arbitrariness is not a feature of sign making. Conventionality *is*, because it is the power of the social that keeps these things stable. And of course we kept the Hjelmslevian, but also Saussurian notion of the paradigm, and the paradigm furnishing the resources for the syntagm, which are the effects of choice by a "chooser" – semiosis.

Barthes, of course, was a Saussurian, and *Elements of Semiology* (1967 [1964]) was a very structuralist kind of semiotics. We found the means of accounting for detail of form interesting. We didn't actually use that book as a foundation for our semiotics, but we found his notion of myth as a motivated sign interesting. The notion of the motivated sign as crucial and central came to me a bit later, actually. It is there in the book called *Social Semiotics* (1988), but it is not so strong. But we wanted to say that it is the social that is generative.

You also mentioned Peirce. I had read Peirce and I had read Saussure as part of a course in linguistics, and neither made much sense to me. But Peirce's notion of the sign became significant for me only once I saw what I had thought, namely the constant interpretation by somebody, the interpretant, in relation to a sign made by somebody else. This really shows that the interest of the recipient reshapes the sign and allows her or him to make a new sign. So the sign newly made in the process of interpretation, but also in the process of initial formation, is really, I think, very much like the notion of the motivated sign. It accounts for a chain of constant remaking in relation to the interest of the maker and the remaker of the sign. So I was slow in understanding Peirce, and I don't think Peirce affected me in how I thought. But I could then see that that's what is central in the Peircian scheme for me: the infinite, kind of constant transformation. And what is important in the Saussurian scheme is the notion of convention, and the notion of reference.

But you haven't taken up Peirce's triad of the icon, index and the symbol. Why not?

Because the only one that makes sense to me is the icon. And, in fact, initially I talked about iconic signs. And then some colleagues kind of niggled me about that: "An icon is visual, and you're not talking about the visual only." Then I realized I was using a metaphor from the visual domain to describe something that is quite general to all semiotic domains. So I thought: well, the sign is actually motivated, it is made as a deliberate act. "Deliberate" is a very strong way of formulating it, but I mean something that is not accidental in the combination of form and meaning. And then I could not really see how, on the basis of the relation of the form and the meaning, one would make a significant distinction between metonym and metaphor, because for me they are just different aspects of making the sign. Symbol didn't fit into that at all. Because either the sign is motivated, or it is not. And the symbol in Peirce, I think, is an odd thing, which is not really motivated, but exists. And the index is just another instance of a motivated sign: that is, it is deictic, it indexes. So it is not a fundamentally different relation, but is, rather, a difference at a different level, maybe more superficial, of the same relation, if that makes sense.

But why doesn't the symbol, the conventional sign, make sense to you?

Because it is established on the same basis as any other sign. You either have a theory of the sign in which you say: "Well, the thing that people call symbol is something which is supported by a lot of power." Like the Red Cross, which is the inversion of the Helvetian white cross. Power is there for good reasons, because we need to keep this kind of thing stable. But its production is not different in principle to the production of the index or the icon, only different kinds of things are related. And you could then say that there are different kinds of things that are brought together in the motivated sign. If you want to call one index because it has more of a deictic effect, and you want to call something else symbol because the power of the social is so strongly expressed to keep it in place, then go ahead and do that. But the principle of their making is the same.

Just to say something else about that: you know, some people use the notion of the motivated sign, and they say some signs are motivated, some signs are less motivated, some signs are not motivated. These are boundaries or decisions which are difficult to maintain. It is a bit like the English saying "being a little bit pregnant". Either you are pregnant, or you are not pregnant. Either a sign is motivated or not. With that premise I have got a means of testing that very strong notion of the motivated sign. If I wanted to use that I would have attempted to describe the conditions that make this particular sign seem permanent, and which would make this particular sign seem more deictic in its effects than these others, without then giving them labels. The moment you have a label, you invent barriers, I think.

So you would rather ask the question: In what way are they motivated?

Yes, exactly.

You talk about signs, but you also talk about semiotic resources. What is the relation between sign, semiotic resource and semiotic system?

I think sign is the basic unit of semiotics. And I think all mammals make signs. But also some non-mammalian animals make signs. When I hear a blackbird make a warning sound it is motivated. It is very different from the song that I love to hear in springtime, in early spring. So making motivated signs is, I think, a kind of given for many species, and certainly mammalians. That's the base, that's the building block.

Resources comes out of a different way of thinking for me. I remember I had been so worried about this constant kind of nagging; the postmodernist, feminist kind of critique of system and structure. I am slow to learn and very reluctant to change. But I thought: of course it is the case that the notion of structure belongs to a particular kind of "the social", or a myth about the social, or an ideology about the social, namely that it is kind of *set*, fixed. It is a late nineteenth-century notion which persisted into the twentieth century for various reasons. And the notion of system–structure had too much of what I think can be shown to be an ideological or a mythic attempt to indicate – and insist on – stability where there isn't actually stability. Things move at different paces, like the dynamics are different, and the viscosity of the social system changes. At the moment, I think things are in more flux than in the earlier part of the twentieth century, despite cataclysms of world wars and so forth. The social actually has not changed that much. I was ready to give up the notion of structure and system, but not that there are certain kinds of regularities. So I am not saying there are no, let's say, morphemes or clauses or sentences or verbs or whatever, in language. But rather that these are resources, and the relations between them are relatively stable and understood by a community.

So in the systemic-functional your emphasis is on the functional more than the systemic, then?

I think so. There is an early paper of Halliday's called "The categories of the theory of grammar", which I think was system–structure, in a Firthian[2] kind of way. But I think by the seventies he had become differently oriented. For me, the system network as a model is too stable. And Halliday himself, when he used to talk in Sydney in seminars he would say: "Well, this morning I heard someone in the weather forecast saying the temperature today will be 27 degrees, that is two above normal", and then he said: "Already the normal is changed." So he was using that as a means of saying that the thing is in constant flux. But he also had drawn a huge system network on the common room wall in the department, a huge thing like a railway goods yard. For me it is not a useful metaphor.

Taking the sign as the central building block, then, is it possible to say what is not a sign?

No. Everything is a sign if it is used as a sign, or turned into a sign. I now just caught myself saying "used as a sign". I think we *make* signs. Just before we started this interview the room got a bit rearranged and it was turned into something that was useable for a particular purpose. We are constantly remaking existing resources to do the job we need to do at a particular moment.

But, then, which role does systemic functional linguistics play in your work now, if any?

Well that goes back to the question you asked me a little while ago about the *kind* of semiotics. Lots of people talk about multimodality, and use the Hallidayan descriptive framework. And Saussure is partly responsible; he said at the beginning of the last century that linguistics will furnish the kind of resources by which we can describe the whole world of meaning, or words to that effect. So Hallidayan scholars have given us this enormously articulated system, and we can pick it up and move it on to architecture, or painting, or Barthes might have done fashion. And Theo van Leeuwen and I, in the *Reading images* (1996, 2006) work we said, rather: What is important about Halliday for our work is the semiotics. But not the semiotics as applied to a particular form. Halliday himself made a distinction between speech and writing. So there is a lot of his work which is about the organization of speech, which comes, I think, from his engagement with Chinese in his early work. He gave much attention to articulating a real distinction between speech and writing, which does not exist all that much in other forms of linguistics. He didn't use the word affordance at all, of course, but he said that speech is organized very differently because of its materiality, and I think he refused to use the word *syntax* in relation to speech.

Theo van Leeuwen and I also said that the materiality of the stuff that gets turned into the resources for communication, semiotic resources, has an effect on how a higher level category such as metafunctions gets articulated. We asked the following questions: What are the semiotic categories, which we need, and which would be common to all the material means which a society turns into the cultural resource of mode? And at what level do they become distinct? Because you can't, for instance, do with marble what you can do with sound.

What do you consider the main difference, then, between the two terms social semiotics and systemic functional linguistics?

Well, Halliday's linguistics was semiotic in conception, as I said, in the relation of the social to the linguistic. That is semiotic, because it points to the basic organization of the sign, and the social origin of the sign, the social production of the sign, by the person who always makes the sign out of existing stuff. On the other hand I think that Halliday remained a kind of a linguist, and I won't put an adjective in front of the linguist. And social semiotics, I think, has taken something from his linguistics, namely the semiotic organization and the semiotic principles, and attempts to apply them to the affordances of materials in specific social environments.

To answer your question specifically, I would say that social semiotics attempts to provide accounts of meaning and meaning making, of all kinds, in all environments. Systemic Functional Linguistics is a specific theory dealing with only one of the very many modes used to make meaning in human social action and interaction.

Summing up what we have been saying about social semiotics; you have talked about the strengths of this as a framework for your thinking. Are there any weaknesses? Anything it leaves out?

Well, the question is, what does it intend to do? And does everything that it intends to do cover what other people might want to do? And the answer is really clear: no. Because there are very many intentions and purposes and things to be looked at in the social. I think that social semiotics is interested in how meaning is *made*. What are the resources for making meaning? Who makes meaning under what circumstances and at what point? How is the resource changed as a result of that?

It doesn't go, as maybe the name says it should, into developing a social theory. It is located in the social, rather than claiming to be an articulated social theory. So should there be an accompanying social theory? I don't know. There are very many different social theories, and maybe that is a question that needs to be answered. I have good relations with people who do real ethnography. At a certain point, what social semiotics might possibly be able to do takes too much effort, and ethnography of a certain kind does it better. And so maybe complementarities of approaches are a better idea than talking about weaknesses, which might lead you to articulate a theory beyond a point of usefulness.

The other question that needs to be answered is: Do we have the right kind of categories at the moment for social semiotics as a theory, or for the very many different modes which come under the frame of social semiotics? And my answer would be no, we don't. And so there is a whole vast field of work to be done. Is that a weakness, or is it a sign of its relative recency? I think at the moment I am too interested in what it can do, rather than what it can't do.

Mode

Let us move to questions around mode and look more closely into multimodality, where you have been doing seminal work. So we will start with the very simple question: What is a mode? And what is not a mode?

Well, the way in which Theo van Leeuwen and I answered it in *Multimodal Discourse* (2001) and the way I would answer it now are different. This is due to the work that has been done between 1996 and 2000. It is important to locate when you have done something, because it reflects what was available, and what the issues were. When we came to write that book, or, rather, when we had talked about it, we said in relation to mode, really the situation is such that the community decides what its resources are. And if a community decides to articulate a particular set of material things, or conceptual things, into mode, then that is a mode for that community. Rather than saying that image is a mode, and photographers come along saying, look, a painting is different from a photograph in ways that we could show to you. And in any case we are talking about materiality, and oil paint is different to digital photography. We would, from the beginning say: *A mode is that which a community, a group of people who work in similar ways around similar issues, has decided to treat as a mode.*

So anything can be a mode, then; is it a socially defined category?

I think anything that is used to make signs, and is understood by others as a sign in a relatively stable kind of way, can be a mode. Going back to social semiotics you can see how Bob Hodge and I, and Theo van Leeuwen and I, would still stick to the usefulness of Halliday saying that every utterance has to fulfil three metafunctions. Then, I would say a mode for me would have to be used by a community as being *modal* and in that it would need to fulfil the three functions of saying something about the world, being able to describe social relations and producing entities which are coherent internally and with their environment.

You have worked quite a lot with visual modes. We would like to challenge you in a different field. How about music as a mode. Does it have all the three metafunctions? How do you treat ideational meaning in music?

Well, let me say – and I think in London that is a sort of common parlance – multimodality marks a domain in which meaning is investigated. It isn't a theory. So different people come with different theoretical frameworks and tools to this field, and therefore the field begins to look very different.

It is a total mistake to say that although every mode would have to meet the requirements of fulfilling these three functions, every mode would do it in the same way. That is, that in every mode there would be something very closely resembling lexis, or very closely resembling syntax as we know it, or morphology or textual organization as we know it from speech or writing. I think that one doesn't have to say that music has the equivalent of words, sentences or paragraphs. My question rather is: What does lexis do, at a somewhat "higher", maybe more general or abstract semiotic level, and how is that done in music, or in gesture or in dance? But ideationally I would say that music has the equivalent of saying something about the world: when you listen closely to any piece of music, it says something about the world if you want to accept that. And not only programme music, say like Beethoven's *Pastorale*, where you have the thunderstorm happening in the middle of the symphony, and the birds singing again after the rain. Every piece of music says something about the world. So Mahler's symphonies say something about the social world on the turn from the nineteenth to the twentieth century. Rap says something about the social world, and it says something about social relations in that world. One of the things that I find really important in this field is the work that Theo van Leeuwen has done in Sydney, in small publications initially and then in his book [*Speech, music, sound*, 1999] which I found totally compelling. He used a lot the work of Alan Lomax, anthropologist of music, where he shows social relations.

Medium

I would like to turn to the concept of medium, because I hear it used in multimodal work as the materiality of the sign, the medium that you use to utter a sign. But we also have the more common meaning of medium in our society as being a technology with an associated practice. So what is the difference? Or what is your take on the concept of medium?

I think this is an area still to be described carefully. I think I am clear about it. Sound, for instance, the physical substance of sound, the compression and rarefaction of air, and its impression on the physiological structure of my ear, or in the production by my so-called speech organs, becomes medium for the kinds of things I want to do in speech. And then, at that level, it kind of finishes. And so the medium of paper is a carrier of kinds of things. And I think the term medium is properly applied at that level. But when I think of a "message", say, I have shifted levels and the term medium now refers to a different kind of "carrier": "carrier" still, but different. The distinction that I want to make shows that there is now a problem with terminology. Partly because we are confusing or conflating quite distinct domains – sound as carrier of meaningful entities, and as a "means for dis-seminating messages" – and partly because of the convergences in technology. So when people talk about *multimedia*, quite often they conflate the resources for representation with the resources for dissemination. They conflate mode as representational resource (where, yes, mode is a carrier of meaningful entities in one sense) with medium as disseminational technology (where the book is a carrier of meaningful entities of a different kind, as is a "poster", as is the "Internet" accessed via Wi-Fi), and I think we need to separate these. Theo van Leeuwen and I wanted to say that there is a relation between these, *and* that they are independent kinds of things. So the little bit of paper with stuff scrawled on it, you know "Cat lost last night" and pinned on a tree in a park, becomes medium of dissemination or distribution of meaning. Generally speaking I would make that kind of distinction between mode (How do I represent things or present things?) and medium (How do I disseminate and distribute things?). When we talk about sound as medium, I think we are talking about it at a very different level. At that point it might be important either to differentiate by occasion or by level; or by asking "What is being disseminated?" I think it needs to be more carefully articulated.

Affordances

Then I would like to turn to the concept of affordances. You talk about affordances of a mode. Could you just start by explaining the concept of affordances, where it comes from and how you use it?

It comes from James J. Gibson's work on biology. He talked about environments as having affordances and its biological and psychological conjunction. I first came across the concept of affordances in work I did with a former colleague, John Ogborn, professor of Science Education here at the Institute of Education,[3] who, in one of our research project meetings said: "Oh, you mean affordances, the affordance of image?" And I thought, it was like Saul on the road to Damascus, the lightning struck, I was blind for a moment, and then after that I saw differently. Of course image can do things that writing can't! And of course sound can do things which writing can't. Of course the infinite variability of the gesture in its sweep or in its pace is not replicable in writing, because we have limited lexis. So different modes allow you to do different kinds of things, and not only *allow* you to do different kinds of things, but insist that different things are done. You can't make a gesture without pacing it.

Would it be relevant to talk about the affordances of the medium too, as medium of dissemination?

Well, people do, and I find myself doing it. And sometimes I use the term facility, because I am not clear whether one should restrict the term affordance to something material, and how it gets shaped by social use and social shape into mode. I am unclear about that. So sometimes I have used it, and when I do, immediately my super-ego chastises me and says that that is sloppy use of terminology. But at the moment I am not clear enough about the distinction.

But you have taken it from a different field and moved it into multimodality. So why should it not be moved into yet another field?

Yes. Why shouldn't it? So the job would be for somebody to say why it shouldn't or why it should. When I talk about the production of the sign I think that there is a signifier which is apt to be the "medium" – let us say just for a moment – for this signified. And I combine them, and now I have got a new sign. But sometimes that metaphoric process is not precise enough. This has the potentials for expressing that, but of course the potentials never absolutely match near enough what I want to do. It is that nearness or aptness that is the metaphor of affordances. The point where I worry is when I see metaphors like *literacy* disseminated promiscuously throughout the world, because I regard that as kind of sloppy thinking.

Literacy

I was going to ask you whether you find the concept multimodal literacy useful or not?

I would avoid it because it says we have got an answer when in fact we have a question.

Yet you have edited a book with that title, in 2003.

Reluctantly. Because we, Carey Jewitt and I, were put at the point where the publisher and the editor of the series said "that's what we want". And at that time – not an ethically strong motive – we thought it was important to have the book published, more important than insisting on the purity of the term.

The same year you published the book *Literacy in the New Media Age*, where you actually discuss the components of the concept of literacy. What would you call it if you don't call it literacy?

I may have said it in that book. The interesting point is that no other language in the world has a term like it; no other society in the world has felt the need for that term. Now, if English was a small language like, with all due respect, Danish or Norwegian, it would not have had that kind of currency or power. It is the significance of the power of English as a language that carries this term along with it. As a metaphor it has been used so widely, even within English, in ways which are uncontrolled. For instance, a former colleague of mine would say that somebody who can't give you a sensitive reading of a Shakespeare play is actually illiterate. And that was an academic who ought to have known differently. So given that the term has such uncontrolled potentials for being used harmfully, I would much rather say let's not use it.

The question is: What do we actually mean by literacy? For instance, in a book I wrote in 1979, which became *Learning to write* (1982), at the very last moment before I sent the manuscript off, driving into Adelaide, I thought: Of course, you have got to put something in on genre. Because when a child learns to write, it has to produce a text, and text has generic form. So I rushed back home in the evening and wrote a not very good chapter on genre, which is for me the beginning of the genre debate in education. Is genre part of literacy? And what is then *not* part of literacy? What is textual form? Where are the boundaries, and who sets the boundaries? Is competence in genre equivalent to competence in literacy? Am I entitled to call somebody illiterate if she or he does not control the generic forms that I do? It's a problem.

But what would be your suggestion then, on how to talk about what a person is able to do with semiotic resources?

Well, in the book *Learning to write*, what had offended me were a number of things. One was the enormous effort in education on reading, and very little effort on writing. This was around 1975–80, and it still persists. PISA (Programme for International Student Assessment), for instance, is much more interested in reading than in writing. So it still persists, and a Marxist might give you a good account of why that may still be so. I would much rather say something that I said in that book: "Children are regarded, in mainstream thinking, as being on the road to competence. And before they reach something, not well defined, that constitutes this competence, they are incompetent." And I thought this was backwards. From a Hallidayan perspective, we look at what people *can* do. From a Chomskian perspective, one would say, with Chomsky, at any time when children learn language, they constantly construct new grammars. What I was wanting to document was that what children do is sufficient in terms of the resources they have for describing the world they want to describe. And I wanted to say that that's the case with all of us: we have certain kinds of resources, which are never fully sufficient for describing what we want to do, but we use them anyway in the best way and as near to what we want to say as we can. This changes our view of the child from being insufficient and incompetent to being always sufficient and always competent, and always expanding the range of their resources, which allows them to do more and more things. To answer your question, at the moment I would prefer to be descriptive and say "that's what this person can do" I might then say that I would want her or him to do something else or more, and I would say what that would be. It would not make negation the basis of evaluation.

Text and communication

Let us start this section with the concept of text. You said that writing is about producing text. So how would you define the concept of text?

Well, it has taken linguistics – never mind other kinds of disciplines – a long time to say that speech also produces text. And it has to do with the fact that we began to be aware that we had technology for making speech storable and examinable and analysable. And I think that that had a big effect, to say that there are spoken texts. And I think we can think of "spoken text" now as relatively normal, although a lot of people who refer to text mean writing. But text etymologically is *texture*, it is things woven together. And if you think of meaning as made multimodally, which I think it is always, then different things are woven together. And so now you have a kind of naming problem, a theoretical issue, whether you want to talk about these woven things that make a relatively coherent meaning entity, whether you want to call that a text, or whether you want to invent new labels for things that are other than writing, or other than speech and writing. Although, for me, speech and writing are so different in organization that already there would be a problem. But at the moment I am happy to call a spoken text a spoken text. So I would use the term *text* for any semiotic entity, which is internally coherent and framed, so that I can see this entity as separate from other entities. I can relate that entity to other entities of its kind in other modes, or maybe even in the same mode. At the moment I am happy to call these things text. But somebody might come along and give me a good reason to say that actually there are too many problems with that. In a book written in 1984, *Linguistic processes in sociocultural practices*, I suggested that *text* was characterized by being socially coherent and complete.

You also use the word communication in some of the titles to your books. Does communication always happen through texts?

I think that in communication we produce texts. I would make that kind of distinction. Text is a material thing, which is a result of semiotic work; communication as semiotic work. Communication is a process, and the result of the process is the production of a text. If it is not recorded, it still is a text, because I have my recollection as a text.

The subtitle to one of your recently published books is *A social semiotic approach to contemporary communication*. I wonder, how closely you would say semiotics is related to communication?

Totally. Semiotics would be the theoretical frame in which I look at communication. But the term *contemporary* is there to say that we live in a period in which, for instance, the whole modal scene is shaken up, with writing becoming less significant. The technologies we use for production and dissemination are having a big effect on the communicational landscape. Social changes have huge effects on semiotic organization. So that was the contemporary, the function of the contemporary as sort of a little red flag.

So would you say our time is different from all other times in terms of how rapidly these things change?

I can't talk about *all* other times, and I can't even talk about parts of the globe where things are still relatively stable. I always feel that when I go to Scandinavia things are less profoundly shaken up, or in flux, than here. But fifteen years ago that distance was larger; Scandinavia seemed much more stable in its assumptions, values and organization than England did. And I think that that distance for me unfortunately – nostalgically speaking – is diminishing. I said in something that I wrote (*Writing the Future: English and the making of a culture of innovation*, 1994), and I mentioned it earlier in our talk: despite the cataclysms in two world wars, and the horrors of both world wars differently, the social stayed relatively intact. Of course, what happened was that the underpinnings of the nation state got shaken profoundly. But the nation state more or less stayed intact, and the world that I experienced as a six-, seven- or eight-year-old in Germany, after the cataclysms in that war and all the horrors of that war and before, still allowed me to see the world of my grandmother, as being a world that I would have recognized in its social organization, and in its means of dissemination. And I think that the distance between, let's say, 1950 and now is greater than the previous sixty year period between 1890 and 1950.

Design

In the book that you published with Theo van Leeuwen in 2001, *Multimodal Discourse,* you introduced the concept of "strata". That is a concept we recognize from Halliday's work. Is yours the same way of using the concept of strata?

We had endless problems in saying what these four[4] things that we want to talk about are. They can be described as being in a sequential relation, chronologically. They can be described in a hierarchical relation of some kind. And actually now they are for me insufficient, and I think even at the time we were not actually that keen. In as far as it suggests the kind of structural linguistic notion of stratification, I would not actually be very happy with that now. Have I got a better way of labelling it? No. Maybe they are in the way that Halliday always insisted on the metafunctions. He said, "these are simultaneous". He always insisted. And people would say, you know, isn't the ideational prior, or the interpersonal prior. But he always wanted to say they are simultaneous, and maybe that's the way of thinking about it. These are simultaneous semiotic domains.

But do you think you came any closer to describing how they interplay?

Well, I do think design precedes production, for instance.

It seems like design is the concept that has lived on from that book, and been developed further.

Well, design is an alternative to prior concepts. I had a life in Critical Discourse Analysis, and in Critical Linguistics before then. And I became dissatisfied with the notion of *critical* discourse analysis and critique, because critique is backward look-ing. Design is prospective, and in education that seems to me essential. Critique says: What has happened? Usually what it analyses is not the work of the power-less, but the work of the powerful; that is one problem. The other problem is when we did critical linguistics in East Anglia in the early seventies, the world was a different kind of world. Although it was already beginning to be shaky, certain social forms were still in place, and power relations were still in place. We thought that if we could show how these worked, then everybody would want to change their relation to power and their use of power. And, of course, linguists would see that they need to talk about power. We would do this by bringing the situation, the contemporary period, into crisis. Critique was a means of producing crisis, and out of crisis would come change. By the time we were in the mid-to-late eighties there was crisis all around; you didn't need to produce it. And also with my move to education I thought, well, what you need to give young people is a means to understand what others are doing by showing them how these resources *can* be used in relation to design. We wanted to send them into the world with tools, which would allow them to design the imaginations that they have about the world, in an ethical frame. So that entered into the New London Group[5] work and became a feature there, and I think it appealed to people. Design is about the resources that these young people need in order to function in relation to their own wishes in society.

Would it be right, then to say that the shift from talking about competence to talking about design also empowers the sign-maker in a different way?

Yes, absolutely. Competence is always limited by what is socially regarded as competence – quite a strict framing – whereas design is not limited by a framing. You can make new things and, of course, my notion of the sign is that signs are always newly made, and they are used in designs that will always be, in some ways, different.

Then how do you analyse design? It is there, behind everything, but how do you get a grip of it? How do you know what the available resources are?

You change things. What happens if I put this element not in the centre, but on the margin, or on the top or on the bottom? Or what happens if I change what is written here into an image, or vice versa? And then you can see that these things will come to look different. And they will have different meanings. Sometimes they will become incoherent. And then you ask: Why was it coherent before? Well, somebody designed coherence. This is what the school should teach, and therefore we would need to have a teaching that shows what the affordances of these resources are, and what the affordances of these resources put together in ensembles can be. Then the student may ask: What is around me, and how can it be used, in relation to my purposes.

In your work you display a great engagement in the interests of the sign maker. And in your book *Multimodality; A social semiotic approach to contemporary communication* (2010) you write about the rhetor. Could your theory be termed a multimodal rhetoric?

Rhetoric, I think, has to be provisional, given what I said about our contemporary world. You therefore need the notion of rhetoric replacing convention. Conventionality did what rhetoric now has to do. So rhetoric has newly come to the fore. Not that it was ever absent, but it was invisible because of the relative stability of conventions. Now the set of choices modally are so much more. The set of choices in terms of media as means of dissemination are so different. So design comes into it.

So what would rhetoric contribute to the field that semiotics can't?

Semiotics is a theoretical orientation that says: How do people act to make meaning? Rhetoric says that people act to make meaning by assessing the environment in which they make meaning: in terms of resources, in terms of intentions, in terms of what is to be communicated, in terms of who the others are. So semiotics is the larger, conceptual theoretical frame, in which rhetoric has a particular place.

How about aesthetics, does that have a role to play in the understanding of multimodal communication?

Well, I will give you my opinion, which will not be repeated by anybody else. I want to make the things I do accountable in terms of the social. I should say that in 1984 I wrote a little book called *Linguistic processes in sociocultural practices*. Not a snappy title, but I did not want to have the reification of a title such as "language and society". In there I was very keen to get away from a Marxist notion of "discourses speak us", the kind of Althusserian notion that we are entirely shaped by the social. Being a father of altogether four children I have experienced that children come into the world already different. And I didn't want that to be eliminated, or ironed out, or suppressed. Because they remain different, they engage with the world differently. So I want to have an accountability to the social while not forgetting about individual difference.

Aesthetics in the world I came from, a degree in English literature, naturalizes certain kinds of things as being evidentially, naturally, outstanding. But I would like to have an aesthetics which says that everything is the product of social action, which is then socially evaluated. So in my little book I called aesthetics "the politics of style". Because style is, for me, the politics of choice, and I make certain kinds of choices, and people respond to these choices and say: "Well Gunther dresses like a kind of scarecrow. He can't be an academic, surely, dressing as he does." So the choices I make are valued, but they are valued by somebody assuming a certain social power. So if style is the effect of my choices, there then follows the social evaluation of it; that is, the politics of style. I want to be able to have aesthetics that allows me to describe anything that is socially produced, and then to understand why something is socially placed high up, rather than at a lower level. So yes, do I think that some people take much greater care about writing, or have a facility in music, or can draw three lines and they are kind of moving. But I would not separate that into an aesthetic domain. I would say all expressions are subject to the politics of style.

So you would emphasize the social construct of aesthetics, or of taste?

Yes, I think taste is a social construct. Nobody comes into the world liking wine, or certain kinds of cheese, or "surströmming".[6]

But you also emphasize the individual, and the materiality of signs. Wouldn't that be another inroad into aesthetic experience?

Of course. That is why I say I don't want to do without that. If I say: "Listen to the fourth movement of Mahler's fifth symphony, doesn't that absolutely break your heart!" and they say, "Well, actually, no" it is because their path, through roughly the same kind of social experiences as mine, has nevertheless been different right from the beginning. As human beings we come into the world differently. I have a memorable experience of one of the four children of which I am a parent, coming into the world, and hearing the midwife say: "Oh, she's a cheeky little thing!" I think one can recognize something of the demeanour of a person, even at the moment of coming into the world. Even if it disappears under a layer of the social, it remains there.

Applications

Now I would like to turn to areas where you have applied your theories. For two decades you have been working at an Institute of Education. How closely do you think education and learning is connected to semiotics and communication?

Learning is, of course, communication, and if you called it teaching and learning, it would be one specific instance of communicational processes. It can't be otherwise. So there is no question that the pedagogic relation is a relation of communication, with certain forms of power, assignations of responsibility and possibility. Learning happens, the way I see it, through one's own making of signs in relation to the world in which one is. *I* remake the world in my making of signs from the world, and in doing that *I* change the resources I have. In changing the resources I have, I change my potentials for action in the world. I call that learning, a constant change in my resources and an accumulation in transformation: an expansion, an extension. That is what I call learning. It is a result of semiotic action. So I can look at it in terms of meaning. You utter something, I engage with it – not all of it, but part of it. I can never engage with everything, representation is always partial. So I take something from there, I transform it for myself, and that changes my inner resources. I have changed meaning for myself. In making the change in my meaning into a new sign, I put something in the world which might have an effect on changing meaning resources in my community. So you can see from the point of view of meaning that in that process also I have changed my capacities for action. I have changed my identity. These things are *so* closely related. What changes is what position you take on that particular experience.

Your projects within education show a very broad range of interests from the English classroom to the operating theatre. So how broad is your concept of knowledge?

Knowledge probably is an effect of the changes in our resources, and what I can bring as a result of their change into my next engagement in the world. Ten years ago I happened to be in Stockholm stumping through the snow at night. I came from a conversation with Staffan Selander about learning, and I thought: Am I learning at the moment? What am I learning? And, of course, I am learning something. I am learning something about the temperature, about the depth of snow, about how long the snow had been lying on the ground. What is *not* learning? When are we not learning?

Then your concept of knowledge seems to be quite different from what is defined in a curriculum.

Of course. You then look at the social environment in which this happens. Has somebody set the curriculum, or are you setting the curriculum? I would say eighty-five per cent of what I have learned has been as a result of me setting my curriculum. Me setting my curriculum in language learning: in order to be successful with these young women around me I had to speak English better! Nobody said, you know you must speak English better before we let you loose on these young women. So I think lastly, by and large, we set our own curricula. And of course we come into the institutional settings of learning with that.

At a time when power in the social was organized in a relatively strict way, and the classroom was organized in a relatively strict way, my own disposition towards learning got changed by the power of the institutional situation in which I was. Now that has changed completely because the state has given up its power. The market is dominant, young people enter into the market at an incredibly early age: six, seven, eight. As consumers they have choice. They come into the classroom not expecting to be weighed down and oppressed by somebody else's authority, but thinking: I have choice. So you see it in the social environment and then see what that social environment is like, and see learning in that particular way. Young people now learn the most complicated things, and James Paul Gee has written about that kind of very extensive learning very persuasively; the most complicated things are learned of their own accord. Much more complicated than anything they learn in the school.

Still, we often think of cognitive processes like learning as closely linked to linguistic conceptualization. Do you think we underestimate other modes in learning?

Yes, totally.

Can knowledge come in other shapes than concepts and words?

I am not a connoisseur, but I can differentiate four or five different types of wines. I can *taste* whether a Chardonnay has had a long life in an oak barrel or oak shavings have been added to the wine in the barrel. Is that knowledge? And can I communicate it? With difficulty, because we haven't got the lexis for those kind of things, which is knowledge learned through taste, through our mouth. Can you differentiate smells? Can you say, that's a lovely smell that reminds me of the rose I smelled in the garden? Is that knowledge?

We end up asking the same question again: What is not knowledge?

Exactly. And there I think the boundaries have been set so strictly: that which I can't discuss in speech or in writing, the extra linguistic is regarded as irrational. I think it is time we said excuse me, but I think I will knock that fence down.

Education seems to cater for all your interests, but are there other domains that you would have wished to explore?

I think my life has been a series of accidents, really. I am very glad to have moved into education. When I was in Sydney, before I came here, I was in a place that focused on media studies and media production, cultural studies, cultural production. Of course that is enormously important; it's a vast educational site, but not seen in those terms. And then I came here, and because of the Neoliberal agenda matched with its profound social changes, education has been in the firing line since then. And so I was forced to think very hard about those kind of things. There is less need for serious consideration or the same intense consideration when you are looking at an advertisement, or a film or something; even a debate on pornography or violence is less severe. What is happening in terms of the government's response to curricular things is deleterious to social futures, in a much more significant way than, say, the things that might appear within cultural studies or media studies. Not that they are unimportant. Not that they are not educational, but they are seen differently.

And then the accident that somebody here, John Ogborn, who was professor of Science Education, had a kind of encounter with Halliday in linguistics in the seventies, and found it useful in particular ways. He approached me and invited me in to do research projects with him. We had three long projects, nine years of intensive research in science classrooms. The science classroom is a very, very good laboratory for semiotics and multimodality, because all of those things are there, most of them actually not recognized in the formal descriptions and curricula of Science Education.

We have talked quite a bit about rapid changes. Are we in the midst of a paradigm change?

Since I was a person partially responsible for introducing the notion of multi-modality, and because I am given to sort of provocative statements, I have been saying things about a diminishing significance of writing, at least in certain domains. Sometimes I have been thinking, have I unchained something that I should not have unchained? Have I taken the stopper out of the bottle and let the genies out, and what damage will be done? Is it a paradigm change if we go away from an acceptance of the notion of centrality of writing – which says that we are constituted as rational beings through the affordances of writing – which has enormous effects on those groups who do not use writing. Is that a paradigm change? I think it is. Is it a paradigm change to say that we are not users of signs but we are makers of signs? Lots of people have said that in all sorts of different ways, but it actually makes the kind of cliché of learner centred education different. It is not just the question if we really are interested in learners, and we will video them running round the classroom. But, it says, we need to attend to the principles that this person brings to their interpretation of the curriculum, and take that ser-iously. And then we need to change our pedagogic stance and pedagogic activity in relation to what we have discovered about the principles that this person has brought to the engagement with the curriculum. That is a learner centred approach. Is that a paradigm change? Does it distribute power differently? I think so.

So, I think, the social does stuff anyway, and academics always run behind the horse that has left the stable. We are not leading anything; we are attempting to understand what has happened. I am not politically active, except in the sense that I attempt to produce a theory of learning which gives significance and dignity to the work of very, very many people in a way it never did before. Is that a significant political action? Yes it is. That is how I would think about that.

The future

Let us finally turn to the future. You did mention that there is a lot of work to be done in developing multimodal semiotics. Can we really hope, or aim for, developing a general semiotics that will be relevant to all modes?

If semiotics is to do with making meaning in communication you could ask, what can be transferred? For instance, in writing we have now accepted that we need to pay attention to a general conception like genre. There are a million different definitions of genre, as many people are concerned with it. But, for me, genre is the instantiation in more or less material form, in writing or in speaking, but in other forms too, of social relations. So it is a materialization or inscription in some way of social relations. In which mode would that not be important? In which mode would I be able to say we will drop for the moment concern with the interpersonal? Or the social? I wouldn't.

I would say: What kinds of categories are essential? If we go to the smaller features, for instance, in linguistics in English we have a distinction between a plosive and a non-plosive, a continuum between a voiceless plosive and a voiced plosive, between intensity and non-intensity in < t > as against < d >. Is intensity a general semiotic feature? Is it a feature of colour? Is saturation related to intensity, and desaturation to lack of intensity?

These are general semiotic features because this society decides that these things are important. For example, somebody who buttons up the top button on his shirt is "buttoned-up" because they do something which constrains. Is constraint a general semiotic feature or not? It depends on the society: if I haven't got clothes, I cannot button up the top button of my shirt. Look at the social and see what kind of things are significant in the social. Are they expressed in everything that I call a mode? Yes, but very differently in different modes. And it is the very different which makes us think that it actually might not be there. This is relevant to everything that has become modal, which is recognized by at least a group in the social as being a means of communication, a resource with some degree of regularity that is understood by its members in some way. I think then we can say what kinds of semiotic categories are essential. *Not* – and this is the difference on my part to other forms of semiotics – not: Does it have clauses? Or does it have clauses of this kind or that kind; morphemes of this kind; does it express past time morphemically or lexically? Not those questions, but: Is it important to have deixis? What would it be like not to have deixis? Those are my questions.

So it seems like you are trying to move away from the view of language as a "prototype"?[7]

As I said earlier, Saussure prophesied that the twentieth century would be the century of semiotics. And he said that linguistics had elaborated and articulated tools that would allow us to do descriptions of the semiotic beyond language. When you look at the kind of linguistics that had been elaborated by the end of the nineteenth century, the focus was on historical linguistics, history of sound changes, history of lexis, not all that much on syntax, only some of it. So it was already kind of optimistic given what in hindsight seems like a somewhat restricted assembly of tools. But, more importantly, the materiality of speech, which was really underlying Saussure's work on the history of sound changes, wasn't attended to in relation to other things. Is there a history of the visual in European history? Of course there is. Can it be related to the social? Of course it can, but differently. Important thinkers often have a way of phrasing things so that everything they say can be turned around, and the negative form, its inversion, is more interesting than the positive. So Saussure said arbitrary and conventional, well, let's drop the arbitrary. Linguistics is a model for semiotics, let's drop that. But there are some things in what linguistics has done: the relation between the social and the formal, in Halliday's linguistics, well, let's keep that.

Do you think there are other theoretical perspectives that might shed light on multimodality?

I said quite some time ago that people come to multimodality with different questions. Psychologists talk about multimodality, but they have different kinds of questions. It is less about meaning in the semiotic way than about the question: is something remembered better if it's visual? Is something for instance, remembered more easily in television than in radio news which is spoken, or news in the newspaper? Do these modes have an effect in terms of memory? That is just one question that a psychologist might ask. Anthropologists might ask a different question. So they come to the field of multimodality, but with different questions. And I would say that that is important.

Finally a very open and difficult question: What do you expect will be the central topics for future research on multimodality?

I think one of the central problems is that people too readily use the label without investigating the domain that seems to be named by the label. That's a problem. So everybody now does multimodality: "I have always done multimodality, because you know, I have always looked at images – although my main interest is in writing." This is a use of the label instead of an intense concern with what the domain is that is being described by the label.

The other is then the need to have intense descriptions of what these things are, and what they afford, and what they can't do. Affordance and constraint: what is better done for this audience with these kind of resources? We need to work more on these sorts of relations of the social and the modal, of the social and the substantial. For instance: Is knowledge about an elbow joint better shown in a three dimensional model or in a drawing or in a written description? I had broken my arm at the elbow playing squash, this is why I ask. And the doctor said, well, we ought to operate because it will always be bent if we don't. But the problem is that the nerves go through a very small point, and it might be damaged and then you can't use your fingers. And I was thinking, would I prefer a doctor who had read a lot about elbow joints, or a doctor who had actually encountered elbow joints in some material form, in an anatomy class or even as a kind of model? Do you see what I am saying? The written can do certain things that maybe the model can't do, but the model can do something that the written can't. So it is those kinds of things we need more of in the future: What can these things do, how are they used in the social? Why were Western societies content for so long to use writing as the central means of communication, even when it seemed inapt?

So you are asking for more specific descriptions in more specific contexts?

Absolutely essential.

Notes

1 Oxford University Press.
2 John R. Firth was a British linguist and one of Halliday's teachers.
3 University of London.
4 Discourse, Design, Production, Dissemination.
5 A group of ten scholars from all over the English-speaking world who met in the American town of New London in 1994 to discuss the future of literacy pedagogy. Their manifest "A pedagogy of Multiliteracies; Designing Social Futures" was published in *Harvard Educational Review* in 1996.
6 Fermented herring, a Swedish dish.
7 Scollon & Scollon, 2009. p 179.

References

Barthes, Roland, 1967 [1964]. *Elements of semiology*. London: Cape. (First published in French, 1964).

Chomsky, Noam, 1965. *Aspects of the theory of syntax*. Cambridge, MA: MIT Press.

Halliday, M.A.K., 1976. *System and Function in Language: Selected Papers*. Oxford: Oxford University Press.

——, 1978. *Language as a Social Semiotic: The Social Interpretation of Language and Meaning*. London: Edward Arnold.

Hodge, Bob & Gunther Kress, 1979. *Language as ideology*. London & New York: Routledge & Kegan Paul.

——, 1988. *Social semiotics*. Cambridge: Polity Press.

Kress, Gunther, 1984. *Linguistic processes in sociocultural practices*. Oxford: Oxford University Press.

——, 1994. *Learning to write*. 2nd edition. London: Routledge. (First published by Routledge and K. Paul, 1982).

——, 2003. *Literacy in the New Media Age*. London and New York: Routledge.

——, 2010. *Multimodality: A social semiotic approach to contemporary communication*. London and New York: Routledge.

Kress, Gunther & Theo van Leeuwen, 1996. *Reading Images: The Grammar of Visual Design*. London: Routledge. 2nd edition 2006.

——, 2001. *Multimodal Discourse: the modes and media of contemporary communication*. London: Arnold Hodder.

Kress, Gunther & Carey Jewitt (eds.), 2003. *Multimodal Literacy*. New York: Peter Lang.

New London Group, 1996. "A pedagogy of multiliteracies: Designing social futures", *Harvard Educational Review*, Spring 1996; 66(1): 60–92.

Scollon, Ron & Suzie Wong Scollon, 2009. Multimodality and language. In: Carey Jewitt (ed.), *The Routledge Handbook on Multimodal Analysis*. London: Routledge.

Van Leeuwen, Theo, 1999. *Speech, music, sound*. Basingstoke: Macmillan.

5

THEO VAN LEEUWEN

Background

When did it all start? How did your career begin?

It was a mixture of design and serendipity. I became a student of the Amsterdam Film School in the late 1960s. It was a time of enormous cultural change in the Netherlands. The three things that interested me at the time were film, jazz and semiotics. I was already reading Roland Barthes and others at film school, and we started a magazine where we wrote about semiotics and film. So already at that time my interest in semiotics existed. But what was going to be the main stream in my life was not yet clear.

By going to film school I was engaging in things that were very different from the background that I came from. I am a son of a protestant minister. There were barely any images in our house at all, and no images at all in the churches. So by choosing film I went in a different direction from my upbringing. I loved my father very much, but while he was full of praise when I wrote poems, when he saw my first film, which I made in my first year at film school, he looked at it and said that he found it rather superficial, and I was deeply hurt. It was a film portrait of a friend of mine, not a bad film – it actually won two prizes. So, coming from a logocentric world, I wanted to prove that images and film could be as good as language. The idea of the language of image, and the language of film, already attracted me, as did French filmmakers like Chris Marker, who talked about the *caméra stylo*, film as writing, doing intellectual work with film. That fascinated me enormously at the time, to the dismay of one of my most admired teachers who thought I risked my creativity by being so intellectually interested. Much as I admired him – he was a very good novelist as well – I never believed that. I don't think the mind and the emotions need to be in each other's way at all. Creativity and intellect can be combined.

So that was stage one. Then later I married an Australian and moved to Australia with her, and although I made quite a lot of films there in those years, and wrote scripts as well, it is hard to get into film in another country, another language, another culture – particularly because in the seventies Australian films were very much concerned with national identity and Australian themes. One film I made, which also won a prize, got reactions like "it is very well made, BUT so European" or "BUT so Kafka-esque" and various similar things which showed a certain distance.

Meanwhile, to make money, I was teaching film production at Macquarie University and I started studying linguistics in the evenings. Still with the idea that it would lead to my original idea of writing about the language of the image, and the language of film. But I thought that if I learned more about linguistics I might be able to do something new instead of just imitating the French writers with a kind of second-hand Saussurean view on things. But the course was all Chomsky and generative grammar. So I started looking for other things and I did my research master's thesis not at all about images, but about intonation. I learned an enormous amount from that. So it took some time before I started writing about images, and meeting Gunther Kress was the catalyst.

In 1983 Gunther Kress had examined my research master's thesis. I later met him at a conference. We talked, and he said "We must do some work together", very generously. Not long after we sat together in his garden in Newtown, and he said "Well, what shall we do, then?" I said it had always been my interest to write about the language of the image, and he said he had realized for years that it no longer makes sense to analyse media texts, text books and so on without taking account of images. Then he walked up the stairs to the bedroom of his two-year-old son and came down with two little books, and said "What do you think of those?" And so we started talking. And the two little books are now in *Reading Images*: the Ladybird book and the Dick Bruna book. But my PhD, which I did at the same time, was still not on images. It is called *Language and Representation* (1993). By this time I had discovered systemic linguistics, as Gunther of course already had years earlier, and my thesis was a way of working through that. That is how that started.

In the eighties and the early nineties I did less filmmaking work, particularly after one film became a financial disaster because of a terrible line producer who had spent all the money before the crew and the actors had even been paid. I just wanted to go easy on the filmmaking side of things for a while, and I returned to working as a jazz pianist alongside my university work. But I also felt that the kind of film and the kind of music I loved was past its peak, while semiotics was just at the beginning of an upwards curve. Here I could possibly contribute something new. So, in my late thirties, I decided then that semiotics was going to be my main activity, and started to engage more seriously in academic work, especially the work with Gunther and my PhD thesis.

What roles did your experiences from being a TV producer and a jazz musician play?

I think that knowing is based on doing, so it is good to be able to calibrate my semiotics with what I know about how things are actually physically done. More generally, I think that our knowledge is grounded in what we do, and ultimately draws its meaning from that – this is the core of my theory of discourse as the recontextualization of practice. Knowledge is ultimately based on doing. I am always trying to apply that in my work, but now new practices are coming up, of which I do not have as much hands-on experience, and that sometimes makes me feel tentative. Still, there is much I can draw on, also in my practice as a musician. In the case of music and sound, for instance, an important part of my book on that subject is about interaction between different musicians. And that account can be useful for analysis as well as practice. And musicians are experimenting with musical interaction, exploring and expanding it, just as much as thinkers. Film is another example. One of my earliest articles was about rhythm and film editing. From my practical knowledge of film, I was dissatisfied with the lack of articulating the fundamental role of rhythm in film editing. I used my experience as a film editor as well as what I had learnt about intonation and rhythm. It makes me happy when practitioners say "Yes, that exactly puts into words what I am doing here". Every now and again that happens. At the London College of Printing I taught in a master's on photojournalism and documentary photography, and the course leader, a very good photographer, said "Sometimes I think about the things you say when I am in the dark room". I have had comments like that from film editors as well. That, to me, is the best praise I can get. It means that I am doing something meaningful.

From SFL to multimodality

What differences and connections do you see between systemic functional linguistics and social semiotics and multimodality, and what role has SFL played in your work?

There were two stages. The first one was that I definitely wanted to talk about language and image, and also language and media, but I was looking for linguistic theory I could use. Even American Functionalists that I liked, such as Longacre (e.g. 1974) and so on, still saw language as a whole. So the concept of register was a big eye opener, it made it possible to talk about certain ways of using language, for instance media language. That was a first step, the concept of register, being able to talk about the language *of* this, that or the other, e.g. the language of media.

Stage two relates to what was then going on in film semiotics. I actually studied for a year in Paris with Christian Metz, a student of Barthes and a film semiotician. Unfortunately by this time he had abandoned linguistics, which I did not know, and moved to a psychoanalytically inspired approach, so I learned a lot about psychoanalysis, and especially about Freud's theory of humour, which I have never regretted. The reason why Christian Metz did not get very far with his approach to the language of film was because he was looking for equivalents to form classes (Metz, 1974). He was basically asking "Does film have something like the word, or like the sentence?", and of course it hasn't got units of that kind. So when I realized that the systemic linguistics approach is essentially semantic, I saw immediately that now the question could be asked in a different way; not "Does film have words or clauses?", which it does not have, but "Is there something in film that fulfils the function of words and clauses?" Modality is a prime example. Language has specific resources for expressing modality: the modal auxiliaries. Film does not have these, but it can express modalities, degrees of realism, in its own ways. So I could now combine my knowledge of filmic signifiers with Hallidayan semantic-functional concepts. And Gunther and I did the same thing by combining the signifiers described by Rudolf Arnheim (e.g. 1974, 1982) – volumes, vectors, and so on – with Hallidayan transitivity concepts (Halliday, 1994). Arnheim, by the way, was an absolutely brilliant semiotician – he just did not generalize the meanings he linked to these signifiers in his discussion of examples. But it was all there already, waiting for the two sides to be brought together into a semiotics of the image that recognizes specifically visual signifiers as realizing meanings that are neither specifically visual nor specifically verbal, but belongs to the culture as a whole. So that is what we did, and then there comes a point, of course – and Gunther, as usual, got to that point before me – that we have to see that in some areas meaning can only, or at least most easily, be expressed either visually or verbally. You have to look for the similarities as well as the differences between visual and verbal meaning making, and at that point you might have to ask how far the Hallidayan framework, which has, after all, been designed for language, can reach. But you should always realize that you might not even have reached the point you are at without the Hallidayan framework. In the same way, you could write a systemic grammar of a language other than English, and you can go very far with that, but there also comes a point at which you have to ask "How is this language actually different?", even if it is another European language. There comes a point at which you have to put your Whorfian hat on again, if you are a good analyst. We have now reached that point. So while not at all letting go of what we have gained, what we have learned, we now need to look at those differences. Once I started looking beyond what we had described in *Reading Images* (Kress and van Leeuwen, 2006) I found aspects of visual communication that were less easily representable in terms of the mostly binary system networks. I became ready to draw on other models. This already began to emerge in *Multimodal Discourse* (Kress & Van Leeuwen, 2001) and later found its way into my research, e.g. on the voice, on typography, on colour and so on.

How do you see the relation between your and Kress's work to O'Toole's work?

O'Toole separately and at the same time started applying Halliday's work to other semiotic modes, to visual art as well as to architecture and music (O'Toole, 2011).

He took a slightly different approach, foregrounding the idea of rank, and linking the ranks to specific systems, in a very plausible way, though without working out these systems in detail, as Gunther and I did in *Reading Images*. It has also been important work, and some of his students, like Kay O'Halloran, have gone on to play a big role in multimodality as well (e.g. 2005). I do not think that we have been deeply influenced by each other, but we are on parallel tracks. But I do not think you can just put the two together, and then have the whole package, as it were. O'Toole's work is specifically about figurative images. Our work can also be applied to abstract images, layouts and diagrams. Another thing about O'Toole's work is his background in Prague school and Slavic linguistics. His focus on art is in that tradition. He has also translated and edited a series of formalist and Prague school writings that I have kept drawing on for many years.

Semiotics and social theory

You have been mentioning the European tradition. How do you place social semiotics in relation to other semiotic traditions?

As I said, the semiotics I discovered when I was young and at film school was French structuralist semiotics. After that I discovered the Prague school; it was not referred to a lot at the time, though it deeply influenced systemics. I continue to admire Roland Barthes. He was trying to do things in a structuralist way but he was a critic as well, and always aware of the social and cultural context. Never "specializing" in the semiotics of this or that: there is not a single mode, as we would now say, he has not tackled, especially in *Mythologies* (Barthes, 1973), and in that he was a pioneer in finding a language for talking about other things as if they were language. There are still things from Roland Barthes that are part of my overall framework, for instance a slightly tweaked version of his concepts of connotation and myth (cf. Barthes, 1973, 1977), and his work on fashion (Barthes, 1983), which I still think is very insightful and definitely has a social semiotic dimension to it. Then, of course, later his work changed, but I feel he had every right to stand back a bit and think "Okay, but what have we missed". It is the sign of a good thinker. And now that I try to write about aesthetics, I am re-reading that later work. I became aware of Peirce mainly through Umberto Eco's critique of the structuralism of the 1960s as not paying attention to semiosis, and to semiotic change (Eco, 1976). But I felt that the social dimension was lacking in Peirce (not in Eco). Maybe I should re-read and see if I still think that way. The theory was also more about sign interpreting than sign making. It confused communication and interpretation; it looked at interpreting nature and interpreting human communication more or less the same way. This was not the line I wanted to take, but maybe, in the time of the "prosumer" the relation between sign making and sign interpreting needs rethinking. But in a social semiotic way, Halliday's move to replace Saussure and Peirce as the founding fathers of semiotics with Malinowski is still important. Malinowski very early on had his finger on the key themes for social semiotics, so I keep saying it, "Look, if you really want an early twentieth-century founding father, if that is really necessary, have Malinovsky".

In relation to that, what do you see as the basic major strengths and weaknesses of the Social Semiotic approach?

There are, of course, different varieties of social semiotics now, different accents. Without wanting to generalize too much, I would argue that context is the key. Halliday taught that we need to explain language, and the use of language, on the basis of context – of the situational context as well as the cultural context. I stick to that as the starting point of social semiotics. But sadly these crucial notions have not been developed and fleshed out in a more sociological sense, and in relation to specific discourse and genres. The social in social semiotics is not always sufficiently kept in focus. That is where I find inspiration in critical discourse analysis, with the way Norman Fairclough (e.g. 2001), Ruth Wodak (e.g. 2009) and so on, and earlier Bob Hodge and Gunther Kress (1993), engage with social theory and relate it to the detail of language, in the way that I believe Halliday intended. There are some sociological references in social semiotics, principally Bernstein (e.g. 1981), and Berger and Luckmann (1966), but more is needed. So when I started doing my PhD – I was then 38 – I hesitated as to whether I would do it in sociology or in linguistics. I talked to an excellent sociologist, Bob Connell (now Raewyn Connell). I admired him very, very much, but he simply was not interested enough in language, in the detail of language. And then I talked to Michael Halliday. He was unable to supervise, having too many students already, so I talked to Jim Martin. But he was not interested enough in social theory for my liking. I said "What do you think about so and so?" and he said "Oh, I don't read that stuff". It was a real dilemma. I should add that this was in 1985, and Jim's participation in the Newtown Semiotics Circle changed that attitude. And he did say something at the time I first talked to him that I will always remember. I asked him "What, then, is important to you – what is to you a good piece of work, a piece of work that matters?" And he said, "Something that other people want to use". I thought it was brilliant. I have never heard it before and thought that academic work was about truth rather than usefulness. Jim had a different answer that I actually thought was quite good. In the end I thought "I can probably learn sociology on my own". I had a half year sabbatical and used it to read myself into sociology – you could still do that back then, use study leave just to read. I still use the notes I made then. And I followed the courses Halliday and Jim Martin gave, and never regretted it.

Yes, that is the next step; that is what social semiotics needs to do, to bring linguistics and social theory together, as I tried to do in my thesis, and as Bob Hodge and Gunther Kress had done earlier. Another thing, of course, is history. If you want to understand and explain things, history is fundamental. It has been neglected and it has therefore become a great area of ignorance amongst linguists. Among the semioticians, Eco is an inspiration in this regard.

Gunther Kress has moved in a direction where he argues for using a less critical
approach, and maybe a more strategic approach, but it seems you have not?

Yes, it is true that, at a certain point, Gunther began to distance himself from the
critical discourse group that started in Amsterdam in 1992, in which he had been a
key member. He and Bob Hodge had, once again, been ahead of everybody else
with the book *Language as Ideology* (1993). They actually started critical discourse
analysis, if you discount philosophers like Herbert Marcuse, who wrote very
interestingly about language. Nevertheless, when he moved to the Institute of
Education, Gunther Kress to some extent distanced himself from CDA, and began
to propagate the idea of design, which is a contribution that had to be made,
though for myself I cannot see why it should be antithetical to criticism. If you
want to change things, you need to analyse what is wrong with the way things are
now. And being critical is not necessarily being negative, it just means that you are
critical, and you are open to what the outcome of that will be. I find this idea of
"positive critical discourse analysis" a distraction. Why should you decide beforehand
whether to be positive or negative? Why should you not first investigate what you
investigate and then come out with a grounded, motivated, evidence-based critique that can make a positive contribution to thinking about what needs to be
done differently, and *then* move to the stage of design? But if people are scared of
being critical, that is scary itself. Quite a few people now say they are doing critical
discourse analysis and yet are not really critical, or they write critical with a small C
or put it between brackets, which are all forms of distancing. I have done it myself
once or twice, but I have now come to the conclusion that it is unacceptable. In
the humanities we are supposed to educate critical citizens – how can you do that
if you are not game to critique yourself?

Sign making

Back to basics – In your work you have used the notion of sign, but not a lot,
and maybe not in the same way as some others do. What is a sign to you, and
what is not?

The concept of sign has a history of being looked at separately from context – that
is the problem, and the reason why I prefer "sign making" – the practice in
which signs are resources – over sign. Sign making means that the relation between
the signifier and the signified is not that of the two sides of a coin. It is much more
flexible and fluid than that, and whenever it is *not* fluid, that is because people have
made rules: "You have to use this signifier to make that signified", and such rules
are made in and for specific contexts. In another context people will use the signifier in other ways. So that is why I am a bit worried about the sign and the traditional discourse of the relation between the signifier and the signified, rather than
between practices of sign making and sign interpreting, in which people do use
semiotic resources. Colour is a fantastic example of that, and that's why I am so

intrigued by it. There are contexts in which colour codes are very precise, for instance safety codes, traffic signs, uniforms. And there are contexts in which colour meaning is fluid and malleable, and in which colour meanings may be more freely (but never entirely freely) interpreted on the basis of shared cultural associations or of the qualities of colour, which I have been describing in my book on colour, rather than on rules, or on "codes". So it's a good example of why you cannot simply take out the sign away from its context. You have to describe it as a semiotic resource with a meaning potential which get actualized in a specific context, rather than a kind of lexicon of colour meaning. For all these reasons I do not really use the word "sign" a lot these days.

What do you think about the concept of a motivated sign?

Signs are always motivated. If people decide to have arbitrary signs, they will have it. If you give people identification numbers, you create arbitrary signs. But it is not because the *sign* is arbitrary, it is because people have decided they want an arbitrary system, and in a sense not even that is arbitrary. People do it for a reason. There is a motive. With language we forget, over the years, how and why signs were originally motivated, so they appear arbitrary, but they are not. If you take the trouble to go back in time, you will find the motivation, so long as some records exist. Language is a great preserver of the past, and understanding its history as a history of social practices, rather than some kind of evolution, can only add to our appreciation of its richness.

How do you define communication and text?

I have not thought a lot about defining communication. I have simply used "communication" as a term for semiotic practices. It is a word with which we indicate the *semiotic* practice that people are engaged in. Text is more of a problem. The meaning of the term "text" has been extended so much in, and applied to, so many things. I have not actually written anything about this as yet, but I have begun to say here and there that maybe the use of the term should be restricted back to actual "textual artefacts". So a conversation would not be a text. It would be a practice, done by people in specific contexts. It only becomes a text when we turn it into an artefact (e.g. by transcribing it) and insert it as a key resource into another *interpretive* practice (e.g. conversation analysis). Thus texts become resources, either normative resources, as when we use a recipe in the practice of cooking, or oracular resources, as in the conversation analysis example, where we use it as a resource to distil truths from, truths about conversation, in this case. The same text can then be used differently in different contexts, e.g. different interpretive practices. A film is used in one way when you go to the cinema, in another way when you give a lecture in film studies. So texts are resources for practices. And, of course, text making itself then also becomes a practice. "Text" was a useful word in the seventies: as with many of our terms, like literacy and grammar, it served to legitimize a field, to say "We are just as legitimate as you, we also analyse texts". The text linguistics of the seventies was an important move. We moved from the sentence to the text. But then "text" became a ubiquitous and very loosely applied term, and now, in relation to the new media, is even confused with resources. So I prefer to talk about practices, and about communicative practices as one kind of practice, and about the text as part of that – sometimes a big part, sometimes a small part.

Multimodality and mode

Now we turn to the notion of multimodality and modes – what is multimodality actually?

"Multimodality" and "mode" have also been used rather loosely and defined rather perfunctorily. We can say, as Gunther Kress does in *Multimodality* (2010), that multimodality is a phenomenon rather than a discipline – the phenomenon that communication integrates a range of means of expression simultaneously. But perhaps this is not entirely correct, because other disciplines use other terms for the same phenomenon, like intermediality and multisensoriality. So "multimodality" is also a disciplinary position, an approach to the study of the phenomenon that hails from linguistics and semiotics.

With "mode" there is a similar problem. Most of the time it is quickly and perfunctorily defined by a few examples, as I have done many times myself: "Modes", and then between brackets, "(e.g. image, music and text, or image, music and language)". Such examples belong to an era in which, despite multimodality, we could conceive of modes as being able to exist separately as well as in combination. Hence we could write a grammar of images as though images could exist separately as well as in combination with "text" ("image-text relations"). But now we have realized that many modes, despite being able to realize all three metafunctions, cannot be used on their own. Colour for example, has to go with something else that it is the colour of – with dress, with architecture, with images and so on. If it is a mode, then it is a different kind of mode from, say, the image or architecture. At the same time we began to discover that some of the things we thought were specific for images are not, and that many of the principles of the so-called grammar of images, for instance framing and salience, could also be applied to other "modes". They are semiotic principles, resources or ways of doing things that cut across modes. So what are they? As I mentioned before, modality is also one of these. It can also be applied across modes. We have a problem here that needs to be addressed theoretically, better than we have done so far.

These things, again, began to dawn on Gunther and myself in *Multimodal Discourse* (2001) without being fully resolved there. We defined mode essentially as an immaterial semiotic resource, a semiotic resource that is abstract enough to be applicable across different means of expression, or different media, as we called it. And, of course, we said that language is such a resource because it can use writing or speech. Narrative, too, would be a mode, because it can be realized in many different media.

It still begs questions that have not been completely resolved, and again I have to insist on the importance of history. At the time we thought that text and image could convey "messages" on their own, as well as together, they actually could and were used separately as well as together. Photography books had no captions other than the place and time the photos were taken, e.g. "Madrid, 1956". Now photographs are part of something else, and take forms that would be less meaningful on their own: low contrast backgrounds, thumbnails, and so on. Practices are changing, and as a result our theories have to adapt. Roland Barthes was not wrong when he distinguished the "linguistic message" and the "photographic message". That is how it worked, and how it still works in older media; in newspapers for example. But in other places things now work differently, and new technology is a vital part of that. It works with principles that cut across modes and that can be equally applied to text, image, graphic symbols – in short to any kind of "object". So, in social semiotics, what are we going to call these? How are we going to reconfigure these two elements – the semiotic principle of narrative, that cuts across media, and the media and combinations of media that it will operate on? A complex question, because all this is probably quite recursive in its own way. So I think that with mode we have to catch up with what has happened with the semiotic practices around us and readjust our terminologies and theoretizations accordingly, and in a way that can both capture the traditional idea of mode, since it still exists, and the new types of semiotic resources that are coming into being.

What is grammar?

From a social semiotic point of view, grammar is a system that prescribes how language is used. Of course, we thought in the past that we were describing language, but were we actually? That is a good question. We were prescribing it. We worked in the service of national languages – that was our role. We were appointed as lexicographers and codifiers, as regulators of the national language and its orders, with a dominant "language" and "dialects". We can now see this as national languages become destandardized. When we used the word grammar in the subtitle of *Reading Images* (Kress & van Leeuwen, 2006) it was a political move in a way, to give status to the study of the visual. But, when a very early version of *Reading Images* was circulating in Sydney, Paul Gillen, a colleague and a philosopher, wrote us in some dismay and said "You're making rules where none existed". Sometimes I think he was right. We did make rules. I visited a high school in Western Sydney, a very tough school where there had been riots, and to my astonishment there were *Reading Images* charts on the wall and they were quite openly prescriptive. Paul Gillen foresaw this. I am not totally against making rules. I have often said that images have become so important that we cannot leave their interpretation entirely open, we need to come to some agreements about how we shall give them meaning – think of scientific visualizations, the regulatory use of spreadsheets, flowcharts, highly visual strategic documents and so on in organizations, or of the continuing use of sexist, racist and colonial imagery in comic strips, advertisements, movies, tourist brochures, and so on. And anyway, language has many rules, but poems have nevertheless been written. So we can make visual rules, but art can still be made. Emilia Djonov, Kay O'Halloran and I did a study of works from an exhibition by David Byrne (Djonov, O'Halloran & Van Leeuwen, 2014), where he created artworks with PowerPoint, astonishing artworks, very perceptive, very interesting: another clear example that intellect and creativity can work together. Even a highly rule-bound, clunky semiotic resource such as PowerPoint can be used to do something creative. We need not be too worried. The same happened with genre in the 1980s when genre theory began to be taught in schools in New South Wales and children would come home and say "Mommy, I've done a recount today". And literary people for whom "genre literature" was inferior to high literature, were concerned. We should not be too dismissive. As social semioticians we are responsible for what our ideas do to the world.

In *Multimodal Discourse* you and Kress said you did not make grammars of any new modes in that book. Why not?

Originally the book was meant to show how to do multimodal analysis, to produce more "tools" that people could then happily jump on and apply to a pile of texts. Instead we got into discussions about multimodal theory. Even then we thought that multimodality should not become a beehive of analytical activity without theoretical underpinnings. The worry was that people would just jump on it and have a bunch of texts, and think "now I've got a tool, and off I go". We were trying to talk about what multimodality actually is, and what its terminologies actually mean. It was difficult, as the new discussion about mode will also be. We went through many byways and hit many dead ends. All these terms – senses, channels, modes – created a universe with blurry boundaries. We tried to bring some order into it – from the social semiotic point of view – from the point of view of communication as a social practice. We did not completely succeed, but at least we made a first step, and that was the strategic move of merging stratification, which is describing language as a layered object, with Goffman's notions of "footing" and "hearing" (Goffman, 1981) which describe the same things, dynamically, as practices in which layerings become divisions of labour. This only gradually emerged. We could have gone another ten years, but we decided that we had better put something out, even though it was not yet perfect. It was at least an attempt to build some theory in relation to where we were at that time more than ten years ago.

How is your notion of stratification related to Halliday's?

It is related to Halliday, but has other influences as well. Stratification is a sort of geological metaphor. It describes language as an object. So the main thought was to reformulate it in relation to practice, so you have a more social semiotic idea in which, as I just said, layers become a process with a division of labour. You could argue that strata are perhaps objectifications, because language is not an object. It does not exist. Language does not exist. It is nowhere to be found, it is an abstract notion. What exists is speech and writing, and these are practices.

Back to modes – you have talked about the evolution of modes. How do they come around, and how do they evolve into being a whole mode? How does it relate to semiotic evolution and technological innovation?

That is a whole set of questions! Important questions for social semiotics, and questions that have not yet been central enough in social semiotics. So you need to go to theories that can help us to understand the drivers and processes of social change a little bit better. This is something that linguistics has been bad at. It has mystified the development of language as a kind of organic, evolutionary process, rather than as a historical human achievement. We have to look at broad social and cultural drivers for change, rather than start with the technology. I could talk about a particular phenomenon, for example diagrams, where there are apparently contradictory tendencies. On the one hand, diagrams are very rigorous, systematic and logical ways of representing things, and, on the other hand, they have also developed as very loose and associative forms of representation. These tendencies have different histories. The first has a long history in science. The other has a history which started in advertising in the early 1950s in relation to the idea of brainstorming for copy-writers – the so-called mindmap. So that relates to drivers such as innovation, but also data analytics. New inventions often have a long period of latency before they really fall into place and move from specific limited uses to much wider application. For instance, Emilia Djonov and I wrote a paper about bullet points (Djonov & Van Leeuwen, 2013), and we found out that in the late 1950s, a fellow employed by Exxon invented the bullet point – it was called a corky dot then, because his name was Corky – and it was propagated as a good way to pitch an idea and write a concise report. There was of course no such thing as a bullet point on the typewriter at the time, it had to be added by hand. Then there comes a point in which these developments fall into place and technology makes them available much more widely. In the age of global corporate culture, everything has to have bullet points, not just business reports, also history and philosophy lectures. So technology now has to have a key place in the study of language and multimodality, and it has to be studied as a resource that makes some things easy to do, other things not so easy, and yet other things impossible. And then we have to study what people do when they want to do something that is not so easy, or impossible. We should not fall into the trap of either seeing everything as determined by the technology, or thinking that you can do really everything you want anyway, if you are technically savvy enough. Certainly, there are no hard and fast rules, and much is possible, yet people's practices are quite similar. Technology to a point now regulates semiotic practices. Software designers design semiotic systems, and it is very sad that we so rarely have a chance of working with them. At exactly the time that Gunther and I thought of the quadrant of given/ new and ideal/real, Powerpoint, too, came up with semantic quadrants that you could put things in that. At that point centre/margin was not yet possible – we also made that comment. Right now centre/margin is totally ubiquitous, most diagrams have something in the centre. In *Reading Images* we wrote about so-called analytical images, which include a wide range of diagrams. Now Microsoft Smart Art provides many more types of analytic diagram than we ever did: nine broad types of diagrams, each with up to forty-eight subtypes, which all have names and come with descriptions of what they are good for. Technology is now centre stage in the development of semiotic resources.

Technology and meaning

We have talked about the importance of technology. What is your concept of meaning? Does it have anything to do with technology?

What we said in *Multimodal Discourse* (Kress & Van Leeuwen, 2001), is that there has been a shift. Certain technologies of recording and distribution were initially intended to have no semiotic impact, to just record and/or transmit things as they are. This has turned out to be an illusion. Contemporary technical media are also means of expression. And if initially they are not, they will soon become so. So therefore I do not really want to make a strong distinction between traditional media and these new media. If you want to think about writing, for instance, it is just as interesting and important to study the technology of the scribes in the Middle Ages and how that relates to what could be said and what could not be said, as it is to look at PowerPoint now. The difference with the new technologies is that they have artificial intelligence built into them. Things that you had to know how to do before can now be outsourced to the machine. This was not reflected in our definition of "medium" in *Multimodal Discourse*. There we saw media as purely material, as tools and materials. In modern media, the immaterial – knowledge – has become material.

But what we had already begun to see in *Multimodal Discourse* was that media do not just "realize" meanings, they add meanings of their own. Yes, in *Reading Images* we provided a grammar that could be applied to texts in different media: photographs, paintings, magazine pages and so on. The next step was to say, but what are the additional meanings that may be realized directly in and by the medium? I think that these are different from the kind of meanings that are independent of the materiality of expression, and that, today, they focus particularly on the expression of identity and on new forms of textual cohesion.

The voice, for example, has long been considered as having no meaning of its own and at most being a marker by means of which you could recognize who a person is, rather than what kind of person he or she is. But now it has become a means of expression, and one that has a lot to do with identities and roles.

Phonology can no longer be construed as merely making meaning possible without adding meaning itself. We have to think of the materiality of the voice and its articulatory potential (along with the way in which technology can now enhance and modify it) as a semiotic resource.

So you have these two levels, and a particular semiotic mode may start out as a medium and then become a mode. An example I have recently been talking about is kinetic typography, the movement of letters, words or even longer stretches of text. Which is definitely a new kind of thing. We now have an alphabet that moves. Kinetic typography begins as an experimental practice that works directly with the affordances of the medium. One of my favourite examples is the title sequence of Hitchcock's film *Psycho*, where the name of Anthony Perkins, who is schizophrenic, splits in the middle. A kinetic metaphor, and an invention of the moment, tied to this particular film. But then people in labs may start thinking up a system to systematically organize kinetic typography, as e.g. in PowerPoint, so that it becomes codified and formalized. And once that happens, all or part of it can become abstract, and realizable – for instance, not just in kinetic typography but also in dance.

Theory building

Do you think we will ever get to such a thing as a grand theory of multimodality? Is that a goal at all?

That is a difficult question. As I said before, I believe it is necessary to have a consistent theoretical framework and a consistent use of key terms such as "mode". That is theory building, and it needs to happen, whether you call it a grand theory or not. On the other hand I very much believe in building up theory case by case, step by step, gradually developing it as you accrue more examples. That is another thing I have also learned from Gunther Kress.

The grand theory is something that we strive for but never achieve, because by the time we have achieved it the world has already changed and the theory is no longer applicable. And if you then continue to work on it, you will be a has been before your life is over. Yes, we need to build theory, but we also need to be flexible and build our theories so that they can move along with the times.

Do you think metafunctions are globally operative across all modes, and what can we do with that? What are the consequences?

The use of metafunctions in thinking about other semiotic modes has been an incredibly important step, and excellent heuristic. And it has still further to go, particularly in relation to the idea of communicative acts, or multimodal acts, whatever you wish to call them. But when I wrote *Speech, Music, Sound* (1999) I commented on the applicability of the metafunctions, because it seemed to me that in sound and music the ideational often has to piggy-back on the interpersonal, because sound is so fundamentally interactional. Then I thought, but what about the visual? Aren't the phenomena we interpreted as interpersonal in images not always representations of interpersonal relations rather than that they are directly interpersonal? Doesn't the interpersonal in images have to piggy-back on the ideational? Close distance to the viewer, for instance, is never actual close distance, only a representation of it. Again, in studying PowerPoint I found that the written language on the slides is often entirely devoid of any interpersonal things. There are just nominal groups. No mood structure. The metafunctions are distributed across the modes in the multimodal mix, and not every one of the modes in that mix has all three. So there are issues to discuss. What kind of work are the different semiotic modes given to do?

Overall I think semiotic modes are very flexible as to what they can and cannot do. I would not want to assert anything as an absolute, fundamental, immutable property of either the visual or of sound or of some other mode. If a need were to occur to make the visual more interpersonal than I think it currently is, ways will be found, but the way it is mostly used now still seems to focus more on the ideational. With sound it is different. Again, when people talk about absolutely essential characteristics of sound, they often comment that sound, in contrast to vision, is omnidirectional. This is true, but if, for some reason, you want it to be more directional, then you invent a directional microphone, and people have managed to do just that. Humans can bend semiotic modes to do things that they originally do not seem to have been designed for, if and when the need of it arises. We need to be alert about the way in which the metafunctional work is divided among the modes in a multimodal text or communicative event, and it can also be the case that certain uses of language are not fully trifunctional, e.g. the use of language on many PowerPoint slides, because there simply are no interpersonal signifiers. It may also be that either the ideational or the interpersonal is, at a given point in time, more developed in one mode than in another, or used less in one mode than in another – that is what I am beginning to think. You could say that in multimodal communication we always need the three metafunctions, so that all three are present in any act of multimodal communication, but which metafunction is mostly or solely carried by which kind of mode in the mix may differ. And when looking at modes separately, you may find that some develop the ideational metafunction more than others, and others the interpersonal. Multimodality requires the metafunctions to be rethought and not taken for granted.

Linguistics in a multimodal world

In your view does language differ from other semiotic modes?

Let me put it this way; there are semiotic modes that are equally shared by all humanity and others that are not, or less so. Speech and singing belong to the former, even though making "graphic" traces and music are also universal. But speech and singing are the only ones that require no tools or materials other than the human body, and that gives them a special place. But when it comes to the things people have said only language can do, I begin to wonder. To give just one or two examples, people have said that only language can be metalinguistic, and only language is capable of generic representation. Not true. There are lexicons of icons that have a true meta-visual function, and are thoroughly generic to boot. Indeed, in the next edition of *Reading Images* we will have meta-images to denote, for instance, the different process types – two boxes with an arrow connecting them representing the transactional narrative process, one box with an arrow emerging from it the non-transactional narrative process, and so on. It is easy to do. And so many of the claims that people have made for the specificity and uniqueness of language are not necessarily true for all times. They may have been true in the practices and beliefs of other periods of cultures, but they are not now.

What about linguistics in a multimodal world?

I am very grateful that I have learnt linguistics. There is nothing quite like it in the humanities when it comes to sharp and systematic analytical training. Linguistics teaches us to describe things very thoroughly, very systematically and very methodically, and that is what I will always be grateful to linguistics for. I made the right decision when I chose it over sociology as the key discipline for my PhD thesis. But certain of the things that were entirely taken for granted in linguistics when I began to study it in the late seventies, e.g. the arbitrariness of the sign, the way that language evolves etc., now need to be questioned. And, by and large, the social was not very strong in linguistics, not even in sociolinguistics, although that is now changing rapidly. Language is as important as ever, but it now needs to be studied in the light of multimodality. We now need a more integral and coherent picture of multimodal communication and all its resources, and all of the ways in which these are integrated.

In the beginning of *Introducing Social Semiotics* (2005) I said that social semiotics needs to describe semiotic resources, the practices in which they are used, as well as the histories of these semiotic resources, their meaning potentials and the discourses that surround them in particular practices – the discourses that regulate them, evaluate them, criticize them, teach them, change them and so on. What linguistics and linguistic discourse analysis can contribute here is, first of all, the fundamental part of describing both the resources, which can be done with the same approach that we use to describe language, and secondly the way in which these resources are used in specific practices, as well as the texts that surround these uses. But social semiotics is, by necessity, multidisciplinary. We need history so we can understand *why*, for example, a particular semiotic resource has poorly developed its interpersonal resources. And to describe practices we need ethnography, or, if they have already been described, documentary research. Social and cultural theory can be good pointers to the issues that make it worthwhile and relevant to look at particular resources and practices. They have less methodological luggage to carry around, and so they get there earlier. But often they just put a flag in the ground and then leave for the next issue. Then we come along and dig a little deeper.

You are a strong proponent of interdisciplinarity. What are the strengths and weaknesses of an integrationalist view in relation to multimodality?

Yes, we just talked about that, how can we still keep the analysis of resources and their uses central – the kind of work linguists and discourse analysts have always done – and at the same time realize that that does not give the whole picture, that you also need social theory, history, ethnography? So the integrationist approach says that your discipline should not be your ideology and your world mission – it should be your craft and your skill only. Then and only then you can work together with people from other disciplines. But there are two buts to that. The first is, how thinly do you want to spread yourself? When I wrote *The Language of Colour* (2011) I used the work of some true specialists, like John Gage (e.g. 1999), who I later had the good fortune of meeting, who spent his entire life studying colour. If everybody was as multidisciplinary as I suggest people should be, then it would become harder to become a John Gage, and we would be much impoverished. I could not have done my book without his work. We need people like that. That is number one. Secondly, even though we need multidisciplinarity, we also need to develop the component disciplines. If we allow them to stagnate, multidisciplinary projects would be much impoverished. So universities and organizations that provide research grants must support both multidisciplinary projects and the disciplines and specialisms that contribute to them. The grant system now is much focused on supporting theme-oriented, national-priority-oriented projects, but they must also support projects that emerge from within the disciplines, without whose frameworks and methods no multidisciplinary projects would be possible. Otherwise we risk academic work becoming automatized and thoughtless, especially now that methodic analysis can be outsourced to computer programs. Corpus linguistics has now become very popular – but where is the theory? I am not against it, but it makes for a very specific lens on language, which, by default, could become a whole view of language, so that we suddenly think of language as an incredible maze of phrases rather than in terms of grammar. What does that mean? Is that actually what language is becoming? Are we thinking about it and debating it, or are we just using corpus linguistics because it is there, has status and kudos, gets grants. I want to ask those questions.

Impact

You have done groundbreaking work and inspired many people. Do you consider yourself an avant-garde scholar?

I think I have been lucky to be in Sydney at a very good time for social semiotics – in the late eighties. It is true, as I explained earlier, that I already had the idea of the "language of the image", but one person having an idea does not make a viable movement. The late eighties was exactly the time when this whole idea of extending Hallidayan social semiotics into multimodality began to blossom in

Sydney. We were very daring; Gunther Kress more so than me. I would still say "Maybe we should look at a few more examples", but Gunther would say "Let's put it out in the world". We did not necessarily read as much as maybe we should have, and instead just charged ahead with daring ideas. And somehow that worked. It was the right moment. Social semiotics was a new thing, at the beginning of an upward curve. I was very lucky to be there and to be part of it, and to help put these new ideas in the world. *Reading Images* turned out to have quite a lot of impact. More impact than *Speech, Music, Sound*, even though I think that that book is by no means one of my worst pieces of work. But less people seem to want to move into that area, despite sonification now creating many new things for sound to do. Maybe its time is still to come – I do not know.

What are you particularly proud about?

That I have been lucky enough to realize that dream; I actually did it, and successfully so. When I look back I feel that something has been achieved. And it all happened in very pleasant talks during early morning breakfasts together. We were just talking, making notes. At a certain point there was a sheaf of notes from our talks and that became the book. Yet at the same time I feel there is much that has not – or not yet – been achieved. I am never completely satisfied with my work and try to look forward rather than back.

How should scholars and students relate to your work? Do you prefer followers or critique?

I am glad you ask that question, because sometimes I wonder whether I created a monster. That happens when I get to see work of people who think that *Reading Images* is a kind of machine: you put images in and then something called analysis comes out of the other end. Or when people think that there is just one exactly right answer to every question, so I get lots of emails from all over the world, even from professors asking "How do I analyse this particular image" – wanting the authoritative answer. That bothers me. To my PhD students, and also to undergraduate students and master's students, I try to explain that my ideas are just made by me, why I made them that way, and that they are not some kind of objective truth I have discovered; that they too can make such ideas, or improve upon mine.

Humanities theories, like scientific theories, can be used in different ways, and for good and bad purposes. Some people use systemics to critically analyse things that are wrong in the world, others use it to try and make machines that do things which humans do better, such as talking or translating or telling stories. That is the problem with methods; and yet they can also do good in the world. I was invited to a critical discourse and multimodality conference in Kuala Lumpur. Almost all of the participants came from the Middle East and Asia, and most of them were fairly young women scholars and PhD students. They felt that multimodal discourse analysis had opened their eyes, helped them to express things they had not known

how to express before – women's issues, consumerism, situations to do with reli-
gion – and they give talks about that. To them, multimodal critical discourse analysis was fresh and new and liberating. But then they would say "I want to learn
more about multimodality, but my professor says I have to do my thesis about
morphology. Can you help?" That makes me less happy, because how much can I
do? And when students say "I now look at things a different way", that makes me
happy too. Makes me think it is worthwhile, what I do.

The future

If we focus on the future, what is so special about our time?
What will the future bring?

Multimodality has only just begun. We started out like the Paris school, thinking
you would need to have the grammar of comic strips, the grammar of graphic
design, the grammar of images, the grammar of theatre and so on, but it is not like
that. The things that matter cross into each other. Everything is connected to
everything else, and that is what we need to learn to deal with. And technology.
We began to include it in *Multimodal Discourse*, but did not yet get very far.
Another issue for the future is interpretation, as not so different from production as
it was made out to be in media theory. We had all sorts of academic divisions, and
while I was too production oriented, audience theory was really the going thing. I
thought that was a rather consumerist approach to media studies. Luckily this
binary division has begun to blur a bit, but all the more important to think about
practices of interpretation and their contexts, and how they work. And to realize
that production and interpretation use the same kind of resources, maybe in the
same way, maybe differently, depending on the context. Those things are top of
the agenda for me right now. Also, creating projects that pay equal attention to
semiotic resources and to their uses, in the context of practices that really matter in
today's world, like consumerism, corporate power, the new poverty, the way
public services change as they are sold out or corporatized even without being
sold – those kind of issues. I believe that our kind of social semiotic approach has
things to offer here that escape the big brush thinkers who do not bother as much
with data as we do.

We could talk about crucial semiotic developments, the new writing, hybrid
between writing and visual design, how it is developing and what that means, and
equally about the new reading, which often is much more interactive than reading
has been ever since the Middle Ages. Or about new media. We can make a distinct
contribution to what Lev Manovich (2001) has called software studies, a contribution from the point of view of socials semiotics, focusing on the semiotic
choices made by software designers, on how they configure layout choices, typo-
graphic choices, colour choices, texture choices and so on. Or about social media.
My social actor theory could be developed multimodally, to see how social media
categorize the people that we interact with, especially in terms of what I have

called relational identification, and in terms of association, the kinds of groups people make. I have no doubt that this would uncover things that have not yet been uncovered in the by now growing literature on social media.

Which patterns can you see now in multimodality that you could not see twenty years ago? What do we know now given the collective development in social semiotics that we did not know when you began? In hindsight, which motifs seem to have been most central during the last decades, and which will be the most central in the future?

If you take multimodality as a phenomenon then there are certainly a number of things that have happened – most of which we have already touched on. One is the greater integration of the visual and the verbal. Another is the proliferation of diagrammatic representation and the developing nature and uses of diagrams. Yet another one is the new modality, particularly in computer-generated images. Remember that twenty years ago we just thought we were talking about images and did not yet know how much would follow from it, how the theory would broaden out, and how much more multidisciplinary multimodality would become. We have come a long way since then, and there is no reason to think that we will not go a long way further still in the next twenty years.

References

Arnheim, R., 1974. *Art and Visual Perception*. Berkeley and Los Angeles: University of California Press.

——, 1982. *The Power of the Center*. Berkeley and Los Angeles: University of California Press.

Barthes, R., 1973. *Mythologies*. St Albans: Paladin.

——, 1977. *Image-Music-Text*. London: Fontana.

——, 1983. *The Fashion System*. New York: Hill and Wang.

Berger, P. & T. Luckmann, 1966. *The Social Construction of Reality*. Harmondsworth: Penguin.

Bernstein, B., 1981. "Codes, modalities and the process of cultural reproduction: A model", *Language and Society* 10: 327–63.

Djonov, E. & T. Van Leeuwen, 2013. Bullet Points, New Writing and the Marketization of Discourse: A Critical Multimodal Perspective. In: E. Djonov & S. Zhao (eds.), *Critical Multimodal Studies of Popular Discourse*. London: Routledge.

Djonov, D., K. O'Halloran, & T. Van Leeuwen, 2014. "David Byrne really does love PowerPoint: Art as research on semiotics and semiotic technology", *Social Semiotics* 23(3): 409–23.

Eco, U., 1976. *A Theory of Semiotics*. Bloomington: Indiana University Press.

Fairclough, N., 2001. *Language and Power*. 2nd Edition. London: Longman.

Gage, J., 1999. *Colour and Meaning: Art, Science and Symbolism*. London: Thames and Hudson.

Goffman, E., 1981. *Forms of Talk*. Philadelphia: University of Pennsylvania Press.

Halliday, M.A.K., 1978. *Language as Social Semiotic*. London: Arnold.

——, 1994. *An Introduction to Functional Grammar*. 2nd edition. London: Arnold.

Hodge, R. & G. Kress, 1993. *Language as Ideology*. 2nd Edition. London: Routledge.

Kress, G., 2010. *Multimodality: A social semiotic approach to contemporary communication*. London: Routledge.

Kress, G. & T. Van Leeuwen, 2001. *Multimodal Discourse: The Modes and Media of Contemporary Communication*. London: Arnold.

——, 2006. *Reading Images: The Grammar of Visual Design*. 2nd Edition. London: Routledge.

Longacre, R.E., 1974. Narrative versus other discourse genre. In: R. Brend (ed.), *Advances in Tagmemics*. Amsterdam: North Holland.

Manovich, L., 2001. *The Language of New Media*. Cambridge, Mass: MIT Press.

Metz, C., 1974. *Film Language: A Semiotics of the Cinema*. New York: Oxford University Press.

O'Halloran, K., 2005. *Mathematical Discourse: Language, Symbolism and Visual Images*. London: Continuum.

O'Toole, L.M., 2011. *The Language of Displayed Art*. London: Routledge.

Van Leeuwen, T., 1993. *Language and Representation*. Unpublished PhD Thesis, University of Sydney.

——, 1999. *Speech, Music, Sound*. London: Palgrave Macmillan.

——, 2005. *Introducing Social Semiotics*. London: Routledge.

——, 2011. *The Language of Colour – An Introduction*. London: Routledge.

Wodak, R. & M. Meyer, 2009. *Methods of Critical Discourse Analysis*. London: Sage.

6

JAY LEMKE

Background

Let us start with your way into academic life and social semiotics.

I was a student at the University of Chicago, first in mathematics and then in physics. I had had an interest even from a very young age in astronomy and cosmology, and that led to an interest in the theory of relativity and quantum mechanics. I knew a lot about those things when I went to university, so in fact I finished my first degree in three years, and was already taking postgraduate courses in my third year as an undergraduate. I had therefore a good head start at a young age in physics, and I completed my PhD at the University of Chicago when I was about twenty-four or twenty-five years old, studying proton and antiproton annihilation. I got interested in the teaching of science, partly because I did not think science was very well taught, even at an excellent university like the one that I was at. Instead of going on in physics where I had an offer of a postdoctoral position, I accepted an offer to go to the City University of New York as an assistant professor in both physics and the field of science education. Because of some retirements of the more senior people, I quickly became the lead person in the field of science education at the university. I initiated a research programme in science education, and I gradually let go of my research programme in theoretical physics. It was very difficult, however, because as a physicist I had been trained to always do research in relationship to a well-developed theory, but there was no well-developed theory in the teaching of science. In that time, Piaget's theory was dominant in education; this theory might have been useful if I was studying young children. However, my area of work was with secondary school students and their teachers. The focus there is more on the content and the concepts of science, and there was no good theory, and there still is no good theory of how to teach and learn science with these kinds of students. I decided to create a theory, and, being a physicist, I was ambitious. I thought that this could not be all that difficult to do. I had created theories in physics. I could certainly create theories about the learning of science. Of course, it turned out to be much more difficult than I had thought.

I had decided from a fairly early time that an important issue was the communication of scientific ideas in the classroom, and this communication was done mostly in the form of oral language, with some additions of diagrams and writing on the chalkboard. I proposed a research project to the National Science Foundation in the US to do tape and video recording of the science classrooms of younger secondary school students to more advanced students and even in some university classes. I wanted to analyse how the meanings of the ideas and the concepts were expressed by the teacher and understood by the students. To do this I needed a theory of language that would enable me to analyse what was being said and to interpret what was being meant conceptually. I talked to some friends of mine who were in anthropology and linguistics, and they asked me if I had read Kenneth Lee Pike or Michael Halliday. I was on vacation in London that summer, and on a shelf in a bookstore I saw Michael Halliday's book *Language as Social Semiotic*. I was very impressed with what I read in that book, and it seemed to me that Halliday had exactly the approach to language that I needed in order to do research on science classrooms. I arranged, therefore, to go to Sydney in 1979. I had a friend who was a young professor in anthropology and linguistics there, and he introduced me to Michael Halliday. Halliday invited me to give a paper while I was there, which I did. It was called "Action, Context and Meaning", which was essentially my approach to language as one component of human action and human communication in a situational context and a context of culture. Halliday and I got along well, and he invited me to come back the following year. My proposal to the National Science Foundation had been approved and I had money to take a year off from my teaching in New York, and to go both to England and Australia to consult with various people about how to analyse the language of science teaching. That really launched my academic career in the direction of studying linguistics and communication as they applied to science, and this was the direction of my work for quite a while.

In the late 1990s, I became interested in some broader issues. My work on language and science education had led me to see the importance of various social and cultural factors in the learning of science that went outside the classroom. I also became interested in the history of mathematical and scientific language, and how it had diverged from everyday language. That was a subject that Michael Halliday was also interested in at that period of time. I was also, by then, dissatisfied with looking only at language. It was clear that you also had to look at other semiotic modalities, certainly diagrams, graphs, maps, charts and pictures. What seemed to me most important was how they were all integrated. Since I had already taken a semiotic approach to language, I wanted to take a semiotic approach to what we today call multimodality, and to expand the application of systemic linguistics from the analysis of discourse, to the analysis of multimodal activity and multimodal texts. I was still a physicist in my habitus, so I turned to the field of complex systems analysis in physics to see if there were any ideas that might be helpful in this regard. I made a little progress, but not as much as I wanted. I turned back again to the study of multimedia and, at that point, computer games. This was around year 2000–02. I studied the nature of multimedia, multimodal interactions in computer games and their applications to teaching and learning. The work on complex systems analysis and computer games mostly took place when I was at the University of Michigan, where I went after New York. Coming here to University of California, San Diego, I began to work with younger children, which was a very new experience; they were playing computer games with undergraduates from the university as a sort of informal learning experience. In studying this, something became very clear to me: you cannot understand the process of learning without including the emotional component. My most recent work is therefore oriented to integrating the analysis of cognitive or ideational dimensions of learning with the affective or emotional and interpersonal dimensions.

How did you develop your contact to Halliday and other social semioticians?

My introduction to systemic functional linguistics and social semiotics came in those early days in 1978–79. I was a visitor for extended periods at Halliday's department in Sydney in 1981, 1982 and 1983, and back in 1985 and 1987 and about every second year thereafter through the 1990s. That was the time when Halliday was writing *An Introduction to Functional Grammar* and using draft versions of it in his MA course in Applied Linguistics in Sydney. I sat in on many of the classes in my summer holiday, which was the middle of the teaching year in Australia. Halliday and I had many conversations, and I also had conversations with Jim Martin, Ruqaiya Hasan and many other people. In that period, we began to talk with people in anthropology, literature and visual arts about possible generalizations of the organizing principles of language as social semiotics to other forms like visual forms, music and dance forms. We organized what we called the Newtown Semiotic Circle. Newtown is one of the neighbourhoods of Sydney that is next door to the university. We had a very interdisciplinary group there, and in fact we pretty much invented the term "social semiotics" in that group. This was really the origin of social semiotics. Michael Halliday and Ruqaiya Hasan participated in that group, and so did Gunther Kress, Theo van Leeuwen, Jim Martin and me. My friend Alan Rumsay was there, Terry Threadgold came from the literature department and there were anthropologists coming too.

It was not so much that social semiotics was an influence on me as it was that I was bringing to this beginning of social semiotics various perspectives that I had already been exposed to. One of the criticisms was that many people who did systemic functional research in those days were too narrowly focusing on the work of Halliday and only on the grammar, and that attention had to be paid to what was going on in the intellectual world around language and society, political analysis, critical theory and feminism. The Newtown Semiotic Circle was engaged in broadening out the enterprise from linguistics to social semiotics. Michael Halliday had already intended that from the beginning, and made it clear in the book *Language as Social Semiotic* (1978) that the purpose of systemic functional linguistics was to provide a tool for critical social analysis. He was all in favour of doing this. He reserved to himself the toolmaker role, but there is no point in making a tool if nobody is going to use it for anything. He wanted to see it widely used in the analysis of ideology in the media and feminist perspectives in literature, which Terry Threadgold was doing, and many other such applications. What I was bringing came partly from my background in physics, which was rather unique in the group. I also brought in my reading in cybernetics and information theory and of Gregory Bateson's work, especially his book *Steps to an Ecology of Mind* from 1972.

I am eclectic and believe in bricolage, where you borrow ideas and tools and ways of thinking from everyone that you can, and you put them together in your own way for your own purposes. Around that time, I began to read about intertextuality from the French theorist Michel Riffaterre (1984), and then Julia Kristeva and Mikhail Bakhtin. I became enormously interested in Bakhtin, especially his ideas about heteroglossia. In the multimodal area, we discussed the work of Roland Barthes, who, as far as I could tell, stole many of his ideas from Hjelmslev without credit. Barthes' work *Elements of Semiology* from 1964 reads almost like a summary of Hjelmslev, especially the ideas about connotative semiotics. Barthes applied these ideas, not only to literature, but also to some very early analysis of multimodality. Foucault was another point of view that I brought in to the discussions in the Newtown group fairly early, especially his work in the archaeology of knowledge. I was also reading Pierre Bourdieu and bringing some of his notions in as well to help give a more solid sociological foundation to social semiotics. The social semiotics in the beginning was very strong on the semiotics, and had only good intentions on the "social". There was not an equally sophisticated social model to go with the sophisticated linguistic model, and you needed both in order to bring them together as social semiotics.

What about American influence?

Bateson worked in the US and a lot of the cybernetics people I was reading were Americans, although most of them originally came from Europe. Heinz von Foerster (1960) and Ross Ashby (1956) were a particularly strong influence for me. In the longer American historical tradition Charles Sanders Peirce has been significant.

The sign

This leads us to your understanding of the sign.

Peirce is significant here. While Halliday's semiotics came from Saussure and Hjelmslev, Peirce had a completely separate and independent approach to semiotics, and in some ways, one that I thought was better. Peirce, for whatever reasons, whether they were logical or just temperamental, liked to have things come in threes rather than twos. So he did not build his semiotics on the signifier and the signified or on a content plane and an expression plane, but he always included a third element. In his scheme, the signifier is the "representamen", the thing that does the representing, and what we usually think of as the signified, he calls "the object". There is, however, a third element, "the interpretant", which I think of as "a system that does the interpreting". In other words, no signifier, no sign in the sense of the material expression points to the signified or the meaning it is supposed to stand for. *You* have to make that connection! You have to do what Halliday calls "construe", and of course you construe according to systems of social convention. Semiotics is very good at describing those systems of social convention. That is in some ways what the grammar is doing for you, but there has to be a third element that actually does this construing. For Peirce, it is not the semiotic relation that is fundamental; it is the process of semiosis. This fits in very well with my own perspective. Coming from physics and from a notion that if meaning making takes place, it takes place because material beings are engaged in material processes and are doing things that make the meaning happen. I certainly understood from a very early point that the Peircian perspective had an advantage over the Saussurian one.

Do you find the central Peircian notions icon, index and symbol useful?

Yes, I do. Like many other people, I have found these notions to be one of the most interesting contributions of Peirce, though you do have to remember that for Peirce icon, index and symbol is only one of three or four different triads that try to characterize the relationship between signifier and signified, representamen and object in terms of different principals of interpretation and different kinds of relationships they can have to each other. In practical terms, I think that *symbol* is the least useful concept because it is the one that is most generic for linguistic science and other kinds of arbitrary science. The other two have, however, proved especially fascinating. If you know Peirce's theory, the most fundamental concepts are *firstness*, *secondness* and *thirdness*. Peirce decided not to give names to them, because glosses would be too misleading. Roughly speaking, *firstness* is a kind of similarity of form, *secondness* is a relationship through causality and *thirdness* is a relationship through convention. In the simplest way of applying this to signifier and signified, you have a similarity of form, as you might have between the map of Norway and the country of Norway. This is iconicity. Many believe that visual representation is more iconic than linguistic representation usually is.

Indexicality is a very fundamental concept for the Jacobsonian functional linguistics tradition. Michael Silverstein's writings about indexicality have made it into a major tool in the thinking of linguistic anthropologists (Silverstein, 1976). They point out that a lot of the meaning that we ascribe to signs or to acts and actions as signs, comes not simply from their denotation, but from another way of thinking of connotation. I may be talking about icons, indexes and symbols, but I am talking about it in English, and that tells you something about me. And I am talking about it in American English, and that says something more about me. You may even hear certain throatiness in my voice because I have been talking a lot, and that also tells you something about me. As a system of interpreting from your point of view, there are many layers of meaning in the words I say, which have some kind of physical or causal relationship to me as the speaker. You can take that even further, not just to me as the speaker, but to the culture and historical period from which I am speaking – Foucault's episteme – the set of conventions of what it is possible to say at this time in history about some things like icons, indexes and symbols. Indexical meaning is therefore a very powerful tool in that way. I would say that indexicality is the number one tool, and iconicity maybe has the tenth of the power of indexicality as a tool. The symbol concept is taken so much for granted that it has almost no power as a tool any more.

Is arbitrariness something you deal with?

I have always regarded arbitrariness as a little bit of an exaggeration. I think degrees of conventionality and degrees of naturalness are more in line. In language in particular, we tend not to see very much of a natural connection, but that is only so when you are looking at the isolated word. If you are looking at the phrasing of a sentence or a long series of utterances, many things are specific to the situation itself, the most obvious things being intonation patterns that you use. Beyond that the ways in which people interrupt and clarify for one another, and the ways in which people hedge and so forth, are not strictly arbitrary or at least they are not arbitrary in the same sense of the arbitrariness of the famous example of the word for a horse in French, Spanish, English or German. Not everything about language is arbitrary in the same way that the selection of lexis is arbitrary. I think it is actually more interesting to think about the ways in which things are less than completely arbitrary. I think conventionality is a safer, less extreme claim about the symbolic relation.

Why do you think that so few of the social semioticians have pointed to Peirce?

I think there are two reasons perhaps, a push and a pull. The push is that Peirce is very hard to read. He wrote thousands of pages, and they are not well organized. And there is more than one Peirce: an early Peirce, a middle Peirce and a later Peirce, and they are almost like three different writers. He had continuity in his thinking, but it is very hard to establish that continuity when reading him. I do not care too much if I am misinterpreting Peirce because I am not claiming to be a Peirce expert. I am claiming to be able to say useful things with ideas that I think I got from Peirce. That is the push away from Peirce. The pull side is that, in social semiotics, there is a very strong sense of loyalty to the Hallidayan tradition and its way of formulating ideas. Halliday did not rely very much on Peirce. He relied a lot more on Hjelmslev, who in turn relied on Saussure.

You have been inspired by Hjelmslev as well.

Yes. I read the *Prolegomena to a Theory of Language* (1953 [1943]) very early on, on Halliday's suggestion. I was very much influenced by it, especially by the connotative semiotics, and I saw the relationship to Roland Barthes. Through Barthes' way of applying connotative semiotics to multimodal texts, I saw how one could apply the general Hjemslevian tradition to such texts. In some ways, connotative semiotics has something in common with my concept of meta-redundancy, and with Peirce's notion of infinite semiosis or chains of signification, where the first signifier points to some signified for an interpretive system, but that in turn can point to another one, and that can again point to another one and so forth. Peirce describes this as linear chains. In Hjelmslev and Barthes, there is a kind of a meta-relation hierarchy, so it is relations of relations of relations of relations. What points to the next connotatively is not either the signifier or the signified of the first sign, but rather the relationship between the two of them, or, in Peircian terms, the meaning-making action. This meaning-making action becomes then the signifier for the next level. This felt very comfortable to me, but I must admit, Hjelmslev's book is also difficult to read. I have said to my students: "When you have finished reading Hjelmslev, start over again from chapter one and read all the way through a second time, because a lot of the things in the first half of the book only make sense once you have read the second half of the book."

Meta-redundancy

Your concept meta-redundancy has turned out to be significant. What do you mean by meta-redundancy?

Meta-redundancy is one of the more difficult notions in my own toolkit. The inspiration comes from Gregory Bateson's work and his notion of meta-learning (Bateson, 1972). In Bateson's own account of his work, the notion developed by watching dolphins in a pool. What Bateson noticed was that, at a certain point, the dolphins caught on to the fact that the trainers did not just want them to learn certain tricks. They wanted them to learn lots of different tricks to impress the audience. The dolphins being quite smart, instead of just doing the next trick, invented a dozen new tricks and behaviours that had never been seen before. The dolphins had, in some sense, learned how to learn. They had figured out what the learning task was about at a higher level, a meta-level. Bateson elaborated this idea in many ways and related it to his theories of communication and to the origins of schizophrenia. The notion of hierarchy relationships – relations of relations of relations – was a big and powerful idea at the time. It was the foundation of French structuralism, and it was important in the analysis of the so-called second order cybernetics. Such ideas were also very familiar to me because of my studies in mathematics and physics. I had also read Bertrand Russell and Alfred North Whitehead on the theory of logical types, which was fundamental for Bateson's work (Russell & Whitehead, 1927).

I tried to construct a systematic version of these ideas in order to basically account for the role of context in meaning. When you study the signifier and the signified, you will see that the same signifier does not always point to the same signified. The same word, the same sentence, the same gesture does not always have the same meaning. So what determines which meaning it has? We usually say that the context determines it. The next question is, what is the context, and how do you know which context is relevant to use to determine the meaning in each case? Logically, you would answer that the norms of your culture tells you which context is the one in which this particular sign should be interpreted as having this particular meaning. You begin to build up a meta-hierarchy. The relationship between the signifier and the signified is itself, mathematically speaking, a contingent probability relationship. In other words, given all the possible interpretations of the given signifier, the interpretations have different probabilities of being the most useful or most shared interpretation, depending on the context.

There are, however, multiple contexts, and for each of those contexts, there is a different probability distribution of the interpretation of the sign. If you are in a different culture, even in the same or the most similar context, there will be a different set of probability distributions. People often misunderstand the term redundancy, taking it to mean 100 per cent redundancy, but that is not what it means. It is a probability. It simply means that A and B are redundant if given A you have a better than random chance of guessing B. It might not be B; it might be C or D, but as long as it is not equally likely to be C or D, we can talk about redundancy. If it is equally likely to be B or C or D, there is no redundancy there. Given the context, then you know which probability distribution to use in interpreting the signs, but, equally, if you know the probability distributions for interpreting the signs, you can figure out which context you are in. This goes both ways. Culture is the next level. If you know the culture, then the rules of the culture tell you in which contexts there are which probabilities assigned to the interpretation of the sign. But you could also go the other way. If you know in which contexts these are the probability distributions, then you know which culture you are in.

Of course you have to make it much more precise. You cannot just set up one culture against another culture. Cultures and contexts are multidimensional, but the principle of the meta-redundancy is there. If the signifier and the signified are redundant in some context, then that is first-order redundancy; the different sets of probabilities in relation to a range of different contexts are second-order redundancy; and the relation of all those second-order relations to the set of different cultural rules about context and interpretation of signs would be an example of third-order redundancy. In principle there is no limit to how far you go, though I do not think human brains operate with more than four or five of these levels of redundancy. As a general term for this, we have the notion meta-redundancy.

Metafunctions, communication, text and genre

You use Halliday's three metafunctions in your work with texts, but you have given them new names: presentation, orientation and organization. Why?

I have done that because I wanted to be able to generalize from the case of lan-guage to the case of other semiotic modalities, and particularly to multimodal texts. I tried to find the common denominator. In art criticism, they talk about icono-graphy, which is the ideational component, about perspective, which has to do with an interpersonal, attitudinal component, and about composition which is more or less the textual aspect. In music, there is another terminology, and so it is for gesture, posture and action more generally. I wanted a common or neutral set of terms that were generic and could be applied across the different modes. I came up with these terms to represent the cross-modal dimensions of meaning making. The claim is that, regardless how you make meaning, with whatever sign-system or combination of sign-systems, you always have a presentational aspect or dimension, something that specifies what the about is, what the content is, what the "what" is; and you have something that is orientational, which expresses your evaluative and attitudinal stance towards it and ultimately towards whoever you are commu-nicating with or co-acting with. You also have an organizational element regardless of how many dimensions and modes that may be involved. These notions are a generalization or an expansion of Halliday's metafunctions.

How do you understand communication?

Communication is one of those terms, like context or culture, that is useful mainly because it is vague. The attempt to give it a precise definition I personally think is counterproductive, although I know many people will disagree with that. I once defined "communication" by saying: "Communication is the creation of commu-nity." For me, that is, in the broadest sense, what communication is. Commu-nication is the processes which bind a community together. People within a community communicate more often and more intensely in more important ways with each other than they do with people who are not part of that community. I do not believe that communication is the transfer of the same meaning from one person to the other. I believe that communication comprises the social processes by which communities bind themselves together, and it does not have to be in language. I think in general it is in joint collaborative or interactive action that communication takes place.

What is a text to you?

Text has a number of different meanings. I have usually distinguished between an *object text*, by which I mean the actual physical, material text, the ink on the paper or the lights on the computer screen, versus the *meaning text*, by which I mean the meanings that are interpreted by some interpreter from the object text. Peirce would say by some system of interpreters given all the contexts, all the intertexts, you know. Halliday of course uses *text* as the fundamental unit of meaning. If an expression or an action has meaning in a community, it is a text. You can then of course ask: "What is not a text?" For me, that is an isolated signifier. You pull a word out of the dictionary, like "rough". "Rough" is not a text. If someone tells me they had bad luck, and I say "Rough!", that, is however, a text.

You also use the notion of genre in your work. What is genre to you?

In the most basic sense, a genre is for me just a *type* as opposed to a *token*. Let me take the most fundamental kind of genre – an action or activity genre. It is people doing things in a way that is typical, recognized, repeated and repeatable in a culture. What we usually think of as a genre, however, is a text genre or a discourse genre, and then you are looking at the language or multimodal expression of that particular activity genre. If you are writing out a text, then the fundamental genre is the genre of the activity of writing, for instance, a haiku. The written haiku itself is a byproduct of the activity, a trace or an index of the action genre that produced it. Of course, it inherits from the action genre certain kinds of features, which is what we usually think of in a more linguistic sense of genre. It tends, for instance, to inherit a division into parts. Each of the parts has a differentiated function within the whole, and there are some constraints on the sequential or temporal ordering of those parts.

Is your understanding of genre close to Jim Martin's notion of genre?

I think it is very close to Jim Martin's notion of genre taken somewhat in isolation. Martin wants to imbed the notion of genre in a sort of stratificational hierarchy. I think that this is sometimes a useful thing to do, and sometimes maybe it is not so useful. Clearly, what is central to Martin's notion are stages, which are, from my point of view, the functional parts of the genre. He is mainly interested in describing what those functional parts are, and what their functions are.

Stratification and text – and time-scales

Is stratification important in your thinking?

Stratification is a notion that seems to be very important to many people in systemic linguistics, particularly Jim Martin. It never struck me as being all that important, and I think the reason for that is that the more strata there are, the more important a notion it is. Originally, there were two strata: the grammar and the phonology. If you take Michael Halliday's three-strata-version, you have meanings expressed in wordings expressed in soundings. This is useful as a way of relating semantics and grammar or meanings and wordings, more useful than the psychological model, in which meanings belong to an immaterial realm of mind, which I do not believe in. That is a fairytale as far as I am concerned. Jim Martin has then added attempts to make context of situation and context of culture or genre into additional strata within the system. Once you start to do that, it becomes an interesting and powerful tool.

You have introduced the concept of text scale.

Text scales is a concept I have created and found useful in my own work. When I started to analyse discourse, my initial interests were in the discourse of science classrooms. At that time, there was still a major debate as to whether there was some kind of grammatical organization above the sentence. Important questions were: What counts as grammatical organization and what does not?; and How is meaning organized above the level of the sentence? Today we all take it for granted that there is a lot of organization of meaning above the scale of the sentence. But what I wanted to know was what kind of meanings you can make with longer texts that you cannot make with shorter texts. This seemed to me to be really a fundamental question. I developed, therefore, this notion of *text scales*, to ask what kind of meaning you can make with a long complex sentence that you cannot make with a single clause, what kind of meaning you can make with a paragraph or a logical argument that you cannot make with a single sentence, with a novel and not with a short story, with a dissertation and not with a fifteen-page article, and so forth. I think that we all recognize that there really are such distinctions of meaning. These differences in meaning are not so obvious, so it is a productive question to ask about text scales.

It is important to be consistent with my larger point of view in which it is always the activity or the activity genre, the people doing things, that is fundamental and not the text. This translates into *activity scales*, or *time scales* as I more recently called it, in which the fundamental question is not just what kinds of meaning can you make over longer periods of activity than over shorter periods, but how do the meanings or the actions that you take over shorter time-scales cumulate and integrate into the meanings that you make over the longer scales. This question has led to a very productive way of looking at things in terms of cross-scale relationships.

The fundamental model that I have used for this work comes indirectly from developmental biology, which is another collaboration field earlier in my career, and also from complex systems theory more recently. The model is essentially a "sandwich" with three levels, in which you put whatever level you are interested in in the middle, and then you look at least one level above it, meaning longer than it, and one level below, meaning shorter than it. The meanings you make or the actions and activities you do that typically take place at the level in focus are themselves organizations made up of smaller activities and actions or units of words or sentences, and they are subject to the constraints and affordances of the longer term activities that are going on at the time. If you are in the middle of the science lesson, those longer scales are represented by the entire lesson or the unit or topic that you are dealing with. The shorter scale is represented by the individual utterances. The level in focus is typically the episode, a series of interactions between students and teachers around a particular topic that achieves a particular aim or objective.

Multimodality

What would you say are your major theoretical contributions to the field of multimodality?

I think the most important tool that I have added is my notion of *multiplicative* or *multiplying meaning*, which, essentially, is an argument from information theory and from the cybernetic approach. If you have several different codes, or several different sets of alternatives, and you are deploying them simultaneously, then the set of all the possible combinations of them is the relevant set for deciding the information value of any particular choice or instance. If I had three sets of three choices each, and if I deployed them separately and independently and I made one choice, I would have one out of three information value for each of them (one out of three plus one out of three plus one out of three). I would have, in effect, what is called a value three of information, whereas if I deploy them in conjunction with each other, so that I have to make a selection from all three simultaneously, I have a space of nine different possibilities. If I choose one, then the specificity of that is one in nine, or an information value of nine. So there is a combinatorial explosion of possible combinations. Because of redundancies and genre constraints, it is not a complete explosion. Not every one of the nine, or nine billion, possibilities is equally likely, but in general it is a lot more than the sum of just adding them up one at a time separately. You can then think about what are the possible combinations that you can multiply. For me, one of the most basic ones is multiplying the presentational by the orientational by the organizational. Even within the metafunctions, there are different sub-dimensions and different modes. So I am also multiplying the linguistic by the visual by the mathematical. At the very least, this gives you a large check list of things to pay attention to. How does, for instance, the orientational aspect of the visual interact and combine with the orientational aspect of the linguistic? It is not always homogeneous, so the orientational aspect of the visual can, for instance, interact with the presentational aspect of the linguistic.

Is the idea of multimodality the largest innovation in social semiotics in the last twenty years?

It probably is. The innovation before multimodality was the critical perspective, I think; the political and social dimension and the ideological dimension of analysis, which still remains on the agenda. But once you look at things in terms of multimodality, there is no going back. Everything is multimodal, even a printed text on a page, the choice of typeface, the bold and the italics, the headers. Most of the texts that we look at online are multimodal. Video is an inherently multimodal text which has auditory dimensions, sound dimensions and in many cases music dimensions in addition to the visual organization dimensions and the talk and language that is going on.

Do you have a brief definition of the term mode?

For me, mode is a short hand for what people will often call semiotic modality, and semiotic modality is a short hand for semiotic resource system, in the original sense of Halliday's in *Language as Social Semiotic* (1978). It is a system of meaning potential, a system of meaningful contrasts between forms in a community that has conventions for the interpretation of those forms and contrasts, as paradigms, as syntagms, and this can be done through multiple expression planes.

How do you distinguish between modes? If we talk about modes multiplying, would you for instance say that colour is a separate mode? Or music?

Some of this, I think, is not so much an inherent feature of the modality of expression as it is a historical product of how people have deployed the affordances, the potentials of the modes of expression. Music, I think, does qualify as a full-fledged semiotic resource system, because historically it has been developed for purposes that have brought out most of its potential in that way. It tends to have a more dominantly attitudinal or emotional function rather than an ideational function, but it can also have an ideational function. Colour, on the other hand, has not been developed historically in our culture in such a way. I do not think we really have colour syntagms that operate as a separate semiotic modality. If I flashed a series of colours at you I do not know if you would make any special sense out of that sequencing. Maybe if I flashed them in the sequence of the rainbow. Or I might be able to flash sequences that are more like female identified colours or male identified colours or darker colours and brighter colours. We have not historically, however, turned colour into an autonomous, or semi-autonomous, system the way in which we have with music.

So, what may fruitfully be analysed as a separate mode might change through history?

Yes, I think so. There is a tendency to conventionally fuse existing modes together, and to some extent to also separate them from each other. I think this is most clear developmentally. For very young children, drawing and writing are not separate modes, yet. They have to be taught how to distinguish drawing from writing and to create one separate semiotic resource system for drawing and a different system for writing. Something that was originally, primordially, developmentally a single system gets split into two. I see no reason why two different systems might not become fused through their redundancy relations moving up towards one hundred per cent. Once they reach one hundred per cent then they are no longer two separate systems, because combining them cannot give you any additional meaning.

What is special to language as a mode?

People have been debating that for a very long time. I have always taken the position that because we are a logocentric culture we have a vested interest in trying to see that language is special, and usually better than the other modes. I remain a sceptic about that. Moreover, it is a pure academic abstraction to say that language exists as a separate mode. It is never deployed, and it cannot be deployed, as a separate mode. There is no expression plane for language which is not also expression plane for some other semiotic modality. In spoken language there is the timbre of my voice, my accent and all the indexical features we were talking about before. In written language, there are typographical features and choices. It seems to me that it is more productive to ask the question: What does language add to the multimodal mix? What are its special strengths or the special purposes for which we tend to use language more than the other modes? I think categorization and sub-categorization is one of those. Language is really good at classifying things and making them into groups, types, sets, categories, sub-categories and overlappings of categories. Language is also very good at separating out processes from participants, which in some ways may be a very artificial thing to do. It is not the way reality actually appears to us or is constructed; we only think it is because we are using language to describe it to ourselves. But if you want to do that, and there are occasions when you do want to do that, language is a particularly good way of doing it.

Now are we talking about affordances?

Yes, indeed, the differential, functional affordances of the different modalities within the multimodal mix. Michael O'Toole (1994) has talked about *mono-functional tendencies* in various genres. One could talk in some ways about *functional speciali-zation* of modes. If you look at mathematics it is really a highly functionally spe-cialized mode. It is extremely good at looking at meaning by degree, quantitative relationships of more and less, and the ways in which more and less of one thing correlates with, or is functionally related to, more or less in something else. That was its original specialized function. Of course it has taken on many other specialized functions too, especially in the last hundred years.

I think that cultures tend to preferentially use certain modes for certain meaning purposes. We tend to use music for emotional and rhythmic kinds of purposes, and language for classifying and also narrative purposes. We use visual representations for showing spatial relationships and so forth.

How would you explain literacy and multimodal literacy?

Literacy like *context* and *culture* is another one of those notions that work best if you do not define it too precisely. The meaning of literacy has changed so much over my lifetime, from being almost exclusively the ability to read print text and gain basic information value from doing so, to the use of written language for your own purposes. Once one goes to a *multimodal* view on literacy, then literacy and multimodal semiotic competence are more or less the same thing. I do not really see how to distinguish them any more. I think one can talk about specialized literacies, like you can have a mathematical literacy in the register of differential calculus, or you can have a literacy in the texts of systemic functional linguistics. To me there are *literacies*, but if you talk about literacy as such it does not mean much more than either the everyday registers of written language or generalized multimodal semiotic competence.

Could we hope to develop a general social semiotics of all modes? And in what ways would that be different from traditional semiotics?

I do not think you can ever really have the modes separately. I think the *only* general semiotics you can have is a fully multimodal semiotics. And I think the main difference from the traditional approach is the social part. Traditional semiotics has been very formalist, with emphasis mainly on forms, relations and contrasts of forms, and constraints on combinations of forms. It has been much less about the functions of those forms and combinations of forms and how they are shaped historically by the kinds of things that people want to do with the forms, including their political objectives, their identity issues and their practical necessities.

Social semiotics, SFL and science

How can social semiotics and SFL contribute to the study of science?

There are many different aspects to science; there is scientific research itself, there is our understanding of science as a social phenomenon, and there is the teaching of science. I believe that perspectives from SFL and social semiotics can contribute to all of those aspects, but in rather different ways. The contribution to the teaching of science is obvious: by helping students to understand that a lot of what goes under the name of scientific thinking or scientific concepts is really specific forms of scientific language, talking science, scientific reasoning and scientific genres – both spoken genres as well as written.

I think that critical discourse analysis is important for understanding science as a social phenomenon. Science is not a purely isolated, neutral, arbitrary or even objective activity. It is culturally and historically situated, and it is deeply interdependent on economic interests and even to some extent on political ideologies. There is a strong gender identity component in many of the ideas and programmes of science, particularly in certain subfields of science. You need tools to be able to persuade people that the things you say are right. Critical discourse analysis, using tools from systemic functional linguistics and perspectives from social semiotics, provides very powerful techniques for actually doing such analysis.

In scientific research itself, I think it depends on the field, and even more on the component of scientific research. One of the areas that is of great interest in scientific research today is representation. How do you represent great, complex data sets and complex interrelationships of different variables? We are in the age of big data, and we have enormous power of representation through computerization, but we have not really invented a lot of new genres of representation, certainly not much in the sense of verbal genres. Scientific articles today reads pretty much as they did fifty years ago, though maybe not like they did 150 years ago. The design of effective scientific representations is a major issue in scientific research today. You cannot understand your data unless you can meaningfully represent it to yourself, and you cannot communicate persuasively arguments about your data unless you have representations that enable you to share your insights and argue about the representations with other members of the scientific community. In particular, I think that multimodal analysis with a grounding in social semiotic approaches, and ultimately in principles deriving from SFL, is potentially a very important tool for the design of better scientific representations and also for new scientific representations.

What is your contribution to this field?

Pretty obviously, my book *Talking Science* from 1990 has had a fairly substantial impact in the fields of science and mathematics education, and to approaches to research on classroom discourse. Some of my notions about the application of the multimodality approach to multimodal scientific text, the integration of mathematics and various kinds of representations such as tables, charts and diagrams, along with the linguistic text in the genre of the scientific article, have been useful. For very many people, this has been a model of how to look at those inter-relationships even in other genres. I have not been in the business of designing new scientific representations, though I might. Some of my social semiotic perspectives have had some small influence in terms of getting people, at least in science education, to have a more sociocultural perspective on the teaching of science. I leave it to other people to try to persuade the scientists to do that.

Halliday has talked about the evolution of the language of science. Is this a field you have worked with?

I think Halliday has probably done more of that, particularly on the language side. His work on the rise of nominalization as a tool in scientific writing and discourse and other changes in the way in which scientists explain the relationships of concepts and ideas that went along with nominalization is historically accurate and very important. My own contribution has been more on the multimodal side, trying to look at the ways in which scientific language and the scientific use of mathematical expressions have become mutually adapted to one another over time as there has been greater and greater use of mathematical representations in scientific writing. If you go back to the 1700s, a lot of the mathematical expression was very verbal, and even some of the diagrams and formulas mixed grammatically normal English or Latin sentences with mathematical symbols and expressions. We do not do it that way any more. There is an almost completely separate grammar for the mathematics, which is ultimately derived from the grammar of natural language, but has become very specialized and diverged from it alongside the special register grammar of different areas of science. I know physics the best, and the way in which the two different grammars accommodate and complement each other has evolved textually over time. Something similar has gone on with visual representations in scientific writing. They are extremely important, more so than people outside sciences realize. There are many scientific articles in which an expert will look first and primarily at the figures and diagrams, and refer to the language only in order to clarify the meaning of what is in the graph, the diagram or the chart. And of course, the ways in which visual elements are accommodated in a complementary way in the creation of the whole multimodal scientific text is an even more complex phenomenon with historical changes, than just the integration of the mathematical symbolism with the text.

Is there a fundamental aim of science text to present one truth, and if it is so how can the truth be represented?

It is certainly true that the genres and register of science have evolved to state precise meanings and in general to imply that there is a true or correct description of reality or of a phenomenon. Scientific texts allow, however, for degrees of certainty about what is being said or claimed, and there are even representational conventions for that. When you represent data in many forms of graphs, you can, for instance, put indicators saying that it could be a little bit more or little bit less than what I think it is, but certainly not a lot more or a lot less. Science does not, however, really have a set of conventions for dealing with multiple points of view about a phenomenon, or multiple interpretations, except to see them as contrastive alternatives, only one of which can be right. There have been certain periods in the history of science when scientists have lived uncomfortably with the notion that there might be more than one correct explanation of what is going on. The most famous recent period of that was the so-called wave/particle-duality in quantum-mechanics, the argument of Niels Bohr regarding complementarity and the notion that reality is inheritably too complex for any one single point of view to be able to explain it all. Then you need to have multiple points of view in order to get a grasp on reality. That only lasted for about twenty years, and it was a very uncomfortable twenty years in the history of science because it went so much against the kind of scientific philosophy that scientists themselves have, which is perhaps a bit more naïve than what many philosophers and sociologists of science have. Scientists do not have a strong motivation for developing multiperspectival approaches, and they are uncomfortable with the notion that you might never be able to resolve a problem. It undermines the identity of the belief system and maybe even the value system of scientists.

Do we need another language and other representations for talking about the future aspects of science, for instance the environmental challenges?

This is a big question. Sciences have for years been convinced about the dangers of climate change and have presented the data and the evidence and representations to decision-makers, who also hear from other people that do not want to give up making more money in order to save the earth. I think the question here is not so much a scientific question as it is a rhetorical and political question. One of the problems is that scientists are not very good at making their case to the public. In designing better scientific representations, a key feature is to find ways to make them more friendly to non-experts, so that, for example, many issues of probability and statistics, which are fundamental to the scientific representation of controversial issues, such as environmental policy issues, simply need to be made more understandable for the average person. Purely in representational and rhetorical terms I think that science could do a lot better, but scientists do not have the time or the expertise to do that. They need people who are good at translating scientific findings of relevance to policy into terms, not for policy makers or experts, or for the staff of people of a congressman or a senator, but for the mass media and for ordinary people.

Cognition, emotions and aesthetics

You have, in recent years, worked with cognition and emotions. How do you combine cognition and emotions?

It goes back to semiotics and natural science, which are the two sources of all my work. The complex systems I was interested in combined human social systems with natural ecological systems. Many of the core theoretical ideas on doing this come from the field of bio-semiotics, which is probably better known in Europe than in the United States. It was the attempt to figure out how meaning-making processes, which, for me, now include feeling processes, take place in material systems; a kind of materialist rather than a formalist view of semiotics. I asked: "Why can't we do for our perspective on feelings and emotions what we've already done for our perspective on cognition?" That is, to go outside of the head, to make it culturally specific, to make it situated in interactions in an environment in a context, and, in effect, to turn it into a social semiotics so that it becomes a social semiotics of feeling.

At the same time, I questioned the traditional distinction between affect and cognition. Reading about embodied cognition for instance, or some of the papers that Paul Thibault (2011) has written about embodied models of language, or "languaging" as he calls it, and works of people like Tim Ingold (2011), an anthropologist from Scotland, and Maxine Sheets-Johnstone (2009), who is a theorist of movement and dance, it became clearer and clearer to me that the traditional distinction between thought and feeling is an ideological distinction. It is a distinction that has to do with gender stereotypes. There is, however, no meaning making without feeling, and there is no feeling apart from its meaningfulness for us. I began to look into the neurological basis of the relationship between thinking and feeling. The so-called feeling centres and the so-called thinking centres of the brain are actually tightly integrated in one another. I looked at bio-semiotics inspired by Jesper Hoffmeyer in Denmark, whose primary interest is in the biological origins of semiosis (Hoffmeyer, 2008). For me, the interest was the biological single unitary phenomenon of feeling and cognition, which we then rip apart, separating them into feeling *versus* meaning, which is not something we should do. I have a chapter coming out in a new handbook on advances in semiotics edited by Peter Trifonas from Toronto which is called *Feeling and Meaning – A Unitary Bio-Semiotic Approach*.

How important is aesthetics in the production and reception of texts?

For me, the aesthetics in the general sense of *aisthesis* in Greek, which means feeling, is fundamental to all aspects of meaning. We tend to associate it with feelings of beauty, but in an earlier generation it was also associated with moral feelings and in the ancient Greeks it was associated with stronger passions, as with tragedy or comedy. In this broad sense aesthetics is fundamental to all aspects of meaning, even scientific meaning or mathematical meaning. Mathematicians find aesthetic beauty in certain kinds of mathematical proofs, and regard other kinds of mathematical proofs, which are equally mathematically valid, as being "ugly". Just like computer scientists will regard certain programming algorithms as elegant and beautiful and they will get all emotionally excited about them, and they will regard others as ugly kludges and *ad hoc* ad-ons that have no real "computer sensibility". In scientific texts, scientists also get quite emotional about a beautifully designed experiment in the laboratory, or a beautiful mathematical formula or expression of an idea or generalization. Perhaps the thing that is most often overlooked is that even the so-called neutral academic objectivity is itself a feeling. It is not the absence of feeling, it is a *particular* feeling that one has and cultivates. There is an aesthetics – if you like – of neutrality, as well as an aesthetics of passion and engagement.

Can aesthetics be integrated in the three metafunctions?

For me aesthetics is a sort of sub-category or a branch more generally within the area of feelings, emotions, evaluations, and stances towards things. Formally it would come within the orientational semiotic function. That is, similar in many ways to Jim Martin's work on appraisal. He sees aesthetics to be an evaluative component within the interpersonal metafunction, and looks at linguistic resources for the expression of attitude and evaluation for which he has the evaluation of objects by aesthetic criteria as one sub-component. I would tend, generally, to go along with that, but it is not just about the semiotic expression and evaluation. It is about the feeling that you get on the basis of which you decide that you are going to evaluate it in this way. I think the feeling in many ways comes first in aesthetic evaluation, and then you look for a semiotic way to justify and explain why you feel that way about something.

I think that the aesthetic, emotional, affective dimension is one of the most important challenges for the future. It has been somewhat neglected and not well integrated. This has a connection to what Jim Martin proposed as *Positive Discourse Analysis*, looking for examples of ways in which discourse represents the best rather than the worst in human beings. It is obviously very easy to find the worst. In his analysis, for example, of the discourse of reconciliation in South Africa, he was striving to find the positive, the aspirational possibilities of humanity. We need to ask what we find inspiring in multimodal texts. How do we use multimodal texts and actions as feeling and meaning mediators to bring out the best in ourselves? I think that is a worthwhile programme for the future.

How do the cognitive and the emotional enter into education and how to design education?

Unfortunately it does not enter in nearly as much as it should enter in. I think that this is another one of our cultural shortcomings. We associate the emotional with women and children and not with men who go to war or rule the world. In education there is an emphasis, to some extent, on emotion and play and feelings for very young children in schools. But then, certainly in American culture, and I think in many other European cultures, a time comes when the only thing we teach children about emotion is how to control it, which means how to suppress it, and how to make it consistent with what the culture considers appropriate emotion in a situation. We do not pay attention to how we can *use* emotion, how it can become a tool in the same way we use meaning as a tool in order to solve problems, to creatively come up with new solutions, to design, create and produce new things, and simply find new ways of enjoying life. If you apply this to science education, some of the students find science education very dull and boring, whereas many scientists find it very exciting and emotionally engaging and inspiring. So there is something wrong, there is something missing in the teaching of science, and perhaps the teaching of many other subjects. This concerns recognition of the emotional and aesthetic dimensions of the subject and the legitimacy of enjoying yourself when you are learning things.

Digital media

You have been especially interested in new digital media and you have worked with these media within the framework of social semiotics. What are your main theoretical contributions in this field?

Initially, I began by taking over concepts that I had used from more traditional media to see how they would need to be changed or extended for new media. My notions of intertextuality led to my analyses of hypertext. The fundamental question was: When you go across a link in a hypertext, what is the meaning relation between the source of the link and the target of the link? Are those relations the same kinds of intertextual relationships that we normally have? Is there a need for clarification or specification of those relationships? How are they organized? How do they appear in different genres? I did some work on that and presented it at a SFL conference in Cardiff a long time ago. I never published very much about it, mainly because I moved fairly quickly into broader analyses of web-based materials such as websites from NASA and comparisons between print text and web-based scientific text.

I kept, however, following the progressions of new media, always looking for the ones that offered the greatest multimodal affordances. Computer games appealed greatly to me around 2000, as they did also to James Paul Gee, who was studying similar things at about the same time (Gee, 2003). Computer games are a dynamic medium, a medium in which events unfold in time in a way that is not as completely under the control of the user as, say, in a website. If I follow a trajectory of links from here to there in a website I control the timing and the pacing of those shifts, but in a computer game, the program controls as much as I do. Sometimes it is even a fight between me trying to slow things down and the program trying to speed things up. I became very interested in issues of pacing and timing and time-scales and the traversals and trajectories over time in dynamic computer multimedia like computer games. That became one of the areas that I published on.

I was also looking at what happens to the presentational and orientational multiplicative model of meaning in this new space. Obviously it gets bigger and more complex, and there are many more different kinds of combinations that take place affected by the temporal dimension. But the thing that struck me as most evidently different was the role of feeling and emotion – though it turned out that it was not really different, it was just more obvious. The pacing was closely related to the anxiety that you had in playing the game. In most of these games you can die, or at least fail in a way that feels unpleasant to you, and you have anxiety about whether it is going to happen. When the pace of the game goes more and more rapidly your anxiety increases. The choices that you make in the game are not based purely on the *meanings* that those choices have; they also are based on the feeling state that you are in at the time you make them. There is developed a feedback loop between the meaning choices you make, the consequences of those choices for your feeling state and the effects of the feeling state on the subsequent meaning choices you make. So the meaning–feeling cycle becomes a single integrated unit of analysis for understanding the trajectory of what you do and what happens in the course of playing the game. The impetus for my most recent work has been trying to articulate a more unified and integrated theory of meaning and feeling.

What, in your opinion, is the role of technology in the new literacies?

I think we are now well aware that technological hype and technological fixes are dangerous. It is too easy to promise too much or to expect too much. No technology is going to make learning better unless it occurs in the context of some genuine motivation for learning, and some thoughtful support for learning from the environment and the teacher. That being said, there is still a lot of opportunity and a lot of affordances. If you replace print text books with multimedia learning support materials or systems, you can use more dynamic media, merely by integrating a lot more video and, in the case of science, a lot more animations and simulations into learning. You cannot pick up your text book and see a diagram about the relationship of pressure and volume, and then push down on the plunger and see pressure and volume indicators change, whereas if you have a well-designed online text book you ought to be able to do that. It is clearly preferable to replace print text books in this way.

More specifically: what is the role of software in designing modern texts?

It depends on what kinds of software one is talking about. There is software behind your ability to push on a plunger in a simulation of a pressure–volume relationship in your online physics text book. There is also more general purpose software to enable you, for example, to create your own simulation of a situation. And there is software that enables students to learn how to programme computers in more fundamental ways. It has been a debate in education, whether learning computer programming should be a fundamental literacy or not. My own view is that general purpose computer programming knowledge beyond the most elementary level is a specialized skill that should be learned by people who have some particular reason or desire to learn it, not necessarily by everyone. But what you might call scripting level programming skills are probably a kind of skill that almost everyone will at some point or other find useful to know. But also in today's reality, such skills are highly specific to particular kinds of genres and tasks, so the conventions that you learn for doing it with one programming system will not necessarily work in a different programming system. I have the feeling that in twenty or forty years from now there will be generic conventions that will apply across many different kinds of scripting. But we are not there yet.

You have used expressions such as hypermodality, multimedia semiotics, meta-media literacy. What are the relations between the mode side and the media side of these concepts?

I use *media* to mean the material technologies of expression and *modalities* to mean the semiotic resource systems, but in choosing the best sounding English word for something I do not always stick rigorously to my own definitions. *Hypermodality* is basically hypertext plus multimodality. Today, in practice, most new multimodal texts or systems are also hypermodal and you probably do not need the term hypermodality any more. It is something that is taken for granted as one aspect or affordance of modern multimodal systems. *Meta-media literacy* is somewhat different. What I meant by meta-media literacy, or meta-media in general, was that the expression plane could be customized to the ways of communicating that you found most comfortable, while leaving the content plane relatively unchanged. Imagine that you had the online multimodal version of your text book and you could request the text book to present a concept to you using more language and less mathematics, or more visuals and less mathematics, or more mathematics and more language and less visuals, or, to use preferentially, certain kinds of visuals rather than other kinds of visuals. The idea of meta-media was simply the notion of a modally customizable presentation of what was still the underlying same content database.

You previously mentioned that you see the medium as part of the immediate context of the text.

Yes, the *material* medium, meaning the technology and the conventions for operating and using that technology, are a part of the context of the text that we usually background. We usually do not pay attention to it, unless it stops working. A book is a multimodal technology material medium, but if two pages of the book are stuck together or they have not been slit or cut through the paper properly, then suddenly it becomes a relevant context. Some avant-garde authors and publishers have even deliberately played around with the conventions of the book, whether it is the convention that you read sequentially page after page, or even that some pages may be cut away or only half of the page exists. Art books of many kinds play with these conventions, and then you suddenly realize that it is a relevant part of the context. Usually "black boxed", as the Latour terminology has it (Latour, 1987), that is, something so much taken for granted that as long as it is not going wrong you do not actively regard it as part of the context.

Social semiotics and SFL in US

What role has social semiotics and SFL played in the US?

Systemic functional linguistics is not widely used and taught in American linguistics departments. The reason for that is historical. Because Chomsky was American, Chomsky's students became the professors in many, if not most, linguistics departments in the United States. Unfortunately the Chomskyan school had a very exclusionary approach to linguistics. They felt they had the right way of looking at linguistics, and everybody else was wrong. They suppressed and pushed out every other approach than their own, not just SFL. SFL has, however, found its home outside of linguistics, in applied linguistics areas – language teaching, for example, computational and anthropological linguistics, and discourse analysis methods throughout the social sciences – and social semiotics is important in multimedia and multimodal analysis methods. Social semiotics and SFL have a significant footprint in the United States, but not in the linguistics departments, and not in formal linguistics as a discipline.

Where can we go to find social semiotics and SFL on the American continent?

Social semiotics is stronger in Canada than in the United States, because it is a British tradition. Much as the academic world likes to deny these things, national loyalties, which are propagated by who is the student of whom and who goes to which university to get their PhD, has an enormous impact on the different shapes of the schools of thought in the different countries. In Canada, Toronto has been a big centre for this approach, not at least through the communicational linguistic studies of Michael Gregory and his students. Gregory has many of his PhD students in different universities across Canada. The educational linguistic approach is strongly represented in the University of British Columbia.

In the United States, the situation is complicated by the fact that there are other functional linguistic traditions besides SFL. Functional linguistics has become pretty strong in anthropology for instance, in the tradition of Dell Hymes and John Gumperz. Then there is my colleague at University of Michigan, Judith Irvine, and the Santa Barbara tradition from Sandra Thompson. In the east, the University of Pennsylvania where Dell Hymes was for many years, is a centre. The Jacobsonian school from Harvard, represented by Michael Silverstein at the University of Chicago, and all his students must also be mentioned. Many of these scholars went into linguistic anthropology because they would not have been able to get jobs in Chomskyan linguistics departments. The antipathy of the Chomskyans forced all the functionalists to become close allies of one another, and there has been much exchange of ideas. Computational linguistics and corpus linguistics are other areas where there is a large amount of influence from SFL.

SFL – today and in the future

As you see it, what are the major advantages and deficits with systemic functional linguistics?

The major advantage is clearly the paradigmatic orientation to meaning; that you analyse wording choices directly in relationship to differences of meaning, which is certainly not possible in a Chomskyan model of language. It is possible in many of the other functionalist approaches to language, but in most of those it requires a great deal more intuition on the part of the analyst to get a satisfactory analysis. I also think that systemic functional linguistics is probably more teachable to a wider range of users than many of the other approaches are. Systemic functional linguistics takes, however, a long time to learn, and this may be one of the disadvantages. There is a lot of specialized terminology; there are a number of difficult kinds of concepts. Halliday often says that people are not accustomed to thinking grammatically, and this is true. It takes an effort to learn how to think grammatically even enough to be able to use SFL grammar as a tool for discourse analysis. One of the other criticisms of SFL, which I have mentioned briefly before, is that it tends to be rather inward looking. People in the field tend to talk mostly to other people in the field and may not look as much outside to other flavours of functional linguistics. They could look more into cultural anthropology and political sociology, and also into other areas of semiotics like biosemiotics and new paradigms like embodied cognition and embodied meaning making, as Paul Thibault, and not many others, has done.

Do politics or ideology and linguistics go hand in hand as Halliday in his early dream of a Marxist linguistics might have said?

They *can* go hand in hand. Sometimes they go too much hand in hand, as when some people using a critical discourse analysis approach may have already decided about the political analysis before they do the linguistic analysis or the multimodal analysis of their texts. As a result, learning how to understand the political situation from the analysis of the texts will not be the case. Instead they are merely trying to prove that their political analysis was correct all along by the evidence that they gain from the text. Rhetorically, perhaps, this could be a useful strategy; sometimes you do need to beat people over the head with evidence for some things that are obviously true. From a research point of view, however, I think this is not a good strategy.

In your view, what are the most important current and future trends in social semiotics and systemic functional linguistics?

One of them certainly is the move towards integrating a semiotic approach with an embodied approach, taking up the implications of a basically materialist model of communication and language, and taking them a step further to talk about what it means to have animate bodies moving, touching, interacting, doing while speaking, gesturing, drawing and writing and so forth. A second one that has some affinities with that is a greater emphasis on feelings and emotions and the integration of feeling and meaning, and how to take that into account, to get richer forms of analysis that do not simply describe what it means and how it means it but also give an account of how we feel about it and why we feel the way we do about it in relationship to the meanings that we make with it. Those would be the two that I am most optimistic about having a productive future in the field.

There are a number of other areas that have been going for a while, that may or may not become more productive in the future. Jim Martin's Positive Discourse Analysis that we mentioned earlier may be one of those. I think applications of SFL in corpus linguistics have been going on for a while now, and with the increasing sophistication of computer language models, there may be a further future for that. It may become possible to extend Halliday's programme of looking at the relative probabilities of different choices within system networks as a function of different genres or registers, so that one could even get quantitative models of register in the programme of generative computational linguistics. And of course, there is always the holy grail of being able to parse natural language with the computer, which we still seem to be as far away from as we were fifty years ago.

References

Barthes, Roland, 1964. *Elements of Semiology*. New York: Hill & Wang.

Bateson, Gregory, 1972. *Steps to an Ecology of Mind*. Chicago: University of Chicago Press.

Gee, James Paul, 2003. *What Video Games Have to Teach us about Learning and Literacy*. London: Palgrave.

Halliday, Michael A.K., 1978. *Language as Social Semiotic: The social interpretation of language and meaning*. London: Edward Arnold.

Hjemslev, Louis, 1953 [1943]. *Prolegomena to a Theory of Language*. Bloomington: Indiana University Publications.

Hoffmeyer, Jesper, 2008. *Biosemiotics*. Scranton, PA: University of Scranton Press.

Ingold, Tim, 2011. *Being Alive*. London: Routledge.

Latour, Bruno, 1987. *Science in Action*. Cambridge, US: Harvard University Press.

Lemke, Jay, 1990. *Talking Science: Language, Learning, and Values*. Norwood, NJ: Ablex/ Praeger Publishing.

O'Toole, Michael, 1994. *The Language of Displayed Art*. Leicester: Leicester University Press.

Riffaterre, Michael, 1984. Intertextual Representation: On Mimesis as Interpretive Discourse. *Critical Inquiry* 11: 141–62.

Ross Ashby, William, 1956. *An Introduction to Cybernetics*. New York: Wiley.

Russell, B. & A.N. Whitehead, 1927. *Principia Mathematica*. Cambridge: Cambridge University Press.

Sheets-Johnstone, Maxine, 2009. *The corporeal turn*. Exeter: Imprint Academic.

Silverstein, Michael, 1976. Shifters, Linguistic Categories, and Cultural Description. In: K. Basso & H.A. Selby (eds.), *Meaning and Anthropology*. Albuquerque: School of American Research, University of New Mexico Press.

Thibault, Paul, 2011. Language behavior as a catalytic process. Parts 1 and 2. *Public Journal of Semiotics* 3: 2–79; 80–151.

von Foerster, Heinz, 1960. On Self-Organizing Systems and Their Environments. In: M.C. Yovits & S. Cameron (eds.), *Self-Organizing Systems*. London: Pergamon Press, pp. 31–50.

7

CENTRAL THEMES

In this chapter, we shall take as the point of departure some central themes covered by the interviews *in toto*. These themes shall be discussed by combining answers from the five interviewees, and, as such, this concluding chapter shall create a (kind of artificial) dialogue among them. If used as an entry to the interviews, this chapter will serve as a guide to the various thematic similarities and differences among our five scholars. At the same time, the discussion of similarities, differences and nuances highlights major motifs in the thinking of the five scholars, and, as such, this chapter may function as a more generally usable companion for understanding the somewhat diverse field of social semiotics. The themes in this chapter cover such diverse areas as systems and concepts; multimodality; social critique and design; functions and applications; future challenges; and hopes and aspirations. We close the chapter with some meta-reflections.

Key figures, new directions

The scholars we have interviewed are all inspired by Michael Halliday's work, and three of them did their doctoral work under his supervision. In their own academic careers, however, they have taken this inspiration in different, new directions. Christian Matthiessen is the one who has worked most closely on developing Halliday's systemic functional linguistics along the lines thought by Halliday, expanding and clarifying it with a strong emphasis on the systemic part; as Matthiessen states in relation to the latter: "in Halliday's grammar, it is dimensions all the way. I find the relational-dimensional thinking very appealing. [...] I think the great power of relational-dimensional thinking is that you have to work out how everything is placed in relation to everything else in terms of a small well-defined set of dimensions, and if you posit something, then you have to see how it relates to other phenomena." Matthiessen has, since his early academic life, been inspired to "read around", and he lets himself be inspired by many different perspectives on human meaning making, but he is not "fond of eclectic models", so he generally puts a lot of effort into translating findings into systemic functional terms, simply because "once the insights have been translated into SFL, I know how they fit into the overall model".

For Jim Martin, it is the more functional part of Halliday's systemic functional linguistics he identifies most strongly with, and Halliday's idea of the intrinsic and extrinsic functionality of language has been a major source of insight in Martin's work. Jim Martin's contribution to social semiotics includes discussions and (re)formulations of context and discourse semantics, and development of a nuanced theory and description of the language of evaluation. Martin's work has, to a large extent, been done in the realm of education; an interest that he shares with Halliday. For Martin, good scholarly work is work that gets used by others, and, as he says, from the very beginning he "wanted to make a contribution to society through my linguistics; and Halliday's aspiration to have a socially responsible linguistics motivated me". Martin's extensive work with experienced teachers over the years has resulted in practical and inspiring models for teaching reading and writing, such as the genre pedagogy presented, for example, in the book *Learning to Write, Reading to Learn* published in 2012 together with David Rose. Genre pedagogy is used in the teaching of both beginning and advanced literacy in schools all over the world.

The other three scholars represented in this book associate most closely with the social semiotic legacy from Halliday. Jay Lemke, himself a scientist, has entered the field of discourses of learning from the inside, as it were. In his search for a theory of language that would enable him to analyse communication and meaning in the science classroom, he found Halliday's book *Language as Social Semiotic*: "and it seemed to me that Halliday had exactly the approach to language that I needed in order to do research on science classrooms." From Halliday's linguistic approach he could develop tools for critical social analysis of the interaction and communication in science classrooms. This led on to work with other modes that are central in science communication, such as diagrams, graphs, maps, charts and pictures, and how they are all integrated. The semiotic approach was the core he could employ "to expand the application of systemic linguistics […] to the analysis of multimodal activity and multimodal texts". Following the development of technology, Lemke added an interest in computer-based communication and game research, moving into informal sites of learning. This has led him to further reflections on the connections between cognition and emotions in meaning making: "you cannot understand the process of learning without including the emotional component. My most recent work is therefore oriented to integrate the analysis of cognitive or ideational dimensions of learning with the affective or emotional and interpersonal dimensions."

Gunther Kress and Theo van Leeuwen have been in the lead of developing the field of multimodal research based on Halliday's understanding of how the social underpins all kinds of meaning making. In other words, Kress, and to some extent van Leeuwen, connect more with the semiotic than the linguistic perspectives from Halliday's theory, as this has been described in *Language as Social Semiotic* (1978). Gunther Kress explains his move into social semiotics with his interest in other modes than language. One result, among others, was the book that he co-authored with Robert Hodge in 1983, where they aimed at exploring "all the other ways in which meaning was made". As a tribute to Halliday and his influence on their work, they chose to title their book *Social semiotics*, thereby emphasizing the links to Halliday's seminal 1978 publication. Kress comments, in afterthought: "That was for me then a kind of decisive step. Really, now I was doing semiotics more than linguistics. Because linguistics could not provide the tools that we needed in order to account for the whole domain of meaning."

Van Leeuwen pays tribute to linguistics as a way into his work within multi-modality, since for him it has been a training of the mind to analyse things very thoroughly and very systematically. However, like Kress, he is concerned with domains of "meanings that are neither specifically visual nor specifically verbal, but belong to the culture as a whole". Therefore, especially the systemic functional emphasis on meaning and semantics (over form) has intrigued van Leeuwen. He claims that "what social semiotics needs to do, [is] bringing linguistics and social theory together". This points to a major motif in van Leeuwen's thinking, namely the idea of semiotics as part of social practices, and he is regretful that too often "[t]he social in social semiotics is not always sufficiently kept in focus" and that "crucial notions have not been developed and fleshed out in a more sociological sense". Tying in with this interest in sociology and ethnography, he has made contributions in critical discourse analysis, and he is strongly concerned with making a "positive contribution to thinking about what needs to be done differently" in society as a whole.

In short, the legacy of Michael Halliday's work on language and semiosis has been developed in what could be regarded as three main directions: a) further work on the *systems* for describing language and meaning making, b) *multimodality research*, i.e. taking semiotics into modes other than the verbal, and c) *discourse as social practice*. In addition, these perspectives have been applied to a variety of social fields. *Systemic* work can be seen in the further refinery of Halliday's grammar. Christian Mathiessen is a key figure in this direction, particularly contributing to a detailed description of linguistic systems. Jim Martin's interest in systemic perspectives is mainly directed in a more overarching level, expanding the systems of stratification with register and genre.

Halliday's social semiotics has been expanded both in terms of a more general semiotics and a social critique. The linguistic system has been expanded into other modes of expression in *multimodality* research, where the semiotic perspectives are foregrounded and more or less cut loose from the linguistic systems, though still inspired by the connections between meaning and form in SFL. Gunther Kress and Theo van Leeuwen are the key figures in this direction, working closely together in both Australian and European contexts, with Jay Lemke entering the scene from his American and natural sciences background.

The third direction we will highlight is inspired by Halliday's ambition "to provide a tool for critical social analysis", as Lemke puts it. This is a logical expansion of the "social" in social semiotics, and it has developed into various forms of discourse analysis, coined respectively as "Critical Discourse Analysis" with Theo van Leeuwen as one of the key figures, and "Positive Discourse Analysis" with Jim Martin as a key figure. In the work of Gunther Kress we see a move from analysis to design as a central perspective on how the individual interacts semiotically with the social world.

The *functional* perspective is underlined by all the scholars in the book and is a basic approach to their understanding of all kinds of meaning making. It enters into their theoretical work, methodologies and analyses in different ways, which come to the fore in various applications of SFL and social semiotics. One very prominent field of applied research is education, with Jim Martin, Gunther Kress and Jay Lemke as central figures. Other fields are health care, computer gaming, music and media discourse.

These directions are not separate in the sense that they develop independently of each other, and the scholars we have interviewed are all involved in more than one direction. But in the following these directions will serve to structure our discussions and the dialogues we attempt to create among the five interviewees.

Systems and concepts

In this section, we shall describe and discuss how Halliday's systemic work on language has been the point of departure for developing SFL and social semiotics into new directions. First we shall approach the concept of *meaning*, which is central to all the directions we shall discuss afterwards.

On meaning

Meaning is at the heart of social semiotics, and meaning in this sense is rooted in the social, in the real life experiences of the people who make meaning. Gunther Kress describes how he was initially drawn to Halliday's kind of linguistics because it did not separate meaning and form in the way that he had found dissatisfactory in transformational grammar. Social semiotic scholars do not enter into philosophical discussions about where meaning is situated or how it can be understood. They seem to take as a starting point that meaning exists in people's lives, and performs its work through their social practices; in Matthiessen's words, "the social, the interactive is central and essential" when we want to explore semiosis. Van Leeuwen is in line with this when he states that "knowledge is ultimately based on doing".

The theoretical anchoring of meaning in the social is shared by all the scholars, but they have slightly different takes on how this works for the individual meaning maker. Matthiessen and Martin do not see the advantage of taking in a cognitive component in the paradigm and connecting with concepts such as mind and cognition; instead they advocate a holistic, all-encompassing semiotic approach to meaning making: the cognitive component gets embedded in a social framework, and there is a tendency to talk about brain, not mind. This resonates with Firth's idea:

> ... such dualisms as mind and body, language and thought, word and idea (...) are a quite unnecessary nuisance, and in my opinion should be dropped.
>
> *(Firth, 1957, p. 227)*

Matthiessen states that he and Halliday connect language with the brain, but put the mind aside, and try to explain the functioning of the brain through language instead of assuming something like the mind or cognition, and using that to explain language. Their approach resonates with the ideas of a number of neuroscientists like Gerald Edelman. Matthiessen goes on to suggest that "knowing and thinking are semiotic processes. From this follows a semiotic understanding of sensory motor systems".

Martin is in line with Matthiessen in this sense, since he objects to a tripartite model of semiosis (a model where you have brain, mind and language) and advocates for "a Hallidayan project, which develops a rich theory of social semiosis alongside a rich theory of neurobiology and interfaces those two directly". For Martin, the dialogue with cognitive theories is futile, and in this sense he is critical towards the efforts made by Halliday and Matthiessen in their book *Construing Experience Through Language* (1999) to build a semantics that might convince cognitive linguists and psychologists that the semiotic project is a reasonable alternative. In Martin's opinion, a project like that is never going to succeed because it is impossible to convince people who believe in the mind that there is no mind. Martin pinpoints his position when stating that: "Halliday is more tolerant of cognitive approaches than I am. He has tried to position his relationship with Lamb as a complementarity; but I am a radical Hallidayan, so I do not do that."

Jay Lemke does not share the scepticism to the concept of "cognition", but this does not mean that he believes in "an immaterial realm of mind". He is in line with the other interviewees in this book in positioning meaning making as semiotic processes in the social and the material by going "outside of the head, make it culturally specific, make it situated in interactions in an environment in a context". Consequently, when he opens up a discussion on the relationship between cognition and emotion, he anchors his thinking in "a kind of materialist rather than a formalist view of semiotics". His view is inspired by Paul Thibault's work on embodied cognition and also by bio-semiotics as it is outlined by Jesper Hoffmeyer. This way of thinking leads to questioning the traditional distinction between affect and cognition, and Lemke concludes "that the traditional distinction between thought and feeling is an ideological distinction. It is a distinction that has to do with gender stereotypes. There is, however, no meaning-making without feeling". Lemke gives examples from the field of academic work: "In scientific texts, scientists also get quite emotional about a beautifully designed experiment in the laboratory, or a beautiful mathematical formula or expression of an idea or generalization. Perhaps the thing that is most often overlooked is that even the so-called neutral academic objectivity is itself a feeling. It is not the absence of feeling, it is a *particular* feeling that one has and cultivates."

This socially grounded way of looking at meaning also connects to the understanding of learning, and may account for the common interests in educational matters among the five scholars. Kress states that learning is a result of semiotic action. Learning he understands as engaging in semiotic resources in a way "that changes my inner resources. I have changed meaning for myself. [...] in that process also I have changed my capacities for action. I have changed my identity. These things are *so* closely related". Talking about meaning and learning in these terms, Kress does not use concepts such as thinking and cognition, but rather he explains this process in terms of external resources being made to inner resources. He does not explain the concept of "inner resources" or connect it to established theories of cognition.

Summing up, we can say that all five scholars share an understanding of meaning as rooted in the social, which can be seen as a fundamental conception of meaning in social semiotics. We find some differences when it comes to how this takes place in and around individual meaning makers, with Kress and Lemke representing an interest in the individual. In Kress's work this is articulated as the interest of the sign maker, while Lemke understands cognition and emotion as embodied processes situated in the social. In Matthiessen's and Martin's work, concepts such as mind and cognition are not deployed; instead, they connect the brain directly to socially organized semiosis.

On the sign

The sign is a fundamental concept in all kinds of semiotics, although Halliday is more concentrated on the notion of sign system, not on the sign itself (see the next section). The concept of the sign was primarily taken up in the interviews with Gunther Kress, Jay Lemke and Theo van Leeuwen, and they approach the concept of the sign slightly differently. For Kress, meaning ties very closely in with sign making: "making motivated signs is, I think, a kind of given for many species", and he regards the sign as "the basic unit of semiotics". In his view signs are *made*, and anything can be made into a sign: "We are constantly remaking existing resources, to do the job we need to do at a particular moment." Theo van Leeuwen is more reluctant to use the word "sign", mainly because it has a history of being understood as stable and divorced from the context. He goes along with Gunther Kress in talking about the making of signs. His point is to underline that the relations between signifier and signified is "much more flexible and fluid". In many cases he prefers the notion of "semiotic resources" because they are not seen as signs, which have specific meanings.

We find more difference in opinion between the two when it comes to the understanding of *how* signs carry meaning, though this is a matter of nuances.

Gunther Kress has made it his mission to reject the notion of arbitrariness in sign making: "[T]he notion of arbitrariness in the Saussurian sign just didn't fit with a social notion. It fitted in one respect, namely that the power of the social was essential to keep the relation of form and meaning together. So we kept the conventional part, and we developed the notion that arbitrariness is not a feature of sign making. Conventionality *is*, because it is the power of the social that keeps these things stable." This notion of the motivated sign first appeared in *Social semiotics* (1988), and later Kress found inspiration in Charles S. Peirce's notion of the iconic sign, when he understood it not merely as a visual sign, but as a metaphor for a more general phenomenon: "So I thought: well, it is actually motivated, a deliberate act. Deliberate is a very strong way of formulating it, but I mean something which is not accidental in the combination of form and meaning." Theo van Leeuwen agrees: "Signs are always motivated. If people decide to have arbitrary signs, they will have them. But it is not because the *sign* is arbitrary, it is because people have decided they want an arbitrary system, and in a sense not even that is arbitrary." Jay Lemke also regards arbitrariness as "a little bit of an exaggeration", and prefers to talk about "degrees of conventionality and degrees of naturalness".

Jay Lemke is the only one of the five interviewed scholars who is significantly inspired by Charles S. Peirce's semiotic thinking. This includes his distinction between icon, index and symbol, picked up by many who are interested in multimodal semiotics. Lemke makes the connection to Peirce's thinking about "firstness" (similarity of form), "secondness" (relationship through causality) and "thirdness" (relationship through convention). While Kress, as mentioned above, connects to iconic signification in his reasoning about all signs being motivated, Lemke is particularly interested in the indexical basis of meaning making: "[A] lot of the meaning that we ascribe to signs or to acts and actions as signs come not simply from their denotation, but from another way of thinking of connotation. I may be talking about icons, indexes and symbols, but I am talking about it in English, and that tells you something about me. And I am talking about it in American English, and that says something more about me. You may even hear certain throatiness in my voice because I have been talking a lot, and that also tells you something about me. As a system of interpreting from your point of view, there are many layers of meaning in the words I say, which have some kind of physical or causal relationship to me as the speaker. You can take that even further, not just to me as the speaker, but to the culture and historical period from which I am speaking." He concludes that indexical meaning is a very powerful tool.

Lemke points to Peirce's tripartite model of the sign, including not only a signifier (the representamen) and a signified (the object), but also "a third element, 'the interpretant', which I think of as 'a system that does the interpreting'. In other words, no signifier, no sign in the sense of the material expression points to the signified or the meaning it is supposed to stand for. *You* have to make that connection! You have to do what Halliday calls 'construe', and of course you construe according to systems of social convention." Lemke claims that semiotics is very good at describing those systems of social convention. That is, in some ways, what the grammar is doing, but he underlines that there has to be a third element that actually does this construing. For Peirce, it is not the semiotic relation that is fundamental; it is the process of semiosis, something Lemke agrees with. Coming from physics and from a notion that if meaning making takes place, semiosis takes place, because material beings are engaged in material processes and are doing things that make the meaning happen. "I certainly understood from a very early point that the Peircian perspective had an advantage over the Saussurian one", Lemke says. He explains the lack of interest in Peircian semiotics among social semioticians as "a strong sense of loyalty to the Hallidayian tradition and its way of formulating ideas. Halliday did not rely very much on Peirce. He relied a lot more on Hjelmslev, who in turn relied on Saussure".

Kress does not, in the same way, choose between Saussure and Peirce. He finds points he supports and points to criticize within the work of both. Like Lemke, he finds the process of semiosis as described by Peirce interesting, and connects it to the interpretant, introducing agency in the act of interpretation: "I could then see that that's what is central in the Peircian scheme for me: the infinite, kind of constant transformation. And what is important in the Saussurian scheme is the notion of convention, and the notion of reference."

On the semiotic system

One axiomatic idea in Halliday's thinking is to operate with semiotic systems, not in the sense of systems of signs, but in the sense of systems of meaning; as he states: "'semiotic' means 'having to do with meaning' rather than 'having to do with signs'." (Halliday, 1995b, pp. 198–99). In other words, in a Hallidayan perspective, there is no usage of the concept sign. Instead, meaning and form – content and expression – are treated in the light of stratification.

Stratification is an interesting and debated concept in the sense that the five scholars in this book have approached it differently, and for different purposes. The one who is most true to Halliday's own thinking of stratification is Matthiessen, who organizes the description of language according to the stratal organization as it is theorized by Halliday, i.e. through the following strata: context, semantics, lexicogrammar and phonology. Martin evaluates Halliday's idea of stratification in the following quotation, which also points to the areas where his description of stratification has expanded upon Halliday's and also where it is different from Halliday's: "There was quite a lot of ambiguity in Halliday's writing about strata during the seventies. You could perhaps see the ambiguity reflected in the Cardiff grammar tradition, where the difference between semantics and grammar is conflated with the difference between system and structure. That is a reasonable reading of some of Halliday's writing in the 1970s. What perhaps evolved under my influence, and under the influence of Christian Matthiessen in Sydney, were distinct system/ structure cycles on the different levels of language." Martin points to Firth and says that Halliday reworked Firth's ideas about phonology into grammar. Martin reworks Halliday's grammatical theory into theory of discourse semantics. "If you are a discourse analyst you have to push on and worry about context; co-text is not enough", Martin says.

Martin does not operate with a stratum for semantics but with a stratum for discourse semantics, thereby emphasizing textual patterns and not grammar as his main concern. And he stratifies context into context of culture and context of situation in order to accommodate for purpose in his model (see below for a discussion of context).

Jay Lemke's answer to the question of how context can be described and understood is his concept of meta-redundancy. This can be seen as a reworking of Halliday's stratification model into a hierarchy of relations. Lemke's aim is to give a systematic account for the role of context in meaning: "When you study the signifier and the signified, you will see that the same signifier does not always point to the same signified. The same word, the same sentence, the same gesture does not always have the same meaning. So what determines which meaning it has? We usually say that the context determines it. The next question is, what is the context, and how do you know which context is relevant to use to determine the meaning in each case? Logically, you would answer that the norms of your culture tells you which context is the one in which this particular sign should be interpreted as having this particular meaning. You begin to build up a meta-hierarchy." This provides a tool to consider what the most relevant context is. Given all the possible interpretations of the given signifier, the interpretations have different probabilities of being the most useful or most shared interpretation, depending on the context.

Halliday himself connects to Lemke's notion of meta-redundancy (Halliday, 1992) this, however, is not something that Martin does – instead he builds on Hjelmslev's ideas of a connotative and a denotative semiotic in order to explain interstratal relation. Lemke himself makes the connection to Hjelmslev, but also to Peirce: "In some ways, connotative semiotics has something in common with my concept meta-redundancy, and with Peirce's notion of infinite semiosis or chains of signification, where the first signifier points to some signified for an interpretive system, but that in turn can point to another one, and that can again point to another one and so forth."

Kress and van Leeuwen have transformed the notion of stratification from linguistics to a setting of social semiotics and communication in their book on *Multimodal discourse; the modes and media of contemporary communication* (2001), and they suggest the following four strata: discourse, design, production and dissemination. Van Leeuwen characterizes strata as a "geological metaphor" where "the main thought was to actually reformulate that in a way that is related to practice, so you have a more social semiotic idea". These four strata are very different to the strata – and in fact to the idea of stratification – as suggested by Halliday, since they do not describe the overarching organizing principle of a semiotic system (such as language). Instead, they are a model to understand the practices of multimodal communication. Kress is not happy with the notion of strata, since he is in doubt whether his and van Leeuwen's suggestion of their four strata was indeed a fruitful way to understand multimodal communication: "We had endless problems in saying what these four things that we want to talk about are. They can be described as being in a sequential relation, chronologically. They can be described in a hierarchical relation of some kind. And actually now they are for me insufficient, and I think even at the time we were not actually that keen. In as far as it suggests the kind of structural linguistic notion of stratification, I would not actually be very happy with that now." However, he cannot offer a better way of labeling these relations for the time being. His best suggestion is to draw an analogy to Halliday's way of talking about the metafunctions: "These are simultaneous semiotic domains."

Stratification is a fundamental principle in Michael Halliday's functional linguistics, and so it is in the work of all the five interviewees, although Kress and van Leeuwen are more sceptical of the notion than Matthiessen, Martin and Lemke.

On text

In all five interviews, the concept of text was discussed, and different properties of text were taken up by the interviewees. Matthiessen defines a text according to the systemic functional architecture at large, i.e. as a location in terms of different dimensions: "One dimension is the cline of instantiation, where the text is located at the instance end. Another dimension is the hierarchy of stratification, where the text is located as a unit in semantics, which is in turn realized as acts of wording – so a text is not only meaning, it is also wording, which is in turn realized as sounding – and the meaning and the wording are located within context. So text is meaning, or content, unfolding in a context of situation: language functioning in context".

For Martin, the text is a "unit of meaning", which instantiates systems on all strata – including contextual properties. A text, therefore, is a complex theoretical concept, combining stratification and instantiation, and taking into account the relationship between the paradigmatic properties of the system and the syntagmatic qualities of the instance. Martin explains text – and how this concept is interwoven with the concept of context – with the following words: "Context for me is a higher stratum of meaning on the realization hierarchy; and if we stratify context, we are looking at genre as a pattern of register patterns, register as a pattern of discourse semantics, discourse semantics as a pattern of grammatical patterns, grammatical patterns as patterns of phonological or graphological or gestural patterns as we come down. There is no text there. We are just at the level of system all the way down. The system/structure cycles are specifying the syntagmatic output of the choices on different levels. You have to move to the instantiation hierarchy to talk about the text in relation to system. The text is an instance of all these systems, an instance of every one of them." Martin stresses that, for him "the text is a unit on the instantiation hierarchy and context is a unit on the stratification hierarchy".

Gunther Kress makes the connection to communication when he suggests to use "the term *text* for any semiotic entity, which is internally coherent and framed, so that I can see this entity as separate from other entities". He regards the text as a result of processes of communication: "Communication is a process, and the result of the process is the production of a text."

Theo van Leeuwen sees text as "resources for practices", and he brings a historical perspective into the use of the concept: "'Text' was a useful word in the seventies: as with many of our terms, like literacy and grammar, it served to legitimize a field, to say 'We are just as legitimate as you, we also analyse texts'. The text linguistics of the seventies was an important move. We moved from the sentence to the text. But then 'text' became a ubiquitous and very loosely applied term, and now, in relation to the new media, is even confused with resources. So I prefer to talk about practice, and about communicative practice as one kind of practice, and about the text as part of that – sometimes a big part, sometimes a small part." Today, van Leeuwen questions the way the concept of text has been expanded indefinitely: "'text' has been extended so much and applied to so many things. I have not actually written anything about this as yet, but I have begun to say here and there that maybe the use of the term should be restricted back to actual 'textual artefacts'. So a conversation would not be a text. It would be a practice, done by people in specific contexts. It only becomes a text when we turn it into an artefact (e.g. by transcribing it) and insert it as a key resource into another interpretive practice (e.g. conversation analysis). Thus texts become resources."

Jay Lemke's understanding of text follows on the one hand from his understanding of meaning making based in material action, and on the other hand from his interests in the interpretative sides of meaning making: "I have usually distinguished between an objective meaning of text, by which I mean the actual physical, material text, the ink on the paper or the lights on the computer screen, versus the *meaning text*, by which I mean the meanings that are interpreted by some interpreter from the objective text." Like van Leeuwen, Lemke also places text in close connection with activity. To him texts are placed and function within an activity or an activity genre. To nuance the concept of text, Lemke has introduced the concept of "text scales" as an answer to questions about how meaning is organized above the level of the sentence: "what I wanted to know was what kind of meanings you can make with longer texts that you cannot make with shorter texts. This seemed to me to be really a fundamental question." Text scales are connected to "activity scales" or "time scales". These concepts open up to interesting studies of cross-scale relationships, and Lemke has developed a model for such analyses, which he characterizes as a "sandwich model": "The meanings you make or the actions and activities you do that typically take place at the level in focus are themselves organizations made up of smaller activities and actions or units of words or sentences, and they are subject to the constraints and affordances of the longer term activities that are going on at the time."

The interviews show how the five scholars agree on seeing text as a semantic unit, but they approach it from very different angles. Matthiessen and Martin both define text according to systemic dimensions, and, although especially Martin is committed to bring context into the picture, emphasizing the interdependency

between text and context, both put a lot of weight on the internal – both grammatical and cohesive – structures and patterns of the text. This marks a difference
to Kress and van Leeuwen, who are more preoccupied with the way in which
texts are situated in a social practice. So is Lemke, but he introduces a different
kind of systematic thinking in hierarchies of semantic action through his notion of
meta-redundancy, a kind of thinking inspired by his background in natural science.

On text analysis

Martin and Matthiessen have different – and to some extent complementary – aims
with their work. Taking all the nuances aside – and there are many, of course –
one could argue that Martin is concerned most with the perspective from above,
i.e. working in from context down to discourse semantics and then to lexicogrammar, while Matthiessen more than anything is interested in the lexicogrammar, and therefore working in from below, i.e. from lexicogrammar to
semantics and then out to context. Martin justifies his position as follows: "What I
do is to try to reinterpret cohesion as a higher stratum of meaning. This is different
from Halliday's 'grammar and glue' model. He is a grammarian and as a grammarian you work with clauses, and you think beyond grammar in terms of how
you can stick those clauses together. This gives rise to what I think of as the
grammar and glue perspective. I think not in terms of glue sticking clauses together, but in terms of discourse semantic system/structure cycles realized through
lexicogrammar. The unit of meaning we need to worry about in semantics is the
text, an unfolding discourse, so we need to think about systems at that level."
Martin regrets that "most systemic work considers, however, texts to be bags of
clauses. People analyse the clauses and add up the results and divide them by the
number of clauses, and think they have the meaning of the text. That is rather
ridiculous, but it is standard practice in SFL meetings. It comes in part from Halliday's comment in his grammar book that if you are not doing a grammatical
analysis of the text, you are just doing a running commentary on the text." For
Martin, therefore, there is "too much clause semantics floating around". To this,
Matthiessen responds: "I would say: 'not too much clause semantics, but too little
text semantics' […] I think it is important to develop semantic descriptions 'from
above' (top-down), from context, as well, but I do not actually see much of that
happening: truly locating oneself in context and thinking about semantics strategically, thinking in terms of context, but also in terms of other systems, including
sensory motor systems – sort of semantics as strategies for transforming what is not
meaning into meaning." Matthiessen advocates that "as far as accounts of semantics
are concerned, we have to find a way to make them as detailed and explicit – as
'hanging together' – as accounts of lexicogrammar; if we are serious about our
understanding of the centrality of language, if, as Martin said to me over three
decades ago 'I don't think we think, we mean' […] then we have to have
accounts of semantics that are explicit enough to support this." This is a missing
piece in the systemic functional puzzle. Matthiessen states: "There has been a

certain tendency among SFL researchers not to value explicitness and modelling of this kind, and this has been detrimental to progress in work on semantics and context."

Van Leeuwen stresses the importance of a contextualized understanding of texts, and in his view, contextualizing means connecting to insights not only from within social semiotics but also from academic fields adjacent to social semiotics: "what social semiotics needs to do, to bring linguistics and social theory together, as I tried to do in my thesis, and as Bob Hodge and Gunther Kress had done earlier. Another thing, of course, is history. If you want to understand and explain things, history is fundamental. It has been neglected and it has therefore become a great area of ignorance amongst linguists."

Jay Lemke stresses the importance of intertextuality in the work with texts. Early in his career, he read Riffaterre, Kristeva and Bakhtin. Lemke says that the notions of intertextuality led him to his analyses of hypertexts. His fundamental question in such analyses was whether the meaning relations between the sources of the link and the target of the link are the same as the intertextual relationships we normally talk about in analyses of verbal texts.

In his work in semiotics Gunther Kress is advocating perspectives more independent of the linguistic model. When asked about important challenges for the future he notes that he is searching for general semiotic features that can be deployed across modes: "This is relevant to everything that has become modal, which is recognized by at least a group in the social as being a means of communication, a resource with some degree of regularity that is understood by its members in some way. I think then we can say what kinds of semiotic categories are essential. *Not* – and this is the difference on my part to other forms of semiotics – not: Does it have clauses? Or does it have clauses of this kind or that kind; morphemes of this kind; does it express past time morphemically or lexically? Not those questions, but: Is it important to have deixis? What would it be like not to have deixis? Those are my questions."

On context

The theoretical modelling of the notion of context has played a central role in the work of both Martin and Matthiessen, and their work differs significantly in this area. While Matthiessen largely has stayed loyal to Halliday's ideas of context, re-modelling context and applying the concept to text analysis and text production has been a major motif in the work of Martin throughout his entire career. Martin has stratified what is one contextual stratum in Halliday's thinking into two contextual strata, which he labels register and genre. Unfortunately this labelling has caused a lot of confusion in systemic functional circles. Martin explains this terminological confusion as follows: "I could not call my approach to context 'context', because I have two strata. Halliday has one, so he calls it context. I had split it up and so had to give the levels different names. I chose genre and register to be those two names." Martin states that a further confusion arises because, for Halliday, register is a linguistic notion and refers to the way in which systemic probabilities in language are pushed about by field, mode and tenor systems. It is only the realizations of his context stratum that he calls register. "The only really substantial issue is whether you stratify context or not. I do; Halliday does not", Martin says.

Matthiessen, whose approach to context and the notion of register is similar to Halliday's, also sees a terminological problem in the changing sense of the term register: "[…] register was a functional variety of language in terms of what you do relative to settings of contextual variables – field, tenor and mode […] But then Martin exported the term register up to context and took register to mean field, tenor and mode, rather than the functional variation that lives in the environment of varying settings of values of field, tenor and mode."

Taking the terminological confusion aside, Martin argues for his dual stratification of context, and explains that his notions of genre and register were developed in his teaching. When he started to teach in the MA Applied Linguistics programme in Sydney, he offered a course called "Functional varieties of language", in which he introduced Gregory's model with field, mode, personal tenor and functional tenor. Halliday used in his courses field, mode and tenor. The students found the alternative views confusing, and two of Martin's students, Joan Rothery and Guenter Plum, suggested to push functional tenor deeper because it seemed to influence all of ideational, interpersonal and textual meaning. They wanted to keep Halliday's notion of ideational meaning construing field, interpersonal meaning enacting tenor, and textual meaning composing mode, which was difficult if purpose (functional tenor) got in the way. According to Martin, stratifying could solve the problem. There were, however, still two terms – personal tenor and functional tenor – on two different levels of abstraction. To avoid confusion, the term functional tenor was changed to genre. For Martin, Halliday's neat model of the relations between the three metafunctions and the three context variables was not sustainable. Martin's genre model has been widely used and discussed. A genre is, for Martin, a configuration of all three kinds of meaning, and the configurations themselves can then be organized into systems. We can map a "level of emergent complexity" beyond field, mode and tenor, and so Martin articulates a culture as a system of genres. Martin points to Matthiessen and says that he has more recently developed a "pie model" where he maps the genre relations as slices of a field pie, where he assumes that ideational meaning construes field. Martin disagrees with this: "I think that decades of work show that ideational integration of genre families of this kind is not the case. The slices are not tied together because they are ideationally related; they are tied together as configurations of all three kinds of meaning. So either you stratify context and stop trying to put genre into one of the three register categories or you give up the intrinsic and extrinsic functionality hook-up notion. I want to hang on to this hook-up as part of our heritage." Martin claims that he and his colleagues have pushed harder at the question of genre relations and, by doing this, the systems of relations started to sort themselves out as four systems, not three, with one system – genre – as more abstract than the three others: field, tenor and mode.

Matthiessen's evaluation of Martin's model of genre and register is – not surprisingly – different to Martin's. Matthiessen sees the notion of genre as something coordinating field, tenor and mode problematic for two reasons: "One problem is that the purposes are functionally diversified, not unified as in genre theory. So I think there is insight into exploring them in terms of field, tenor and mode." Matthiessen says that until someone has worked out an explicit model of how genre actually relates to field, tenor and mode, he will not reify the model. In Martin's work, there are certain combinations of genres occurring together with certain combinations of field, tenor and mode. Matthiessen claims that there are other ways of accounting for co-occurrence: "The closest to genre seems to me to be situation types, which are somewhere mid-region on the cline of instantiation, between context of culture and context of situation." According to him, there is a tendency for genre to become synonymous with text structure, which leads to confusion. Matthiessen emphasizes, however, that the confusion is not Martin's fault, but comes from the way in which people have used the concept of genre. On Martin's critique of his (and Teruya's) recent "pie model", Matthiessen comments that he and Kazuhiro Teruya have discussed the fields of activity, and worked with the rich amount of papers on genres and genre agnation, and differently from Martin have come to the conclusion that the account of genre is to a large degree field oriented, and that there is a kind of complement in tenor and in mode.

In light of stratification and instantiation, Matthiessen explains the theoretical difference between his (and Halliday's) model and Martin's by emphasizing that Martin and his colleagues have mainly explored the questions of context, ideology, genre and register through the hierarchy of stratification. For Matthiessen, another dimension is also of great importance: the cline of instantiation that Halliday explored in an early work, *Explorations in the Functions of Language* (1973). Matthiessen says: "it is true of Michael Halliday, Ruqaiya Hasan and a number of us, that we have not stratified context, but instead, in our work, context is, just like language, extended along the cline of instantiation; it is extended from the context of culture at the potential pole of the cline via institutional and subcultural domains and situation types to contexts of situation at the instance pole. So, different contextual patterns have different locations along the cline of instantiation; interpreted contextually, genre corresponds roughly to the range of the cline of instantiation explored under the heading of situation type. This is a way of exploring the same territory, but in a two-dimensional way."

On communication

Kress sees communication as closely linked to the production and reception of texts: "I think that in communication we produce texts. I would make that kind of distinction. Text is a material thing, which is a result of semiotic work; communication as semiotic work."

For Lemke, however, the result of communication is a community: "Communication is the processes which bind a community together. People within a community communicate more often and more intensely in more important ways with each other than they do with people who are not part of that community. I do not believe that communication is the transfer of the same meaning from one person to the other. I believe that communication comprises the social processes by which communities bind themselves together, and it does not have to be in language. I think in general it is in joint collaborative or interactive action that communication take place."

In the section on meaning, we highlighted how Matthiessen suggests that interaction is central and essential when we want to explore semiosis. It is therefore striking that Matthiessen – as Halliday – is not comfortable with the notion of communication: "when people link language and communication they tend to operate with this notion that language is there to 'clothe' ideas that arise somewhere else, so it leaves out the ideational component; it misses out on what Whorf has emphasized: language as a resource for construing experience. Communication is the exchange of meanings, and part of what meanings do is to construe our experience." The last bit of Matthiessen's statement contains a definition of communication that takes into account both interpersonal and experiential meaning; the exchange of meaning points to the interpersonal perspective, while the construal of experience points to the ideational perspective on meaning. Matthiessen's definition bears some resemblance to the way that Martin defines communication, although Martin stresses the interpersonal perspective on communication rather than the ideational perspective, when he states that communication "is using your semiosis, using your semiotic systems to negotiate meaning".

In line with Matthiessen's reluctance to theorize about communication, van Leeuwen prefers to talk about semiotic practices over communication. Gunther Kress has included the concept in some of his titles, e.g. *Multimodality: a social semiotic approach to contemporary communication* (2010). He uses "communication" and "semiotics" more or less as synonyms, explaining communication as semiotic work (similarly to van Leeuwen), and states that "[s]emiotics would be the theoretical frame in which I look at communication". Both Kress and Lemke see teaching and learning in the classroom as a form of communication. However, Lemke admits that "[c]ommunication is one of those terms, like context or culture, that is useful mainly because it is vague".

On the Sydney grammar versus the Cardiff grammar

In systemic functional linguistics, there exist two main approaches to the description of lexicogrammar: the approach known from Halliday's and Matthiessen's *An Introduction to Functional Grammar* (2014), which is sometimes labelled the "Sydney grammar", and the approach known as the "Cardiff grammar", whose main exponent is Robin Fawcett.

Martin and Matthiessen may disagree on how one most appropriately may theorize the concept of context, and they may have different takes on the stratum between context and grammar – discourse semantics for Martin, and semantics for

Matthiessen – but they agree that Halliday's approach to grammar is the one to advocate. Comparing Halliday's approach to the approach taken by Fawcett and the Cardiff grammar, Matthiessen states: "a key difference between the Cardiff grammar and the Sydney grammar is that in Halliday's grammar it is dimensions all the way. I find the relational-dimensional thinking very appealing."

This view can be seen as a contrast to modular-based grammatical thinking, which has been and still is prominent in many linguistic models. Matthiessen sees greater advantages in a relational-dimensional thinking that allows you to see how every unit is in a system, and where one phenomenon always is related to other phenomena, both globally and locally. For Matthiessen, the Cardiff grammar is closer to modular thinking.

Martin also points out that the dimensions in Halliday's thinking provide for a richer description and model of language than does the Cardiff grammar, since the Cardiff grammar "conflates axis and stratification (with system conflated with semantics and structure with grammar)". To Martin, the advantage of stratifying language into two distinct strata – discourse semantics and lexicogrammar – is that it gives room for both clause semantics and text semantics: "if we conflate axis with stratification as in the Cardiff model we can only have a clause semantics", Martin states. Another issue with the Cardiff grammar is that its semantic categories are neither motivated by grammatical structures, nor co-textual patterning. Martin says: "If you look carefully, Fawcett's systems for MOOD and TRANSITIVITY, or whatever he calls them in a particular phase of his research, are not based on or motivated by structure (in the way that they are for Halliday and Matthiessen and others)." Martin points at Fawcett's recent MOOD networks (e.g. Fawcett, 2008), where he has speech function labels for what Halliday would classify as imperative, interrogative, declarative and exclamative clauses. Such labelling does not, according to Martin, make generalizations about structural patterns, and a wide variety of grammatical syntagms realize most of Fawcett's features. Martin also criticizes that there is no co-textual reasoning either by Fawcett in terms of the discourse semantics of exchange structure. This turns Fawcett's description into a kind of speech act theory. The advocates of the Cardiff grammar have a philosophical notional perspective on meaning, not a social semiotic one, and of course, naturally enough, this is set in a cognitive framework.

The Sydney and the Cardiff grammar both build on a systemic and functional approach in their description of language, and they are often labelled as "two dialects of the same language". Matthiessen and Martin, however, find this labelling misguiding, since the two approaches to language description hold significant differences. While Matthiessen mainly criticizes the Cardiff grammar for being too modular oriented, Martin, among other things, takes up the lack of co-text reasoning.

Multimodality

Among the scholars in this book, Kress and van Leeuwen are the main exponents – and to a large extent the founding fathers – of multimodal social semiotics.

Multimodality has played a central part in Jay Lemke's work too: "once you look at things in terms of multimodality, there is no going back", he states. With his interest in the history of mathematical and scientific language, and how it had diverged from everyday language, he soon became "dissatisfied with looking only at language. It was clear that you also had to look at other semiotic modalities, certainly diagrams, graphs, maps, charts and pictures. What seemed to me most important was how they were all integrated".

Kress and van Leeuwen have taken up the semiotic perspective in Halliday's work and applied it to several forms of expression; Kress acknowledges this legacy in this way: "social semiotics, I think, has taken something from his linguistics, namely the semiotic organization and the semiotic principles, and attempts to apply them to the affordances of materials in specific social environments." He points to Halliday's distinction between speech and writing as one inspiration for this move. Van Leeuwen, coming from a background in film production, originally searched for a way of theorizing language and image, and also language and media, and he found inspiration in the systemic functional concern with meaning over form: "now the question could be asked in a different way; not "Does film have words or clauses?" which it does not have, but "Is there something in film that fulfils the function of words and clauses?" Modality is a prime example. Language has specific resources for expressing modality: the modal auxiliaries. Film does not have these, but it can express modalities, degrees of realism, in its own ways."

Both Kress and van Leeuwen stress that multimodality is a field of research, rather than a theory or a discipline. As such, it can be approached from different theoretical perspectives. Choosing to coin the phenomenon as "multimodal" creates an expectation of explanations from language and semiotics, van Leeuwen points out. This leads him to look for "a more integral and coherent picture of multimodal communication and all its resources, and all of the ways in which these are integrated". He found (in *Introducing Social Semiotics*, 2005) "that social semiotics needs to describe semiotic resources, the practices in which they are used, as well as the histories of these semiotic resources, their meaning potentials and the discourses that surround them in particular practices – the discourses that regulate them, evaluate them, criticize them, teach them, change them and so on".

Working with multimodality may shed light on similarities as well as differences between modes, Kress claims. One side of semiosis that becomes apparent when one looks at meaning making across modes, is that the materiality of the sign makes a difference: "Theo van Leeuwen and I also said that the materiality of the stuff that gets turned into the resources for communication, semiotic resources, has an effect on how a higher level category such as metafunctions gets articulated."

Van Leeuwen notes how *Reading images* has become a reference work for the multimodal, especially visual analysis, and he admits being proud of that: "the idea of the 'language of the image' […] I have been lucky enough to realize that dream, I actually did it, and successfully so. When I look back I feel that something has been achieved".

Jay Lemke presents his notion of multiplicative or multiplying meaning as his most important contribution to the tool box of multimodal analysis. This accounts for the "combinatorial explosion of possible combinations" in multimodal communication, in short pointing out how multimodal communication does a lot more than adding up modes. He says that if you have several different codes, or several different sets of alternatives, and you are deploying them simultaneously, then the set of all the possible combinations of them is the relevant set for deciding the information value of any particular choice or instance.

In the section above on meaning, we touched upon Halliday's view that it is from language and language use that we understand cognition, not the other way round; in his own words, what is at stake is the following:

> When people reason through talk, they are actually reasoning with **meanings**; but these meanings are not a separate "cognitive" universe of concepts or ideas – they are patterns of semantic (that is, linguistic) organization brought about, or "realized", by wordings.
>
> *(Halliday, 1995a, p. 246; orig. emphasis)*

So, to Halliday, language is fundamental to man as a semiotic being, although he occasionally takes other semiotic systems – or modes – into consideration:

> Some people claim that [...] anything that can be meant in any way at all can also be meant in language. ... *I am not sure.* Some semiotic systems may be incommensurable with language; witness the sometimes far-fetched attempts to represent the meaning of a work of art in language (but, again, cf. O'Toole, 1994). But while the question is important, and deserves to be tackled much more subtly and fundamentally than this rather simplistic formulation suggests, it is not necessary for me to try to resolve it here. All that needs to be said in the present context is that other human semiotics are dependent on the premise that their users **also** have language. Language is a prerequisite; but there is no need to insist that language can mean it all.
>
> *(Halliday, 2003, p. 4; orig. emphasis; cf. Halliday, 1978, p. 99, and Halliday, 1989, p. 10)*

As Halliday's close associate, Matthiessen, too, is primarily concerned with language, but he reaches out to other semiotic systems and advocates for the idea of multimodality: "We certainly know things in other semiotic systems as well. I think probably people vary in terms of the nature of the complementarity of the semiotic systems they operate with, but obviously there has been research into image schemata and so on, and I think mathematics is a way of knowing. It is obvious that these semiotic systems differ considerably in terms of the extent to which we share them across the human family. Some are very specialized in terms of human cultures and the division of labour within a given culture, while others are much more general: language is a very general kind of semiotic system." As

Matthiessen, Martin has also primarily worked with language as a mode of meaning, and he reiterates Halliday's point that language is the only modality that can talk about other modalities. Language is also, according to Martin, the only mode that is a stratified system. Attempts have been made to impose concepts like rank, metafunctions and strata on other modes of meaning, but Martin is of the opinion that we do not really have system/structure cycles for, for example, images. When Martin talks about the future challenges for social semiotics he raises among other questions the following: "How can we build the theory that enables us to understand how the meanings from different modalities come together into a single text?" Martin thinks that we are still stuck in a linguistic theory.

On mode

The definition of mode is functional and rooted in the social in the thinking of Kress and van Leeuwen. Gunther Kress's definition is: "A mode is that which a community, a group of people who work in similar ways around similar issues, has decided to treat as a mode." Jay Lemke relates his definition to a semiotic resource system in the original sense presented by Halliday (1978): "It is a system of meaning potential, a system of meaningful contrasts between forms in a community that has conventions for the interpretation of those forms and contrasts, as paradigms, as syntagms, and this can be done through multiple expression planes." In this way Lemke connects mode to Martin's thinking presented previously on paradigmatic properties in a system, and syntagmatic qualities of the instance.

It has been debated whether modes, regarded as systems of semiotic resources should be defined in terms of certain systemic features. One possible requirement would be that a mode should be able to express all three metafunctions. This can be seen as a question of what the basic unit of analysis is: the single mode or an instance of multimodal communication. Theo van Leeuwen makes this point: "You could say that in multimodal communication we always need the three metafunctions, so that all three are present in any act of multimodal communication, but which metafunction is mostly or solely carried by which kind of mode in the mix may differ. And when looking at modes separately, you may find that some develop the ideational metafunction more than others, and others the interpersonal. Multimodality requires the metafunctions to be rethought and not taken for granted."

The point that the multimodal ensemble is the most fruitful unit of analysis is also made by Jay Lemke when discussing the problems of analysing language (rather than speech and writing) as a separate mode: "It seems to me that it is more productive to ask the question: What does language add to the multimodal mix? What are its special strengths or the special purposes for which we tend to use language more than the other modes?"

A possible disagreement between Kress and van Leeuwen appears in the further theorizing of the concept of mode. As we have seen above, Kress stresses the materiality of modes, and how that affects the affordances of modes. Van Leeuwen, on the other hand, calls for a rethinking of the concept of mode in *Multimodal*

Discourse: "We defined mode essentially as an immaterial semiotic resource, a semiotic resource that is abstract enough to be applicable across different means of expression, or different media, as we called it. And, of course, we said that language is such a resource because it can use writing or speech. Narrative, too, would be a mode, because it can be realized in many different media." Van Leeuwen points to history when he claims that multimodality may work in different ways in new and old media: "I think that with mode we have to catch up with what has happened with the semiotic practices around us and readjust our terminologies and theorizations accordingly, and in a way that can both capture the traditional idea of mode, since it still operates in practice, and the new types of semiotic resources that are coming into being.

Matthiessen's concern is mainly of a practical kind. He notes that "'mode' has come to have so many senses: it is one of the variables in context, but we also have modes of meaning, modes of expression; and we have it in description – we talk about modes of a verb". Therefore, he is not comfortable with the term multimodality and prefers the term "multi-semiotic systems", which originally is coined by Eija Ventola. Martin normally uses the term "mode" as a register category parallel to field and tenor. He refers to meaning-making systems not as "modes of meaning" but as "modalities". There is, according to Martin, confusion in the use of terms here because, as "mode", "modality" is used in different ways. Halliday uses, for example, "modality" for probability and usuality. Martin emphasizes that there is a need for more precise terms in this area.

To the ambiguity of the definition of mode, van Leeuwen adds that, with mode, there lies a theoretical problem in the fact that "[m]ost of the time it is quickly and perfunctorily defined by a few examples, as I have done many times myself: 'Modes', and then between brackets, '(e.g. image, music and text, or image, music and language)'." Van Leeuwen thinks that this is now becoming far more complex because, despite multimodality, the modes are both able to exist separately as well as in combination.

Social critique and design

Theo van Leeuwen reiterates Halliday's strong impetus that we need to explain language and the use of language through an understanding of context, and he stresses the necessity of understanding and analysing context in terms of social practices, as do sociologists; this gives a deeper understanding of (the social) context than is available if utilizing only systemic functional/social semiotic concepts. To van Leeuwen's regret, such a deep sociological understanding is missing in a lot of social semiotic work. In his own work, he finds inspiration in critical discourse analysis, and he mentions scholars such as Norman Fairclough and Ruth Wodak who "engage with social theory and relate it to the detail of language, in the way that I believe Halliday intended. There are some sociological references in social semiotics, principally Bernstein, and Berger and Luckmann, but more is needed".

Gunther Kress agrees with van Leeuwen that social semiotics does not have a fully articulated social theory to account for the social context: "It is located in the social, rather than claiming to be an articulated social theory." Instead of developing such a theory on its own, he suggests that a complementarity of approaches is the best solution. Then the social semioticians may collaborate with social scientists of different kinds, depending on the aims of each particular project. In his own work, he has worked with ethnographers who have provided a fruitful social framework for understanding the context. Where Kress turns to ethnography, van Leeuwen turns to sociology in search for a complimentary approach to fill in the gaps in social semiotics. This choice may mirror a slight difference in emphasis in their work: Kress combines an interest in the sign maker, and what motivates individual semiotic choices, with an understanding that all meaning making is situated in the social. Van Leeuwen has shown an interest in sociology from the very beginning of his academic career, which can be seen from his dilemma whether to choose linguistics or sociology as the subject of his PhD. He points to social theory, and also to history, as helpful disciplines for understanding the social practices in which meaning is made.

Jay Lemke also underlines the social, and comments how the lack of social theory was an initial weakness: "The social semiotics in the beginning was very strong on the semiotics, and had only good intentions on the 'social'. There was not an equally sophisticated social model to go with the sophisticated linguistic model, and you needed both in order to bring them together as social semiotics." This can be seen from the very first paper he presented in Michael Halliday's linguistic department in Sydney, entitled "Action, Context and Meaning". This sums up how he understands "language as one component of human action and human communication in a situational context and a context of culture". In contrast with Martin and Matthiessen, he pays tribute to eclecticism: "I am eclectic and believe in bricolage, where you borrow ideas and tools and ways of thinking from everyone that you can, and you put them together in your own way for your own purposes". Lemke, as well as van Leeuwen, points to the Newtown Semiotic Circle as an important arena for "broadening out the enterprise from linguistics to social semiotics", as Lemke puts it. To this arena Lemke brought his background in physics and cybernetics, as well as readings of Gregory Bateson's anthropology and Pierre Bourdieu's work in the sociology of culture.

Jay Lemke points to critical perspectives as the most important innovative perspectives through the last decades, besides multimodality: "the political and social dimension and the ideological dimension of analysis, which still remains on the agenda." In particular he has turned these perspectives towards his own field of science: "I think that critical discourse analysis is important for understanding science as a social phenomenon. Science is not a purely isolated, neutral, arbitrary or even objective activity. It is culturally and historically situated, and it is deeply interdependent on economic interests and even to some extent on political ideologies."

On analysis in relation to design

Van Leeuwen and Kress both support the idea that knowing is based on doing (as van Leeuwen puts it), and that social semioticians look at what people can do (as Kress points out). Therefore, design and reflections on design play a crucial role in their work. However, there is a difference to their views on design in relation to analysis. Van Leeuwen propagates a practice where both design and analysis play a role, while Kress has distanced himself from critical analysis and today is only interested in design; this is summed up by van Leeuwen as follows: "when he moved to the Institute of Education, Gunther Kress to some extent distanced himself from CDA, and began to propagate the idea of design, which is a contribution that had to be made, though for myself I cannot see why it should be antithetical to criticism. If you want to change things, you need to analyse what is wrong with the way things are now. And being critical is not necessarily being negative, it just means that you are critical, and you are open to what the outcome of that will be."

Kress justifies his practice by saying: "Design is prospective, and in education that seems to me essential. Critique says: What has happened? Usually what it analyses is not the work of the powerless, but the work of the powerful; that is one problem." Kress also sees another problem, and he refers to his own experiences doing critical linguistics in East Anglia in the early seventies. At that time the world was more stable. Although it was already beginning to be shaky, Kress says, certain social forms and power relations were still in place. The aim of the critical analyses was to show how these relations worked, and "then everybody would want to change their relation to power and their use of power". Critique was, according to Kress, a means of producing crisis, and out of crisis would come change. Time has changed, and in the mid-to-late eighties there were crises around, and nobody needed to produce them, he claims. When Kress moved to education, he rather wanted to give young people the tools that they needed to design their imaginations about the world so that they could function in relation to their own wishes in society. Kress says that this also became a feature of the work in the New London Group.

We see that, for van Leeuwen, a critical approach is still needed and such an approach can be combined with an interest for design. For Kress, the concept of design is, to a large extent, related to his work in the field of education, and the aim is to give young people the tools that they need to be active voices in the modern society. Kress has used the concept "design for learning" in recent publications. Critical analysis is not necessary to reach this aim.

Functions and applications

There is a strong tradition in social semiotics for working closely with real life problems in applied research. In this section, we shall reflect upon examples of such applications, and how they, in turn, have inspired further theoretical development. Jay Lemke and also Christian Mathiessen have been involved in work on new information technology, Mathiessen in computer assisted descriptions of language and Lemke more in the field of computer assisted learning and computer games. Theo van Leeuwen has applied social semiotics in the study of software, film and toys. Jim Martin and Gunther Kress have both applied their insights in studying health communication; Martin has studied the discourse of schizophrenic speakers while Kress has used multimodal communication in the operating theatre as case. These are but a few examples of how the application of social semiotics has entered into dialogue with a broad spectre of social experiences.

On education

First and foremost, social semiotics and SFL have proved applicable in studies of education, and studies on the construal and communication of knowledge. In this field, especially Jim Martin, Gunther Kress and Jay Lemke follow in Michael Halliday's footsteps. Kress makes a clear connection between learning, semiotic processes and communication: "Learning is, of course, communication, and if you called it teaching and learning, it would be one specific instance of communicational process. [...] Learning happens, the way I see it, through one's own making of signs in relation to the world in which one is." Kress points to education being "in the firing line" since he moved into the field of education in 1990: "What is happening in terms of the government's response to curricular things is deleterious to social futures, in a much more significant way than, say, the things that might appear within cultural studies or media studies. Not that they are unimportant. Not that they are not educational, but they are seen differently."

Jim Martin started his work with education in the 1970s, and over the years he has developed a genre-based pedagogy in close collaboration with school teachers, inspiring teachers all over the world. The stratified model of context was the basis of the pedagogy, and the starting point was a reaction to process writing, which strongly dominated the teaching of writing in the 1970s and 1980s. In certain varieties of this paradigm, knowledge about language is seen as useless and even harmful, and the teacher is seen as a guide more than a teacher. Martin and his colleagues were inspired by the work Halliday had done with young children in the 1970s, and by the work of Clare Painter in the 1980s and 1990s. Halliday and Painter both studied how adults were scaffolding young children in their language development. Scaffolding became a principle idea of the genre pedagogy as well. Through the use of model texts in a wide range of genres, the students develop their writing together with the teacher. The teaching of writing should, according to Martin, be explicit, and the teacher should actively teach, not only guide, the students. "[T]alking about language is a part of learning language", Martin says. He makes the point that knowledge about language and genres is necessary; and that students need "resources of knowledge that they could draw on", and not only diffuse ideas of what texts look like. The genre pedagogy also has a social side as students from less privileged classes need more explicit teaching to master the school genres, normally built on middle-class ideas and ideology. In the interview, Martin talks about a "socially responsible linguistics" inspired by the visions that Halliday had for SFL from the very beginning.

Jay Lemke defines his perspective on the teaching of science as a "sociocultural perspective". Gunther Kress also points to the science classroom as an interesting field of study: "The science classroom is a very, very good laboratory for semiotics and multimodality". Both of them have felt the need for a multimodal approach to the semiotic processes going on in the science classroom. When asked about his contribution, Lemke states: "Some of my notions about the application of the multimodality approach to multimodal scientific text, the integration of mathematics and various kinds of representations such as tables, charts and diagrams, along with the linguistic text in the genre of the scientific article, have been useful. For very many people, this has been a model of how to look at those interrelationships even in other genres."

In Gunther Kress's work on the role of texts in education "literacy" seems to be an important concept, appearing even in book titles such as *Literacy in the New Media Age* (2003) and *Multimodal Literacy* (Jewitt and Kress, 2003). Yet today he tries to avoid using the concept because he is worried about "metaphors like *literacy* disseminated promiscuously throughout the world, because I regard that as kind of sloppy thinking". Lemke seems to share this scepticism in his comment that "literacy" is one of those notions that work best if you do not define it too precisely: "The meaning of literacy has changed so much over my lifetime, from being almost exclusively the ability to read print text and gain basic information value from doing so, to the use of written language for your own purposes. Once one goes to a *multimodal* view on literacy, then literacy and multimodal semiotic competence are more or less the same thing." He suggests to talk about *literacies*, and mentions specialized literacies, like a mathematical literacy in the register of differential calculus.

Education and politics

There is a social drive in social semiotics that we will discuss further below. This has played a particular role in the interests in education. Behind Jim Martin's work on educational genres as well as Jay Lemke's interests in formal and informal sites of learning, there is a deep engagement in empowering young people. Gunther Kress regards his move to education as moving into a field that is shaping the future: "I am very glad to have moved into education. When I was in Sydney, before I came here, I was in a place that focused on media studies and media production, cultural studies, cultural production. Of course that is enormously important; it's a vast educational site, but not seen in those terms. And then I came here, and because of the Neoliberal agenda matched with its profound social changes, education has been in the firing line since then. And so I was forced to think very hard about those kind of things. There is less need for serious consideration or the same intense consideration when you are looking at an advertisement, or a film or something; even a debate on pornography or violence is less severe."

This is also an area where Christian Mathiessen sees the benefits of collaboration across fields of expertise: "Later on in the 1980s, people came from education with real expertise in education and worked with Martin, Halliday and Hasan. I am thinking of people like Joan Rothery, Frances Christie, Beverly Derewianka, Geoff Williams, Len Unsworth and a number of other people. These are people who worked specifically on what got identified as educational linguistics. So you had very good conditions for a dialogue between different areas of expertise, and you had people who understood the important and essential move from basic research to the development of materials to implementation. I think understanding these phases is very important, also for other areas."

The engagement in education illustrates Halliday's thinking about the purpose of academic research in a more general sense, Christian Matthiessen explains: "the engagement with education issues was very central from early on; it was very much part of what those who were members of the linguistic group in the British communist party were concerned with. They were concerned with what Halliday has now found a term for: appliable linguistics – meaning that linguistics, just like other branches of science and scholarship, could actually have an engineering application, address problems in the community and make a positive difference to the human condition. It was part of the thinking from the beginning that SFL should be scientific in the theoretical sense, but also in the engineering sense and, as Halliday said somewhere along the line, there should be more emphasis on the engineering sense of science than the philosophy sense of science. In that sense, it was appliable, and so it should be appliable to the education context."

Academia and politics

Some of the scholars presented in this book are clearly driven by social consciousness in their work, mirroring as it were Halliday's communist/Marxist upbringing. It is very explicit in Martin's work, and also in his answers in the interview. He says: "I have always wanted my linguistics to do something in the world. This is very different from Chomsky, who is very famous for his politics but claims his linguistics has nothing to do with that work." We have also seen that social consciousness was an important motivation for his work in school and in the development of genre pedagogy. In addition, the recent studies of young offenders in New South Wales show his social engagement. Also van Leeuwen's work – he has had a long run in Critical Discourse Analysis – was driven by social consciousness. In CDA – and in Martin's idea of Positive Discourse Analysis – discourse is, among other things, defined by the way it articulates aspects of power and oppression in a society. When looking into future challenges, van Leeuwen underlines a motivation for projects that may make a difference: "projects that pay equal attention to semiotic resources and to their uses, in the context of practices that really matter in today's world, like consumerism, corporate power, the new poverty, the way public services change as they are sold out or corporatized even without being sold – those kind of issues. I believe that our kind of social semiotic approach has things to offer here that escape the big brush thinkers who do not bother as much with data as we do."

Gunther Kress also wants to be in dialogue with social development, even though he realizes that academic understanding often lags behind in a rapidly changing world: "So, I think, the social does stuff anyway, and academics always run behind the horse that has left the stable. We are not leading anything; we are attempting to understand what has happened. I am not politically active, except in the sense that I attempt to produce a theory of learning which gives significance and dignity to the work of very, very many people in a way it never did before. Is that a significant political action? Yes it is. That is how I would think about that."

Jay Lemke is more engaged in how scientific knowledge can be communicated to the public, not only in education, but also in matters of relevance to political decisions: "One of the problems is that scientists are not very good at making their case to the public. In designing better scientific representations, a key feature is to find ways to make them more friendly to non-experts, so that, for example, many issues of probability and statistics, which are fundamental to the scientific representation of controversial issues, such as environmental policy issues, simply is understandable for the average person." However, he warns against too close relations between academic analysis, politics and ideology: "Sometimes they go too much hand in hand, as when some people using a critical discourse analysis approach may have already decided about the political analysis before they do the linguistic analysis or the multimodal analysis of their texts. As a result, learning how to understand the political situation from the analysis of the texts will not be the case."

The social indignation/motivation is less salient in Matthiessen's work; he seems, to some extent, more occupied with language description, typology and the more systemic part of SFL, and lesser occupied with the more broad, contextual issues. And Matthiessen's definition of the concept discourse as "text in context" (Matthiessen, 1992, p. 18) does not in any way emphasize power relations; it is not a purpose-driven definition, it is a definition that is generally applicable to all context-sensitive studies of text.

Future challenges, hopes and aspirations

The scholars interviewed in this book have contributed immensely to social semiotics and systemic functional linguistics. Even though they can all look back over a long academic career, they do not give the impression that they have arrived at an end point; there is still more work to be done to develop the fields that they have devoted their lives to. There are new areas to cover, previous concepts to reconsider and new challenges to be met. In this section we will sum up what the scholars see as important challenges for the future.

Refining theories and concepts

Theories and concepts prove their usefulness when tested in analytical work on semiotic and social practices, which may in turn lead to revisions. After two decades of work in the field of multimodality, van Leeuwen believes that it may be time to reconsider some of its concepts from a more principal and theoretical point of view. He points to historical and strategic reasons for some of the choices made in an early phase, such as when concepts like *text*, *grammar* and *literacy* in the field of multimodality were used to claim a field. After an indefinite expansion of the concept of text, he calls for a more well-defined and theoretically grounded understanding of this concept. Gunther Kress, too, is open to reconsider the extent of the concept of text. When giving his definition of a "text" as an internally coherent and framed semiotic entity, he adds: "At the moment I am happy to call these things text. But somebody might come along and give me a good reason to say that actually there are too many problems with that." Jim Martin also takes up the concept of text and mentions intermodality as one of the major challenges for the future. He says: "We have created a huge crisis for ourselves by proposing simultaneous realization hierarchies for the different modalities, and then you are faced with the problem that you have a multimodal text." Martin asks how we can, in the future, build a theory that enables us to understand how the meanings from different modalities come together into a single text as it unfolds.

Another central concept that needs rethinking, van Leeuwen claims, is the concept of *mode*. The semiotic resources contributing to the multimodal ensemble are mostly explained through examples, which leave theoretical understandings of how they work as a semiotic system in the obscure. Kress, too, reflects that the way he defines mode has changed: "It is important to locate when you have done something, because it reflects what was available, and what the issues were." In the early stage the important point was to situate the understanding of mode in the social: "if a community decides to articulate a particular set of material things, or conceptual things, into mode, then that is a mode for that community", Kress says with reference to his and van Leeuwen's work in the late 1990s. The wide range, including both the material and conceptual in the understanding of what makes up a mode, seems to be one of the reasons why van Leeuwen calls for rethinking. Through his own work on modes, ranging from sound through image to colour, he has encountered problems with defining single modes with an independent material base: "But now we have realized that many modes, despite being able to realize all three metafunctions, cannot be used on their own. Colour for example, has to go with something else that it is the colour of – with dress, with architecture, with images and so on. If it is a mode, then it is a different kind of mode from, say, the image or architecture. At the same time we began to discover that some of the things we thought were specific for images are not, and that many of the principles of the so-called grammar of images, for instance framing and salience, could also be applied to other 'modes'. They are semiotic principles, resources or ways of doing things that cut across modes. So what are they? As I mentioned before, modality is also one of these. It can also be applied across modes. We have a problem here that needs to be addressed theoretically, better than we have done so far."

Other concepts may enter into the field and need to be theorized in a way that makes it possible to integrate them into the larger theoretical framework; in other words, to translate them into a concept with a clear place in the relational-dimensional thinking, which Matthiessen advocates. Typically these are concepts used in a very general sense across scholarly fields. A case in point is the concept of *medium*, which tends to be taken for granted, Lemke states: "the *material* medium, meaning the technology and the conventions for operating and using that technology, are a part of the context of the text that we usually background. We usually do not pay attention to it, unless it stops working." In multimodal semiotics it has been used on several levels, as "semiotic media", the material substance of expression, but also about media for production and distribution (Kress & van Leeuwen, 2001, pp. 6–7). When reflecting on this, Kress calls for differentiation of levels and more careful articulation: "The distinction that I want to make shows that there is now a problem with terminology. Partly because we are confusing or conflating quite distinct domains – sound as carrier of meaningful entities, and as a 'means for disseminating messages' – and partly because of the convergences in technology. So when people talk about *multimedia*, quite often they conflate the resources for representation with the resources for dissemination. They conflate mode as representational resource [...] with medium as disseminational technology."

Van Leeuwen also points to how changing technologies lead to the need for further theoretical development. The challenges from new technologies may also lead to new understandings of the traditional media, in a historical perspective, van Leeuwen states. One point, which appeared already in *Multimodal Discourse*, was that media do not just "realize" meanings, they add meanings of their own. "The difference with the new technologies is that they have artificial intelligence built into them. Things that you had to know how to do before can now be outsourced to the machine. This was not reflected in our definition of 'medium' in *Multimodal Discourse*. There we saw media as purely material, as tools and materials. In modern media, the immaterial – knowledge – has become material."

Another concept to reconsider is identity. In the postcolonial, globalizing world, Martin claims that identity becomes a major issue. He says that resources that enable us to work more seriously with identity are needed and have to be developed. We need to be able to talk precisely about how people negotiate their identity through discourse. This may be an important trend in SFL in the future.

On the idea of social semiotics as a grand theory

The scholars interviewed to this book have different opinions as to whether social semiotics – and systemic functional linguistics – should be regarded and deployed as an all-encompassing theory and methodology, or whether it is one perspective among a number of equally fruitful perspectives. Matthiessen propagates systemic functional linguistics as an all-encompassing model: "I like to translate findings into systemic functional terms, since I am not very fond of eclectic models – Frankenstein models where you are not quite sure how the parts fit together." This is also Martin's position: "I personally like to bring as much as I can into our orbit."

Kress and van Leeuwen represent a contrast to this position. Van Leeuwen states that "The grand theory is something that we strive for but never achieve, because by the time we have achieved it the world has already changed and the theory is no longer applicable. And if you then continue to work on it, you will be a has been before your life is over. Yes, we need to build theory, but we also need to be flexible and build our theories so that they can move along with the times." Kress explains his and van Leeuwen's position as one of asking questions of a general kind that call for complementary approaches, including social theories: "At a certain point, what social semiotics might possibly be able to do takes too much effort, and ethnography of a certain kind does it better. And so maybe complementarities of approaches are a better idea than talking about weaknesses, which might lead you to articulate a theory beyond a point of usefulness." Within multimodal research he points to the need for more detailed work on modes. He claims that we need "intense descriptions of what these things are, and what they afford, and what they can't do. Affordance and constraint: what is better done for this audience with these kinds of resources? We need to work more on these sorts of relations of the social and the modal, of the social and the substantial."

Jay Lemke also advocates a greater openness to perspectives from outside SFL: "it tends to be rather inward looking. People in the field tend to talk mostly to other people in the field and may not look as much outside to other flavours of functional linguistics. They could look more into cultural anthropology and political sociology, and also into other areas of semiotics like biosemiotics and new paradigms like embodied cognition and embodied meaning making, as Paul Thibault, and not many others, has done."

Matthiessen's devotion to the systemic functional project means that he holds the idea of the system axiomatic; hence the descriptive model of the system network is central. One could argue that he represents the most systemic thinker among the scholars in this book. His thinking is contrasted by Kress, who finds the notion of system problematic; as he points out: "the notion of system–structure had too much of what I think can be shown to be an ideological or a mythic attempt to indicate – and insist on – stability where there isn't actually stability." Martin is somewhat in line with Kress – though not so sceptical about the notion of the system itself, more about the way systems are depicted – when he states that "[o]ur representations of system and instance right now are very static and synoptic. We use essentially a two-dimensional page to configure the systems and a two-dimensional page to show the structure of a text – both as synoptic 'fait accompli'. We are stuck in our linguistic theory now, and I think we have fallen far behind where the biological and physical sciences are in terms of animated modelling and multidimensional visualization".

As we have seen, the key figures in the generation after Michael Halliday have taken his social semiotics in several directions, developing ideas on meaning in systems, modes and social relations according to their own interests. In the interviews they demonstrate reflections which may lead to reworking of established concepts, as well as a constant scholarly curiosity which may lead to further development.

References

Fawcett, Robin P., 2008. *Invitation to Systemic Functional Linguistics Through the Cardiff Grammar: an extension and simplification of Halliday's systemic functional grammar.* London: Equinox
Firth, J.R., 1957. *Papers in Linguistics, 1934–1951.* London: Oxford University Press.

Halliday, Michael A.K., 1973. *Explorations in the Functions of Language*. London: Edward Arnold.

——, 1978. *Language as Social Semiotic: the social interpretation of language and meaning*. London: Edward Arnold.

——, 1989. *Spoken and Written Language*. 2nd edition. Oxford: Oxford University Press.

——, 1992. How Do You Mean. In: Michael A.K. Halliday, 2002. *On Grammar. Collected Works of M.A.K. Halliday* volume 1. London & New York: Continuum, pp. 352–68.

——, 1995a. Computing Meanings: Some Reflections on Past Experience and Present Prospects. In: Michael A.K. Halliday, 2005. *Computational and Quantitative Studies. Collected Works of M.A.K. Halliday* volume 6. London & New York: Continuum, pp. 239–67.

——, 1995b. On Language in Relation to Fuzzy Logic and Intelligent Computing. In: Michael A.K. Halliday, 2005. *Computational and Quantitative Studies. Collected Works of M.A.K. Halliday* volume 6. London & New York: Continuum, pp. 196–212.

——, 2003. Introduction: On the "architecture" of human language. In: Michael A.K. Halliday, 2003. *On Language and Linguistics. Collected Works of M.A.K. Halliday* volume 3. London & New York: Continuum, pp. 1–29.

Halliday, Michael A.K. & Christian M.I.M. Matthiessen, 1999. *Construing Experience Through Language: a language-based approach to cognition*. London: Cassell.

——, 2014. *Halliday's Introduction to Functional Grammar*. 4th revised edition. London: Routledge.

Jewitt, Carey & Gunther Kress (eds.), 2003. *Multimodal Literacy*. New York: Peter Lang.

Kress, Gunther & Theo van Leeuwen, 2001. *Multimodal Discourse. The Grammar of Visual Design. The Modes and Media of Contemporary Communication*. London: Hodder Arnold.

Kress, Gunther, 2003. *Literacy in the New Media Age*. London: Routledge.

——, 2010. *Multimodality: a social semiotic approach to contemporary communication*. London: Routledge.

Matthiessen, Christian M.I.M., 1992. *Lexicogrammatical Cartography: English Systems*. Sydney: University of Sydney. "Draft V".

Rose, David & Jim R. Martin, 2012. *Learning to Write, Reading to Learn: genre, knowledge and pedagogy in the Sydney School*. London: Equinox

Van Leeuwen, Theo, 2005. *Introducing Social Semiotics*. London: Routledge.

INDEX

Note: Page numbers in *italic* refer to figures and photographs.